"What is so great about this annual series is that editor Holly Hughes curates articles that likely never crossed your desk, even if you're an avid reader of food content. Nearly every piece selected is worth your time." —The Huffington Post

"There's a mess of vital, provocative, funny, and tender stuff . . . in these pages." —*USA Today*

"Some of these stories can make you burn with a need to taste what they're writing about." —*Los Angeles Times*

"The essays are thought-provoking and moving. . . . This is an absolutely terrific and engaging book. . . . There is enough variety, like a box of chocolates, that one can poke around the book looking for the one with caramel and find it." —*New York Journal of Books*

"Stories for connoisseurs, celebrations of the specialized, the odd, or simply the excellent." —*Entertainment Weekly*

"This book is a menu of delicious food, colorful characters, and tales of strange and wonderful food adventures that make for memorable meals and stories." —*Booklist*

"This collection has something for connoisseurs, short story fans, and anyone hungry for a good read." —*Library Journal*

"Browse, read a bit, browse some more, and then head for the kitchen." —*Hudson Valley News*

"The finest in culinary prose is offered in this new anthology . . . these pages delight and inform readers with entertaining and provocative essays. . . . This book ultimately opens readers' eyes to honest, real food and the personal stories of the people behind it." —*Taste for Life*

"Longtime editor Hughes once again compiles a tasty collection of culinary essays for those who love to eat, cook, and read about food. . . . A literary trek across the culinary landscape pairing bountiful delights with plenty of substantive tidbits." —*Kirkus Reviews*

"A top-notch collection, Hughes brings together a wonderful mix that is sure to please the foodie in all of us." —*San Francisco Book Review*

"An exceptional collection worth revisiting, this will be a surefire hit with epicureans and cooks." —*Publishers Weekly*, starred review

"If you're looking to find new authors and voices about food, there's an abundance to chew on here." —*Tampa Tribune*

"Fascinating to read now, this book will also be interesting to pick up a year from now, or ten years from now." —Popmatters.com

"This is a book worth devouring." —*Sacramento Bee*

"The cream of the crop of food writing compilations." —*Milwaukee Journal Sentinel*

"The book captures the gastronomic zeitgeist in a broad range of essays." —*San Jose Mercury News*

"There are a few recipes among the stories, but mostly it's just delicious tales about eating out, cooking at home, and even the politics surrounding the food on our plates." —*Spokesman-Review*

"The next best thing to eating there is." —*New York Metro*

"Spans the globe and palate." —*Houston Chronicle*

"The perfect gift for the literate food lover." —*Pittsburgh Post-Gazette*

best ***Food*** WRITING

2015

best
Food
WRITING
2015

edited by

Holly
Hughes

Da Capo

**LIFE
LONG**

A Member of
the Perseus Books Group

Design by Jeff Williams
Set in 11 point Arno Pro by the Perseus Books Group

Cataloging-in-Publication data for this book is available from the Library of Congress.

First Da Capo Press edition 2015
ISBN: 978-0-7382-1864-9 (paperback)
ISBN: 978-0-7382-1865-6 (e-book)

Published by Da Capo Press
A Member of the Perseus Books Group
www.dacapopress.com

Da Capo Press books are available at special discounts for bulk purchases in the U.S. by corporations, institutions, and other organizations. For more information, please contact the Special Markets Department at the Perseus Books Group, 2300 Chestnut Street, Suite 200, Philadelphia, PA, 19103, or call (800) 810-4145, ext. 5000, or e-mail special.markets@perseusbooks.com.

10 9 8 7 6 5 4 3 2 1

Contents

Someone's in the Kitchen

At the Stove

Life, on a Plate

Introduction

I hadn't been to that Columbus Avenue restaurant in over twenty years, not since we moved twenty blocks north. Frankly, I was surprised it was still there, given New York City's rapid restaurant turnover rate. But there it still stood, and, luckily, they even had a table for us at the last minute.

The menu was the same, too. (Quite possibly, the very same sheets of laminated paper we'd been handed back in the last century.) I ordered *pappardelle al ragu* mostly because the name of the restaurant is Pappardella. I figured, you can't stay in business twenty-plus years if your namesake dish isn't pretty reliable.

My first bite released a flood of taste memories. I realized that this was the same dish I had always ordered—no doubt using the same logic—when we came to Pappardella. I literally closed my eyes in pleasure to savor it. The pasta was toothsome and meltingly fresh, the ragu sauce rich, meaty, and satin-smooth. It warmed my soul in places I hadn't known needed warming.

"I could make this," I thought to myself. "Sure, it would probably take all day. But it would be *worth it.*"

For the next week, I hunted down ragu recipes. Almost all of them called for ground meat, which baffled me—surely that had been shredded meat in Pappardella's hearty ragu. I asked the local boutique butcher for advice. "So improvise," he said blithely. "Throw in chunks of chuck instead of ground beef, and shred them with a fork once they've cooked to tenderness. Sounds pretty good to me." I've never been one for following recipes to the letter; his encouragement was all I needed. Of course he also wanted to sell me an imported brand of pappardelle that only he carries, but I went along with that, too.

And yeah, it took all day, but the pay-off (why do I always forget this?) was that the apartment smelled of glorious meat and garlic and spices for hours, and my family was ravenous by the time I served dinner. "Mom, this is amazing," my younger son said. And then, the clincher: "Why don't you always cook like this?"

Why not, indeed?

Does anybody cook like that all the time? You'd think so, judging from the artfully composed dinner dishes that crowd my Facebook feed. At 6:30 on a busy weeknight, when I still don't know what I'm going to throw together for dinner that night, those photos make me feel so inadequate. That dialectic—between the obsessive quest for flavor and the demands of just getting something on the table— runs throughout this year's edition of *Best Food Writing*. In my yearlong search through websites, magazines, newspapers, bookstores, and blogs, I found the gulf between the culinary haves and have-nots running deeper than ever.

On the one hand, there's the high end of America's food culture, where top chefs are celebrated like rock stars. Several writers in this year's *Best Food Writing* profile high-level chefs of all stripes, from Ryan Sutton's look at Chicago's inventive Phillip Foss (page 84) to Allison Alsup's portrait of New Orleans's "queen of Creole cuisine" Leah Chase (page 113). We join Jeff Gordinier for a road trip with Rene Redzepi and Danny Bowien (page 103), sit with Tom Junod at the closing night of Wylie Dufresne's WD-40 (page 76), and experience an eye-opening event at Dan Barber's Blue Hill with *New York Times* critic Pete Wells (page 72).

For today's food-obsessed audiences, dining out is the ultimate indulgence; foodies compete for a reservation at a "hot" restaurant like birders trying to complete their life list. Other writers in this book scrutinize the ever-shifting paradigms of high-end dining—the essence of service (Oliver Strand, page 54), the subtle racial message of upscale restaurants (Todd Kliman, page 63), and a trend toward focus-group-driven menus (Besha Rodell, page 46). We also get tantalizing (or maybe scary) glimpses of dining's high-tech future from Rowan Jacobsen (page 2) and Emily Kaiser Thelin (page 14).

Gourmet excesses aren't confined to restaurants, of course—home cooks can be just as perfectionistic as chefs. As Russ Parsons (page 134) and Daniel Duane (page 138) meticulously parse the details of such simple foods as roast chicken and a hamburger, other writers travel far and wide in their personal quests for culinary traditions—Keith Pandolfi's gumbo pilgrimage (page 187), Karen Coates's world-wide chicken journey (p. 179), and Matt Goulding's hunt throughout Italy (page 194) for the most authentic ragu. (A man after my own heart!)

Yet there's a counterpoint to all this as well, as a rising chorus of other writers reject the gastro-elite's standards and insist on the local, the simple, the handmade, the just-plain-folks end of things. (It's telling that this year, the *New York Times* changed the name of its Wednesday section from Dining to simply Food, to embrace a much wider range of topics.)

As both Molly Watson (page 40) and Tamar Haspel (page 35) argue, the truth is that daily meal prep can be a thankless chore, even if your kids aren't as bad as the picky eaters Sara Deseran describes (page 31). And as Debbie Koenig reminds us (page 224), the aspirations of modern foodie-cool culture can be downright depressing to a regular home cook.

Luckily, some of this year's writers share their solutions: J. Kenji López-Alt (page 128) demystifies cast-iron cookery, Sarah Grey offers a template for easy family-style entertaining (page 227), David Leite (page 284) meditates upon the therapeutic value of bread-baking, and Chez Panisse chef Cal Peternell (page 144) crafts a shortcut ragu recipe for his son. (Yes, it's officially the Year of Ragu.)

In contrast to high-end dining, we can also admit to loving chain restaurants and takeout joints. John DeVore justifies his passion for Taco Bell (page 271), Jane and Michael Stern rave about Nashville hot chicken (page 167), John Birdsall longs for Mexican street food (page 287), and Jim Shahin swears to the life-giving power of a hoagie (page 278).

When it comes right down to it, it's liberating to confess that our appetites are governed by a great deal more than just a discerning palate. Some foods we love simply because of family connections—like Kim Severson's coconut cream pie (page 237), Steve Hoffman's sausages (page 242), or Zainab Shah's *nihari* stew (page 251). Yet that taste-memory trigger is often complicated—witness Nicholás Medina Mora's yearning for carnitas (page 209) or Elissa Altman's conditioned reflexes about anything high-cal or high-carb (page 267). For Anthony Bourdain (page 291), it's not a single dish but the entire gestalt of cooking and eating at the Jersey Shore.

"Why don't you cook like this all the time?" It was my mistake, of course, to read that as a complaint about my customary culinary repertoire. What my son had really been telling me was that he'd loved the *pappardelle al ragu* that night. Nothing more, nothing less.

The night after the ragu dinner, of course, nothing had changed. I was on a tight deadline, and no one in the family seemed to know when (or even whether) they'd be home for dinner. I slung a pan of prepackaged chicken meatballs into the oven and poured bottled dressing over green salad from a plastic bag. Everyone sat at the table more or less at the same time, and gobbled it down while watching *Chopped* on the kitchen TV.

Still, no one complained. It was a good-enough dinner.

And I'm learning to live with that.

The Way We Eat Now

The Perfect Beast

By Rowan Jacobsen

From *Outside*

Rowan Jacobsen, the author of *American Terroir, Apples of Uncommon Character,* and *A Geography of Oysters,* is our go-to guy on issues of how what we eat impacts the planet. Here, the multitalented reporter, science writer, and environmental journalist—visits a futuristic food lab.

I dumped meat a few weeks ago, and it was not an easy breakup. Some of my most treasured moments have involved a deck, a beer, and a cheeseburger. But the more I learned, the more I understood that the relationship wasn't good for either of us. A few things you should never do if you want to eat factory meat in unconflicted bliss: write a story on water scarcity in the American Southwest; Google "How much shit is in my hamburger?"; watch an undercover video of a slaughterhouse in action; and read the 2009 Worldwatch Institute report "Livestock and Climate Change."

I did them all. And that was that. By then I knew that with every burger I consumed, I was helping to suck America's rivers dry, munching on a fecal casserole seasoned liberally with E. coli, passively condoning an orgy of torture that would make Hannibal Lecter blanch, and accelerating global warming as surely as if I'd plowed my Hummer into a solar installation. We all needed to kick the meat habit, starting with me.

Yet previous attempts had collapsed in the face of time-sucking whole-food preparation and cardboard-scented tofu products. All the veggie burgers I knew of seemed to come in two flavors of unappealing: the brown-rice, high-carb, nap-inducing mush bomb, and the colon-wrecking gluten chew puck. Soylent? In your pasty dreams. If I couldn't have meat, I needed something damn close. A high-performance, low-commitment protein recharge, good with Budweiser.

I took long, moody walks on the dirt roads near my Vermont house. I passed my neighbor's farm. One of his beef cattle stepped up to the fence and gazed at me. My eyes traced his well-marbled flanks and meaty chest. I stared into those bottomless brown eyes. "I can't quit you," I whispered to him.

But I did. Not because my willpower suddenly rose beyond its default Lebowski setting, but because a box arrived at my door and made it easy.

Inside were four quarter-pound brown patties. I tossed one on the grill. It hit with a satisfying sizzle. Gobbets of lovely fat began to bubble out. A beefy smell filled the air. I browned a bun. Popped a pilsner. Mustard, ketchup, pickle, onions. I threw it all together with some chips on the side and took a bite. I chewed. I thought. I chewed some more. And then I began to get excited about the future.

It was called the Beast Burger, and it came from a Southern California company called Beyond Meat, located a few blocks from the ocean. At that point, the Beast was still a secret, known only by its code name: the Manhattan Beach Project. I'd had to beg Ethan Brown, the company's 43-year-old CEO, to send me a sample.

And it was vegan. "More protein than beef," Brown told me when I rang him up after tasting it. "More omegas than salmon. More calcium than milk. More antioxidants than blueberries. Plus muscle-recovery aids. It's the ultimate performance burger."

"How do you make it so meat-like?" I asked.

"It is meat," he replied enigmatically. "Come on out. We'll show you our steer."

Beyond Meat HQ was a brick warehouse located a stone's throw from Chevron's massive El Segundo refinery, which hiccuped gray fumes into the clear California sky. "Old economy, new economy," Brown said as we stepped inside. Two-dozen wholesome millennials tapped away at laptops on temporary tables in the open space, which looked remarkably like a set that had been thrown together that morning for a movie about startups. Bikes and surfboards leaned in the corners. In the test kitchen, the Beyond Meat chef, Dave Anderson—former celebrity chef to the stars and cofounder of vegan-mayo company Hampton Creek—was frying experimental burgers made of beans, quinoa, and cryptic green things.

The "steer" was the only one with its own space. It glinted, steely and unfeeling, in the corner of the lab. It was a twin-screw extruder, the food-industry workhorse that churns out all the pastas and Power-Bars of the world. Beyond Meat's main extruders, as well as its 60 other employees, labor quietly in Missouri, producing the company's current generation of meat substitutes, but this was the R&D steer. To make a Beast Burger, powdered pea protein, water, sunflower oil, and various nutrients and natural flavors go into a mixer at one end, are cooked and pressurized, get extruded out the back, and are then shaped into patties ready to be reheated on consumers' grills.

"It's about the dimensions of a large steer, right?" Brown said to me as we admired it. "And it does the same thing." By which he meant that plant stuff goes in one end, gets pulled apart, and is then reassembled into fibrous bundles of protein. A steer does this to build muscle. The extruder in the Beyond Meat lab does it to make meat. Not meat-like substances, Brown will tell you. Meat. Meat from plants. Because what is meat but a tasty, toothy hunk of protein? Do we really need animals to assemble it for us, or have we reached a stage of enlightenment where we can build machines to do the dirty work for us?

Livestock, in fact, are horribly inefficient at making meat. Only about 3 percent of the plant matter that goes into a steer winds up as muscle. The rest gets burned for energy, ejected as methane, blown off as excess heat, shot out the back of the beast, or repurposed into non-meat-like things such as blood, bone, and brains. The process buries river systems in manure and requires an absurd amount of land. Roughly three-fifths of all farmland is used to grow beef, although it accounts for just 5 percent of our protein. But we love meat, and with the developing world lining up at the table and sharpening their steak knives, global protein consumption is expected to double by 2050.

That's what keeps Brown up at night. A six-foot-five, pillar-armed monument to the power of plant protein, with a voice that makes James

Earl Jones sound effeminate, he became a vegetarian as a teenager growing up in Washington, D.C., after his family bought a Maryland dairy farm. "I began feeling very uncomfortable in my leather basketball shoes," he says. "Because I knew the cows. I'd pet them all the time."

In his twenties he became a vegan. "It wasn't emotional. It was a question of fairness," he says. " 'Why are we treating our dog so well and not the pig?' As you get older, you try to become more coherent." He was already thinking big. "I wanted to start a plant-based McDonald's." Instead, he went into the alternative-energy business, working on fuel cells for Vancouver-based Ballard Power Systems. "Somehow energy seemed like a more serious thing to do. But the food idea kept eating at me, until finally I said, 'You know what, I gotta do this.' "

Brown's aha moment came in 2009, when the Worldwatch Institute published "Livestock and Climate Change," which carefully assessed the full contribution to greenhouse-gas emissions (GHGs) of the world's cattle, buffalo, sheep, goats, camels, horses, pigs, and poultry. An earlier report by the United Nations Food and Agriculture Organization had pegged that contribution at 18 percent, worse than cars and trucks. That's shocking enough, but the Worldwatch study's authors, two analysts from the World Bank, found that the FAO hadn't taken into account the CO_2 breathed out by our 22 billion livestock animals, the forests being felled to make room for pasture and feed crops, or the total impact of the 103 million tons of methane belched into the air by ruminants each year. When everything was tallied up, Worldwatch estimated, livestock were on the hook for 51 percent of GHGs.

That was all Brown needed to hear to put the plant-based McDonald's back at the top of his agenda. Forget fuel cells. Forget Priuses. If he could topple Meatworld, he thought, he could stop climate change cold.

Brown's first breakthrough came when he discovered Fu-Hung Hsieh, a food scientist at the University of Missouri who had perfected a way to turn soy protein into strips that chewed like chicken. (Top secret, can't tell you, but it has to do with heat, kneading, and cool water.) Brown founded Beyond Meat in 2009, and in 2012, its inaugural product, Beyond Chicken Strips, began wowing the gatekeepers of the food world.

"Most impressive," said Food Network geek Alton Brown. "It's more like meat than anything I've ever seen that wasn't meat."

"Fooled me badly," Mark Bittman admitted in his *New York Times* food column. It also fooled Twitter cofounder (and vegan) Biz Stone, so he invested in the company.

So did Bill Gates, whose Gates Foundation backs potentially world-saving innovations. "I tasted Beyond Meat's chicken alternative," he wrote online, "and honestly couldn't tell it from real chicken." Gates quickly realized the blockbuster potential. "Our approach to food hasn't changed much over the last 100 years. It's ripe for reinvention. We're just at the beginning of enormous innovation."

Gates sat down with Brown in 2012 and gave him some tips, which the entrepreneur took to heart. As Brown recalls, "He said to me, 'If you get this thing to cost less than meat, and you get international quickly enough, then this is huge.'"

The scalability is there: Beyond Meat's manufacturing process uses a small fraction of the land, water, energy, crops, and time that making real meat does, and it requires no new technology. And the timing is right. Whole Foods has enthusiastically sold Beyond Chicken Strips, which retail for $5.29 for a nine-ounce bag, from the very beginning. And although Brown wouldn't disclose sales numbers ("Our competitors definitely make use of this type of information," he says), Beyond Meat expanded from 1,500 to 6,000 stores in 2014, including mainstreamers like Safeway.

Even the fast-food industry is coming around. When Chipotle added shredded-tofu Sofritas to its burrito options at a few California restaurants in 2013, sales outstripped expectations. Half the Sofritas buyers, Chipotle found, were meat eaters. Chipotle is now rolling them out across the country, the first new item it has added in ten years. One rapidly growing restaurant chain, Veggie Grill, an all-vegan West Coast eatery, offers seemingly familiar fast-food items like Mondo Nachos and Crispy Chickin' with meat replacements made from soy and gluten.

But you can't fix climate change with fake chicken. Although the 21 billion cluckers around the world consume vast amounts of crops and choke waterways with their manure, their impact is dwarfed by the 1.5 billion head of cattle. It takes about 9,000 calories of edible feed to produce 1,000 calories of edible chicken and 11,000 calories of feed for 1,000 calories of pork—a far cry from the 36,000 calories required for 1,000 calories of beef. More important, cattle and their ruminant cousins—sheep, goats, buffalo—produce geysers of methane during digestion. One molecule of methane traps 25 times as much heat as a molecule of CO_2, so each cow produces the annual GHGs of a car driven about 9,375 miles. Per pound, that's eight times more than chickens and five times more than pigs.

There are, of course, lots of good arguments for raising cattle sustainably: it's easier on both the animals and the land. But it's no solution when it comes to global warming. Grass-fed beef generates significantly more methane and has nearly twice the carbon footprint of its grain-fed kin.

If Brown was going to tackle climate change, he had to hack beef.

Beef flavor has never been all that difficult to approximate—some salt, some aroma molecules, and bingo. The juiciness and the chew are the real challenges. The meat industry acknowledged as much in a 2006 trade publication: "Meat texture is supremely important. Texturized vegetable protein, something that could be quite a commercial threat to us . . . has, so far, made little impact," wrote the meat scientist Howard Swatland, author of *Meat Cuts and Muscle Foods*. "This is because food technologists so far have been unable to extrude their plant proteins into anything resembling real meat. The taste and colour can be faked quite easily, but the texture cannot. In a way, therefore, it is the texture of meat, and the fact that many of our customers love to eat it, that keeps us all in business."

Muscle is made up of bundles of long, thin fibers wrapped in tough connective tissue, like shrink-wrapped logs. Scattered through the fiber packets are tiny pockets of fat, which the body draws on for energy. A lot of the joy of meat is the feeling of your teeth punching through these bundles, the fat and juice squirting as you chomp.

Plant proteins, on the other hand, are not aligned or bundled. They're more like random piles of sticks. They have none of the tensile strength or moisture-retention properties of muscle, which is why earlier generations of veggie burgers fell apart and lacked the release of rich, juicy fats. The only exception is gluten, the protein found in wheat, which has some amazing qualities. It forms a spring-like structure that can expand

and contract, making dough stretchy and retaining moisture in its matrix of interlinked proteins. But those long proteins also like to curl in on themselves like a nest of snakes, which prevents digestive enzymes from getting at them. When that partially digested gluten makes it into the gut of someone with celiac disease, the immune system mistakes the intact proteins for evil microbes, freaks out, and strafes the intestine with friendly fire. Even those who don't have an adverse response to wheat often find the concentrated gluten in veggie burgers to be digestively challenging.

For Brown, gluten was out. Also becoming less popular with consumers was phytoestrogen-heavy soy, the other mainstay of both veggie burgers and Beyond Chicken. But top food scientists had labored for years to come up with palatable soy- and gluten-free meat substitutes, with no luck. Plants just didn't want to be meat.

It was time for a paradigm shift. In the fall of 2013, Brown hired Tim Geistlinger, a biotech rock star who had been working with the Gates Foundation to develop antimalarial drugs and a yeast that makes clean jet fuel out of sugar. Geistlinger fits the Beyond Meat mold: brainiac science geek who bikes on the beach every night and recently completed his first Tough Mudder. ("I was one of the only non-meat-eaters on my team," Geistlinger says, "but with access to compounds like these, it's a no-brainer.")

Geistlinger, chef Dave Anderson, and the other Beyond Meat scientists began a series of marathon sessions in the lab, trying to do what cattle do: transform short plant proteins into long, succulent fibers. Their legume of choice was the yellow pea, whose protein is readily available—both to the body and in the marketplace. Pea starch is used by the food industry as a natural thickener for everything from sauces to deli meats. In the past, after the starch was isolated, the protein was discarded. Win-win.

Pea protein is the new darling of the no-soy health-food set, but it has a powdery mouthfeel and no structural integrity, so it has never starred in its own production. "Without fibers you can have something that's hard and dry or mushy and wet," Geistlinger says. "They're fairly mutually exclusive." Early last year, Beyond Meat released a pea-based product, Beyond Beef Crumble, that approximated the look and feel of cooked ground beef and made a decent taco filling, but it wouldn't hold together and had no chew. Geistlinger decided he had to create fibers from the material—that is, do something to make them line up and link together to mimic muscle.

For a while the team got nowhere. Geistlinger kept tweaking the chemistry—"taking shots on goal in a constructive way," as he puts it—and Anderson kept playing around with the results. Nothing. "Early on we thought we were close," Anderson remembers. "So I brought in an In-N-Out burger. We tried the In-N-Out and it was just chew, chew, chew, and then we tried ours. I was like, 'Wow, we're not even close.'"

Eventually, Geistlinger suggested trying something radical—the big Beast Burger secret, which involves a certain combination of temperature, pressure, timing, and chemistry that he could tell me about only in veiled terms. "The food scientists had been arguing to go in one direction, because that's how things had always been done," he recalls. "And I said, 'Well, this is a different protein. I think we should push this in the opposite direction.' They were like, 'Why would you do that? You can't do that.' And I said, 'Well, let's just give it a shot.' And sure enough, boom. It was immediately apparent. We tasted it right when it came out, and we just went, 'Wow! We've never had that before.' It was awesome. You could see the fibers. You could feel them. And it didn't get dry in your mouth! All these problems that we'd had just went away. Later that day, we met with our CFO and I said, 'Here, try this,' and he said, 'Holy shit! What is that?' And I said, 'That's the same stuff. We just changed two things.' It turned out much, much better than we ever thought it was going to be."

To perfect the nutritional formulation, they worked with Brendan Brazier, a two-time Canadian ultramarathon champion who created the Vega line of vegan performance foods. After playing around with the burger, Brazier became a convert. He liked the taste, but he loved the 24 grams of protein, 4 grams of fiber, and 0 milligrams of cholesterol in every burger, which left beef (19 grams of protein, 0 grams of fiber, and 80 milligrams of cholesterol) far behind.

"It's so nutrient dense," Brazier told me. "I plan on using several per week."

The Beast Burger will have its coming-out party in select Whole Foods in January. Is it as delicious as a quarter-pound of well-marbled, inch-thick USDA Choice? Hell no. Good ground beef, lovingly grilled at home and served piping hot, packs a juicy succulence that this Beast lacks. In flavor and texture, the current Beast reminds me of the Salisbury steak of my youth—not exactly something to celebrate, but not terrible, either. "It's a different kind of chew," Anderson admits. "To me it's a better chew. A beef burger is very gristly."

The prototype Beast was so packed with micronutrients that it smelled like a Vitamin Shoppe kiosk. Taste testers made it clear that they'd gladly sacrifice a soupçon of supplement for a blast of beefiness. The new iteration is good enough that New York Mets captain David Wright, who stopped eating red meat years ago after noticing that it made him feel sluggish, will endorse it—part of Beyond Meat's aim to woo red-blooded athletes—and it's only going to get better.

"Why just look at soy and pea protein?" Brown says. "Why not look at every plant and see what has the best amino acid profiles and what can be produced the most cost-effectively? It turns out there are a lot of things you can get protein from."

"What's exciting to me is that we now have a completely different set of proteins that we can tune," says Geistlinger. "We're looking at yeasts and algae, which both have amino acid profiles that are superior to beef. We made something that used yeast from the brewery across the street. It came out like bratwurst!"

The issue of Frankenfoods raises its head. When I told Geistlinger that I was skeptical of processed foods, especially ones produced by novel techniques, he pointed out that Beyond Meat uses no artificial ingredients and employs the most time-tested of cooking methods (heat and pressure). "Our process is gentler than making pretzels," he said. "Getting that browning on a pretzel requires chemically changing the bonds in the molecules. That's more harsh than what we do."

Grilling meat also involves chemical changes, of course, but ones that have been tested for many generations. Mark Bittman, for one, is going to stay off the faux-meat bandwagon for now. "I think we have to evaluate each of these products individually," he told me. "Some fake meats can easily pass for 'real' meat, but in many cases that's because 'real' meat has been so degraded by the industrial production of animals. Still: the best direction for most of us is to eat unprocessed food of all types; fake meat hardly qualifies."

Health aside, some of my friends were just weirded out. Why turn plant proteins into burgers and dogs? Why not just eat them as peas and soybeans and seeds? To which I say: taco, chimichanga, empanada, crepe, pierogi, wonton, gyoza, stuffed roti, pupusa, pastie, pig in a blanket, croque monsieur, pastrami on rye. Culture is a lump of flesh wrapped in dough. If you want to save the world, you'd better make it convenient.

You're still wondering about that shit-burger, aren't you? Here's what I know. Every year, the Centers for Disease Control and Prevention teams up with the FDA to check for antibiotic-resistant bacteria in the meat sold in American retail outlets. In 2010, the most recent year for which data has been released, they purchased 5,280 samples across 11 states and tested four states' for fecal bacteria. They found it in 90 percent of ground beef and ground turkey, 88 percent of pork chops, and 95 percent of chicken breasts.

If this shocks you, then clearly you haven't been watching YouTube videos of slaughterhouses in action, where the high-speed slicing and dicing of 300 to 400 head of cattle an hour saturates the air with a fine fecal mist. Really, the amazing thing is that 10 percent of our ground beef—even the organic stuff, which is largely processed in the same manner—manages to escape contamination, and that anyone eats it at all.

The part that really terrifies Meatworld? Millennials are already bailing on beef.

Every generation skews toward vegetarianism in high school and college, only to regress as life gets more complicated. But the newest graduates aren't coming back. "We've definitely seen interest in vegetarian as well as vegan food rising steadily on college and corporate campuses, but so has interest in eating less meat in general," says Maisie Ganzler, VP of strategy for Bon Appétit Management Company, which provides food services to many top universities and corporations, including Duke, Johns Hopkins, Yahoo, and Google. If you want to know what America's next generation of thinkers is eating, just ask Bon Appétit. "For us, vegan isn't about niche appeal," Ganzler says. "We try to offer a lot of vegan options in the cafés for our high-tech clients. Millennials are more meat conscious, and vegan appeals to a variety of growing populations."

As vegetarianism goes mainstream, factory meat's one advantage—that it's cheap—disappears. "There aren't any obstacles to us underpricing beef as we scale up," Brown says. "The industry is large and established, yet it's facing huge cost challenges. The price slope for beef since 2010 has been pretty steep. We're already competitive with certain grades."

There's no reason that Beyond Meat can't have extruders all over the world churning out affordable protein patties and even a plant-based "raw" ground beef that's red, pliable, and designed for cooking. Once that happens, Brown won't let U.S. supermarkets slot him into the hippie aisle anymore. "As soon as we have our ground beef ready, they need to put it next to the animal protein."

He'll have to catch Impossible Foods, founded by Stanford University biochemist Patrick Brown and also backed by Bill Gates, which in October revealed a raw "ground beef" featuring bioengineered "plant blood" designed to approximate hemoglobin. The patty turns brown and savory as it cooks. Although the costs are not yet competitive and the flavor is a work in progress, Impossible Foods expects to have its meat going head-to-head with ground beef next year. "Livestock is an outdated technology," says Patrick Brown.

Considering the speed of change, the money and smarts being thrown at the problem, and the desperate need, it seems likely that sometime in the next decade, Beyond Meat or Impossible Foods or another rival will perfect vegetarian beef, chicken, and pork that is tastier, healthier, and cheaper than the fast-food versions of the real thing. It will be a textbook case of disruptive technology: overnight, meat will become the coal of 2025—dirty, uncompetitive, outcast. Our grandchildren will look back on our practice of using caged animals to assemble proteins with the same incredulousness that we apply to our ancestors' habit of slaughtering whales to light their homes.

I was thinking about that on the kind of crackling fall day when absolutely anything feels possible, back at my neighbor's farm, eyeing my four-legged friend. The leaves on the Vermont hills were a shimmering metallic curtain of bronze and rust, the sky limitless, the pasture speckled with goldenrod. A week of daily Beast Burgers had left me wildly energized and clearheaded, and I liked the feeling. "I don't know what I ever saw in you," I told him. He blinked back at me and uncorked a fragrant burp.

Growing a $30 Million Egg

By Emily Kaiser Thelin

From *Food & Wine*

Writing about another high-tech food solution that seems straight out of science fiction, food writer/editor Emily Thelin, who's also a trained chef, spins a narrative that bridges her vegan-friendly home base in Berkeley, California, with the futuristic wonks of nearby Silicon Valley.

W hen I first met my husband, Josh, at a July 4th potluck barbecue in 2009, I had a strict rule against dating vegetarians—too much time spent defending my carnivorous ways. So I was crestfallen when the dashing stranger with whom I had been getting on so well suddenly plopped a veggie dog on the grill. I sighed and pulled out my bone-in rib eye. But as that steak cooked, with smoke swirling and fat spattering, Josh never flinched. When I carved into the medium-rare meat, he even asked how it tasted.

He explained that he'd never renounced meat—he'd just never eaten it. Ever. Since before he was born, his parents have eschewed meat and eggs. His father, Jay Thelin, cofounded the Psychedelic Shop on Haight Street in San Francisco in 1966. Jay was a rigorous idealist (he hoped LSD could expand the collective consciousness and end the war in Vietnam). Later, he discovered a spiritual path that convinced him that meat and eggs (and drugs and alcohol) hindered access to the divine. Out of a mix of habit, loyalty and pride, Josh has remained a vegetarian his entire life. He's always been curious about omelets and steaks—just not enough to try them.

When we started dating, it felt good to eat more vegetarian meals. If I was missing meat, I ordered a roast chicken or braised pork shoulder when Josh and I ate out. Eggs became our only point of contention. On weekend mornings and at the end of a long day, I crave an omelet. Josh valiantly tries to win me over with his scrambled tofu, but, well, come on. Maybe I've succumbed to Francophile propaganda, but omelets, soufflés and other classics of egg cookery have always represented the ne plus ultra of independent adult living to me. And I make good omelets. When we got married, we joked that our lives would be perfect if only someone would build us a plant-based egg.

Last year, we learned that our absurdist fantasy was coming true. Big investors in Silicon Valley put $30 million into a start-up called Hampton Creek, where R&D scientists are building a vast database of legumes and grains (including often-overlooked ones like the Canadian yellow pea and sorghum) to determine which plant proteins can mimic—indeed, outperform—the properties of eggs.

The fact that the company's founder, Josh Tetrick, is vegan has nothing to do with it. A former lawyer who'd worked in international development, Tetrick started Hampton Creek in 2011 to make sustainable food choices easy. "I fully support free-range eggs," he says. "But my dad won't buy them because they cost more. We're looking for better and cheaper alternatives." Industrially produced eggs seemed an obvious first target, he said, because of their many inefficiencies: food-safety scares, animal cruelty, high production costs.

But how do you top an egg? As Auguste Escoffier wrote in *Le Guide Culinaire* "Of all the products put to use by the art of cookery, not one is so fruitful of variety, so universally liked, and so complete in itself as the egg." Eggs poach, scramble and fry. They emulsify dressings, structure cakes, even clarify wine. There are vegan substitutes that can replicate certain facets, but can plant proteins mimic them all?

Just Scramble, Hampton Creek's whole-egg alternative, is the company's most ambitious project. As food scientist Harold McGee explains in *On Food and Cooking*, when raw, a real egg's proteins float like tiny coiled ropes in watery suspension. When cooked (or whipped), the coils unwind and collide with one another to form a three-dimensional web. This web traps the air in a soufflé, thickens the milk in a custard, or suspends the egg's own water in the curds of scrambled eggs. For a proper scramble, a plant-egg needs to create identically elastic and moist curds at the same pace.

Hampton Creek has hired three former chefs from Chicago's avant-garde restaurant Moto who collaborate with its scientists on prototype after prototype. Their goal is to create something finer than an actual egg, with better flavor, more protein and less environmental impact. Recently, they found an iteration close to the real thing; it consists of a half-dozen ingredients, but contains no gums or hydrocolloids and nothing genetically modified. I wrangled an invitation to the facility so I could cook my husband his first omelet.

I was nervous: What if my husband just didn't like eggs? I heated an omelet pan with a dab of oil, then poured in the liquid plant-egg. It looked just like a beaten whole egg, pale yellow and perfectly smooth (it's only a coincidence—the plant strains are naturally yellow). I missed cracking egg shells one-handed, but didn't miss cleaning a whisk and bowl.

As it cooked, the plant-egg gently and slowly transformed from liquid to solid, just like a real egg. I nudged aside the cooked curds with a spatula, and the uncooked parts pooled right in. A few curds on the bottom lightly caramelized but never turned rubbery or dry. I took the pan off the heat when the omelet's center was just this side of runny. I added mushrooms I'd sautéed with garlic and white wine, shook the eggs to the edge of the pan, and then upended the omelet. Airy and elastic, it folded in on itself and slid onto the plate, a perfect package. "I can't believe how quickly it cooks," Josh said. "Scrambled tofu takes an age."

I took a bite. Texturally, the omelet was spot-on. Flavor-wise, it tasted a bit grassy, like olive oil. If I was judging it as an egg substitute, I might have given it a 7 or 8 out of 10.

"We'd probably give this a 5 out of 10," one of the chefs said. "Ours will have to be better than an egg."

One thing I've learned about tofu scramble: It's always better with cheese. I sprinkled grated cheddar on the omelet—the grassiness vanished. Now it tasted fantastic.

It may be months before Just Scramble is ready for market, but I'm happy to pass the time brushing up on omelet recipes: Escoffier's *Le Guide Culinaire* has 31 pages of egg dishes, 11 for omelets and (real) scrambles alone.

OMFG! It's the PSL!

By Allecia Vermillion

From *Seattle Met*

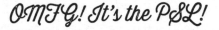

As food and drink editor of this Seattle lifestyles monthly,
Allecia Vermillion had a natural interest in one of the most
popular products of Seattle's wildly successful coffeehouse chain,
Starbucks. What she found was a fascinating inside look at the
R&D process that brought it to market.

H e strode down the narrow beige hallway cradling a pumpkin pie
in one arm—an accessory made all the more strange because
it was April. And because he ferried this particularly autumnal baked
good into a highly secure chamber, one so closely guarded that only he
and a scant few others possessed security badges granting access to the
room within.

The interior looked like a kitchen crossbred with a high school chemistry lab: An array of glasses and cups awaited experimentation; milk and
espresso equipment lined the shelves and filled multiple refrigerators.
Outside it was the season for Easter baskets and decorative bunnies, but
within this secret space fake leaves rustled on tables and paper turkeys
hung on the walls. Someone had draped sweaters over the chairs.

The man—rangy, athletic, thirtysomething—settled in at a table
with a handful of colleagues, each with their own homemade or store-
bought pumpkin pie before them. A few participants sported lab coats.

There, on this spring day in 2003, under the fluorescent lights of this
laboratory at Starbucks headquarters in the heart of SoDo, they picked
up their forks and got down to the serious business ahead. Between

bites, they discussed the question that brought them here: What does an espresso version of fall's most seasonal dessert taste like? They forked chunks of filling into their mouths and debated which elements were most appealing with coffee. The pumpkin? The cinnamon? Everyone sipped espresso alongside each forkful; a few even poured shots over their slices to approximate how it might play with pumpkin pie's texture.

Based on customer surveys and traditional corporate metrics, the bizarre, pumpkin-fueled conclave unfolding here should have never happened. But from it emerged one of the most successful, if sometimes ridiculed, rollouts in Seattle coffee history.

Since the pumpkin spice latte's inception 11 years ago, customers have ordered more than 200 million, each topped with whipped cream and a parting shake of spices. It arrives while the summer sun still beats down hot over most of the country, but a combination of masterful marketing and a fan base with the kind of obsession usually reserved for pop stars has transformed this drink into a national harbinger of fall.

Fans paint tiny Starbucks cups on their nails. They dress their dogs up in latte costumes for Halloween (pug-kin spice latte—get it?). They post online comments like, "Can it be fall now? I am so ready for Pumpkin Spice Latte, pants, warm sweaters & lots of cuddles." The morning after the first presidential debate of 2012, the nation was talking in nearly equal measures about Obama's curiously detached performance and a front-page *Wall Street Journal* article about a temporary shortage of pumpkin spice lattes after an early-season rush.

Plenty of others hate it. Their online comments are more in the vein of "tastes like candle wax" or "How do you make a pumpkin spice latte? Put yoga pants, Ugg boots, a hoodie, an iPhone 5, and a white girl into a blender." But if you partake in any form of social media whatsoever, it's nigh impossible to ignore the drink's return each year. (The Starbucks media team tracks 3,000 tweets a day when the hot beverage reemerges from hibernation, usually around Labor Day.)

Like any larger-than-life figure, the pumpkin spice latte has an origin story. It has also developed a folk hero in Peter Dukes, a lanky former all-metro point guard for the Roosevelt High School basketball team, with long eyelashes, an almost bashful grin, and a sense of humor about his role as the beverage's unofficial mascot. He even totes a Styrofoam pumpkin to media interviews to set the mood.

Back in early 2003 he was a product manager in the company's espresso division. In those days Starbucks' handful of seasonal drinks were clustered around Christmas. The brand new peppermint mocha had performed well, and company higher-ups told Dukes they wanted a similarly successful drink for the fall season.

His team compiled a list of about 20 potential flavors. Most were some variation of chocolate or caramel, but a conversation about the tastes of fall can't get too far before someone brings up Thanksgiving's signature dessert. So Dukes threw the idea of a pumpkin pie latte in the mix. Not that the idea of combining pumpkin pie spices with lattes descended directly from the heavens down to Starbucks headquarters—places like J.L. Hufford Coffee and Tea Company in Lafayette, Indiana, already had one on the menu—but it was definitely unexplored territory in the world of branded espresso drinks.

An online survey invited customers to select the theoretical latte that sounded the most appealing. The results: Starbucks regulars overwhelmingly preferred ushering in autumn with those familiar chocolate or caramel flavors. The pumpkin pie latte fell flat in the survey.

Well, "fell flat" is a little harsh. "Near the bottom middle," Dukes recalls. It should have died there. But something about the idea stirred his imagination. He couldn't let it go.

At 44, Dukes is old enough—barely—to have grown up with Starbucks. As a kid his mom would take him shopping at the QFC in University Village and give him the decidedly adult responsibility of selecting the coffee, plus a piece of chocolate for himself. He left Seattle to study economics (and play basketball) at Stanford, then went on to work in accounting before an MBA recast his path. He arrived at Starbucks in 2001. In the spring of 2003, he found himself pondering pumpkin as he prowled other coffee shops and paced the aisles of local grocery stores in the name of research.

The orange gourd is so tied to our cultural identity that Americans of all backgrounds, in all climates, feel compelled to go pick them in the patch, attend festivals in their honor, or set one on the front porch for an entire month, even though we seldom actually eat it. When you get down to it, the flavor is pretty mild.

Dukes noted a subtle distinction, but an important one: The blend of spices that go into a pumpkin pie—nutmeg, cinnamon, a bit of clove—is deeply familiar, almost primal to consumers, but new ground for flavored drinks . . . or any other flavored product. Not only do the smell and taste of those spices evoke all the nostalgia that goes with the season, Dukes realized, they answered the questions raised back in the liquid lab: "The spice is important because it brings out the pumpkin and the espresso."

Now he had to select which flavors made it to the next step—with his boss's approval. The world of brand management is a jargon-filled one, and *bench top* is the term for what happens next. Product managers like Dukes join forces with the research and development team and prepare actual steaming, frothy prototypes of each drink. Mocking up multiple versions of 20 seasonal lattes would be prohibitively expensive, so it was Dukes's job to put forward four contenders from that original list—four drinks worthy of analysis, scrutiny, and tasting over and over again.

Three of the drinks he presented to a team headed by Michelle Gass, then the vice president of beverages, were unimpeachably logical— they ranked at the top of the customer survey. There was a chocolate-caramel concoction, a latte with orange flavoring and spices, and another dubbed the cinnamon streusel latte that would later be released as the cinnamon dolce latte. Then there was his fourth and final recommendation: that drink with pumpkin pie flavoring.

Gass was skeptical. Those mediocre customer survey results didn't exactly telegraph "wildly successful fall beverage."

Her approval was key, not only because of her title, but because she was a rising star at Starbucks. The former chemical engineering major was just 35 at the time, two years older than Dukes, but had already made a name for herself as the marketing manager for Frappuccinos, expanding the line beyond the original coffee and mocha flavors and taking it from a tiny slice of Starbucks' profits to more than $2 billion. (It was her idea to promote the Frapp as an afternoon indulgence and to add the almost hedonistic cloud of whipped cream.)

But Dukes stood firm against his boss's push back. "Trust me," he told her. "Let us play with it. I've seen what's out there in the market, and there's nothing like it."

What followed was a three-month odyssey of mating pumpkin with spice. The R&D team targeted four possibilities for the drink—high pumpkin, high spice, low pumpkin, low spice—and versions with high and low levels of both components. They tested. They refined. Joined along the way by a few others, the same gang that sampled pumpkin pies beneath paper turkey decorations in the liquid lab gathered again two or three times a week, tasting their way through these prototype versions. They jotted notes on sheets and went around the circle sharing feedback on each drink, book club style. "I've tasted a lot of pumpkin spice beverages," says Dukes. "You just keep narrowing down and narrowing down."

The pumpkin spice cabal decided the flavoring should be a sauce, not the typical flavored syrup. That extra viscosity helped mimic the proper heft of a mouthful of pie. Ultimately the version with high levels of both pumpkin and spice won consensus.

The next question: what to call the thing. "Initially we were being asked to come up with a name that matches the season," Dukes recalls. His team batted around the idea of "fall harvest latte," a name that at best didn't quite explain the drink and at worst connoted sipping on a hay bale. They settled on pumpkin spice latte, a simple name that communicated all the happy-fuzzy feelings associated with pumpkin but reflected the spices' prominence.

Early tests at 100 stores in Vancouver and Washington, DC, in the fall of 2003 portended customers might actually like this wild card of a drink. "You just looked at the sales results and you knew," Dukes remembers. "It clearly separated itself from any other beverages we had tested at that point in the market."

The company's 10-year PSL anniversary hoopla happened last year, oddly enough, but the pumpkin spice latte made its nationwide debut one decade ago this September. The following month, October 2004, company sales spiked 11 percent compared with the previous year, thanks in large part to the new hit drink. But once technology—particularly the nascent quivers of social media—caught up, it would become something even bigger.

"Every year I'll drink at least one to commemorate that it's fall," Melody Overton said of the pumpkin spice latte on a recent evening at the Starbucks on Olive Way. You might say that Overton's a fan of Starbucks. An attorney in Pioneer Square by day, she keeps a personal blog and self-published a book, both dedicated to the coffee company's general doings and her various Starbucks-related adventures—like road tripping to Sacramento to sample test drinks at locations there. She refers to her encounters with Howard (Schultz, the CEO) and Cliff (Burrows, the head of Starbucks in both North and South America) with mononymous awe and even sends Howard a birthday email every year. She'd like to convey those same wishes to Cliff, she just doesn't know his birthday.

Despite her annual pumpkin spice assignation, though, and despite having a poster of the drink hanging in her office, "I'm not actually a huge pumpkin spice latte fan," Overton confesses. "It's a little bit sweet for me."

Laila Ghambari knows what she means. The director of coffee at the local chainlets of Cherry Street coffeehouses (her dad's the founder) and winner of the 2014 United States Barista Championship, Ghambari is not ashamed to admit that she enjoys the occasional hit of pumpkin spice.

The flavor has now infiltrated coffee shops everywhere. In 2012 Cherry Street started making its own sauce, one that ratchets down the sweetness, amps up the spice, and—unlike the original—contains actual pureed pumpkin. (During a three-month window last year, Cherry Street baristas went through 24 gallons of the house pumpkin spice syrup and served up roughly 3,500 of the seasonal lattes.)

America's affection for specialty drinks stems from its collective history of drinking really bad coffee, Ghambari says. The sort that involves a screw-topped tub of granules and a little plastic scoop. "It doesn't taste good, so you put cream and sugar in it. Now, even if the coffee doesn't taste bad, people assume it's going to taste that way. They automatically order something with syrup in it"—the coffee equivalent of salting food before taking a bite.

I finally drank one myself on a chilled afternoon last fall at the Starbucks on Pier 55, in the shadow of the crumbling Alaskan Way Viaduct. When the barista called my name and plunked my order on the counter, the only thing distinguishing it from drinks that don't have their own official Twitter handles is that scrawl of "PSL" in black Sharpie on the side of the cup. (The company trademarked the acronym in 2013.) A strong, sweet aroma wafted out of the tiny hole in the lid.

The formula hasn't changed since those first days in the lab ("We'd have a revolt," says Dukes of the PSL fan base). The version that emerged from those clandestine meetings bears more resemblance to a liquefied glazed doughnut than a piece of pumpkin pie. One flavor that's conspicuously absent is the sharp rap of espresso. It's in there, though, just lurking beneath the sweetness. Perhaps even more conspicuous: the lack of any discernible pumpkin. There *is* pumpkin in the formula. Or, more precisely, pumpkin flavor. But the spices assert themselves utterly over the more delicate gourd. If this were a piece of art, the pumpkin would be formed by negative space.

While chalkboard art in Starbucks stores focuses on the pumpkins, those spices—along with that age-old trick of making something a limited-time commodity (cough, McDonald's Shamrock Shake)—are key to the mania. At least that's the theory posited by Carolyn Ross, an associate professor at the school of food science at Washington State University. "People agree it smells nice across cultures," she says of the nutmeg, cinnamon, and clove blend. "I once had a pumpkin spice latte not from Starbucks that was pumpkin-heavy, and it was awful."

But what really fuels the PSL craze? Adroit marketing and social media. Each year brings an increasingly elaborate rollout plan, involving hashtags and secret codes that "unlock" the PSL at a particular store and Facebook contests where fans vie to have the latte land in their city a week earlier than the national debut. To follow #PSL on Twitter or Instagram this time of year is to be flooded with images of those Starbucks cups, brandished, hoisted, or artfully arranged to showcase that familiar acronym scrawled on the side in black. And then, of course, there are the commercials: the one with the overzealous PSL fan air-drumming with a pair of green venti straws; or the series featuring a fully staged—and completely fake—Pumpkin Spice Days festival in a small, bucolic town, complete with cinnamon-stick-twirling contests and a Miss Pumpkin Spice pageant.

Peter Dukes the man long ago moved on to new projects within the company. But Peter Dukes the homage is 60 miles north of Starbucks HQ, in Skagit County. Just off Route 20, in the old downtown strip of Burlington, population 8,400, dwells a five-foot-tall illustration of Dukes, a deliberately rustic rendering of the sort of portrait that might gaze out from the pages of a high school history textbook.

This oddball tribute is left over from the most recent round of Pumpkin Spice Days commercials, filmed in the area in 2013 for the drink's 10th anniversary campaign. But the staffers at a nearby Starbucks, three miles north, were puzzled when I asked where it was. "I should know," confessed the motherly woman who took my order. "My daughter was in that commercial." The kindly ladies at the town visitor's center, however, received my query as if it were a totally normal one, spun me around, and pointed me toward the sidewall of the DeCamp and Stradford furniture store directly across the street.

Dukes is depicted from the shoulders up, wearing a blue polo shirt. His name is emblazoned on a white banner splayed across his chest. It's an exaggerated likeness; the real Dukes looks distinguished and slightly outdoorsy. Here the artist gave him a less-than-flattering overbite and sort of a *Dumb and Dumber*–meets–business casual haircut. "They emphasized that this was supposed to be a caricature," he had told me. (He once stopped to pay it a visit and snap a few photos while driving his daughters to summer camp in Bellingham.)

Just around the corner from Dukes's smiling likeness, Burlington's old main street still bears the false fronts, sturdy awnings, and backdrop of sloping fir trees that recall its start as a logging town. Though the PSL festival in the commercials was fictional, the town does celebrate Berry Dairy days every June. It's a true-to-life version of the agrarian American ideals the humble pumpkin represents.

What was created in a lab has taken on a life of its own and become a frothy microcosm of how contradictory those ideals can be these days. The pumpkin spice latte is loved and hated. Artificial but genuine. Manufactured by canny marketing, yet legitimately, ardently adored. We have once again become a population accustomed to consuming seasonally, be it the first rhubarb of spring, summertime berries, or a sauce engineered to summon fall from inside a corrugated cardboard sleeve while the summer sun still shines overhead.

Maverick Wine Guru Tim Hanni Rethinks the Pour

By Chris Macias

From the *Sacramento Bee*

Can one man change the entrenched assumptions of high-end wine culture? *Sacramento Bee* critic-at-large Chris Macias— himself an iconoclast who surfs between food, wine, culture, and music writing—spent some time with a wine expert who's willing to break all the rules.

Throw away your Wine Wheel. Disregard the precious pairings from restaurant sommeliers. This Master of Wine insists that much of what you've been taught about fermented grapes is just plain wrong.

Allow Tim Hanni to demonstrate.

In his two-story home on the edge of Napa's tony Silverado Resort and Spa, Hanni lines up a selection of wines on the kitchen island. Notion No. 1 to be debunked: Red wines are "heavier" than whites.

Hanni mixes a pour of white zinfandel with cabernet sauvignon in a glass. The wines quickly separate into two distinct layers, like a bottle of unshaken Italian salad dressing. The cab floats on top, outweighed by the white zin and its residual sugar.

"People say the big, heavy red wine you serve in the bigger glass, because a BIG wine needs a BIG glass, even though it's not bigger than any other wine," he said. "We have legions of wine educators telling people untruths. We need to be more responsible about the information, the expectations and the false judgments we put on people."

Many things in the wine world aren't supposed to mix. Cabernet sauvignon and oysters. Moscato and rib-eye steaks. White zinfandel and good taste. Hanni says that's a bunch of twaddle. People should be empowered to decide what tastes good to them.

In a multibillion-dollar industry that often insists on absolutes—the kind of wines meant to go with certain foods, even the kinds of people qualified to be experts—Hanni, 63, remains one of the highest-regarded and most iconoclastic figures. He's a certified Master of Wine whose anti-establishment notions might raise eyebrows or elicit smirks from colleagues, but they have others in the business reconsidering ideas once viewed as sacrosanct.

He extols the virtues of supermarket-brand moscato, a wine that's a punch line to the Riedel-swirling, first-growth-Bordeaux-collecting crowd. The best wine match for a "supertaster," someone with nature's most evolved taste buds? According to Hanni, it's white zinfandel, perhaps the lowest-hanging fruit in the hierarchy of wine connoisseurship.

"The whole industry needs to be reset," Hanni said on a recent March day. "We say, 'This is wine education and we're going to educate people,' and the information is purely and simply wrong."

There's nothing cavalier in this message. Hanni, a gregarious presence with a hard laugh, has dedicated more than 30 years of his life to the grape. He's a certified wine educator who has lectured in more than two dozen countries about flavor balancing, sensory sciences and culinary history. He's written a book, "Why You Like the Wines You Like," and developed food and wine pairing products. He popularized "umami" as a basic taste.

Much of Hanni's current efforts center on the annual Consumer Wine Awards, to be held Saturday at the McClellan Conference Center in Sacramento. It's the rare kind of competition where wine expertise won't get you a seat at the judges' table. Instead, regular folks pick the winners. It's an event that embraces "diversity of both the wines of the world and the diversity of the people who love wine," according to organizers. In other words, minutiae between a "gold" and "gold minus" sauvignon blanc will not be chin-stroked here.

Hanni co-founded the competition in 2009 as a way for the industry to better understand what people actually prefer. At the core of Hanni's belief system: Matters of taste have too many variables and can't be held to universal truths; it's better to listen to the people, not the wine careerists.

It's a revolutionary philosophy, especially for someone who has made a career in wine. But there's one more detail to know about Hanni, and true to his character, it doesn't pair well with conventional wine wisdom.

He's hasn't had a swallow of the stuff in 23 years.

Clouds in the Wine

An addict's final drink can occur almost anywhere. For Hanni, it happened at JW Marriott Phoenix Desert Ridge Resort & Spa over a glass of Meridian chardonnay, which sells for about $10 a bottle. He was a company man on a business trip, selling wine for Beringer Vineyards. The date was Dec. 16, 1993.

His new wife, Kate, had recently checked into an alcohol treatment center. She'd quit drinking 12 years before, but relapsed after meeting Hanni, already a wine industry legend. In 1989, he became one of the first two Americans to earn the Master of Wine title, the Holy Grail for certified wine professionals. Even an advanced sommelier is a mere mortal compared to a Master of Wine, who must conquer a series of grueling tests that fewer than 10 percent of participants pass.

A founding member of The Young and the Decadent, an influential group of burgeoning wine professionals, Hanni was coming to terms with a tough realization about himself: He was an alcoholic. Like his father, who also struggled with booze, Hanni was mostly a happy drunk, but his mood would darken after too many drinks. By now, Hanni was experiencing blackouts, drinking more and faster than ever. He knew it was just a matter of time before his marriage would crash and burn like his previous one.

Hanni could see his drinking days were coming to a close. The glass of chardonnay in his hand would be his last swallow of alcohol.

"I just knew I wanted to change," he said. "I don't know if I was declaring that I'd had it all—dozens of vintages of d'Yquem, 1947 Cheval Blanc, and eaten at three-star Michelin restaurants. What's next?"

But with this decision came a future as cloudy as a glass of unfiltered chardonnay. A Master of Wine who could not drink alcohol was Mario Andretti with four flat tires, Eric Clapton on a no-string Stratocaster.

Hanni broke the news to his wife once he returned home from Phoenix. She worked in real estate, but Hanni was essentially the breadwinner. "The real estate market was dead at that time, and he's a Master of Wine, which is a rare title to have," said Kate Hanni. "I was frantic that it wasn't going to work out."

Hanni also had to tell his bosses that he was done with alcohol. He had recently been appointed director of international development for Beringer Vineyards, a signature Napa winery which was then owned by Nestlé. Hanni says his employers were supportive, and offered him work in non-alcohol segments of their parent company.

A trained chef, Hanni considered focusing on food. But his heart remained with wine, the subject he knew best, even if a swallow could send him into a downward spiral. Hanni used his vacation time and checked into a rehabilitation facility for 28 days. He hoped he could continue to work with wine, albeit with a different angle.

"By not drinking, maybe I could become a better observer," said Hanni.

But it wouldn't be long before he found himself with Bordeaux glass in hand once again.

New Approach

Some people collect stamps. Others art. Hanni, who was born in Ohio and raised in South Florida, collects flavors: Experimental seasonings from Japan, monosodium glutamate powders, salts, spices, extracts and the sweet-tasting amino acid glycine.

"I have cabinets full of hundreds and hundreds of flavors and things," Hanni said, poking through the garage, where he parks a beloved 2005 Lotus Elise autographed by Andretti. "I'm just so curious. I'm not diagnosed anything, but I am very OCD. I am very ADHD, and also generally to a degree dyslexic and really numerically dyslexic."

Unable to enjoy wine for its intoxicating properties, Hanni obsesses over flavors and how they're perceived, especially in terms of pairing the beverage with food. He's proposing a new paradigm for wine appreciation, one that values personal preferences and accounts for the wide variety of taste sensitivities among people.

Hanni divides wine drinkers into different "vinotypes," ranging from "tolerant" tasters who need big flavors to perk up their taste buds, to "hypersensitive" and "sweet" types who would wince at bitterness and other pronounced tastes. Hanni says you match the wine with the diner, not the dinner. Hard-and-fast rules about, say, a delicate fish requiring a light white wine don't apply to Hanni. Sensitivity to taste is as unique as a fingerprint.

Hanni has worked with sensory scientists around the world to form his conclusions. He's taken pictures of some of the industry's most noted tongues, including those from gourmet grocer Darrell Corti and wine critic Jancis Robinson, to count their taste buds. In his research, Hanni found that some people have fewer than 500 taste buds, others more than 11,000. Hanni found that a number alone doesn't mean much.

"You can count taste buds and make certain generalizations, but how many receptors are there at the end of each bud? Which kind of receptors?" said Hanni. "And at what intensity is the transmission of the connection to the brain?"

This quest to better understand individual taste led Hanni back to a practice that's seemingly incompatible with sobriety: sipping wine. To be clear: He doesn't swallow it. He tastes and then spits it out. It doesn't happen often, he says, and he certainly doesn't recommend this practice to fellow recovering alcoholics.

Though it's dangerous for a recovering addict, Hanni said he felt confident enough in the taste-and-spit approach. Maintaining his marriage and professional standing were enough motivation to keep him from losing control again. His wife had seen him kick a three-pack-a-day cigarette habit and believed in his resolution.

"I can't rationalize what I do," said Hanni. "(But) I've never at any point been at risk at relapsing. I don't know why."

The triggers would seem to be everywhere around Hanni's home: The crystal decanters in a cabinet, the samples of distilled chardonnay under a counter, winemaking equipment in the backyard.

Dr. Michael Parr, a Sacramento addiction specialist, would never recommend this scenario for his patients. But he says maintaining sobriety while working in the alcohol industry can be accomplished under very select circumstances. Hanni's case is definitely the exception, like an open spot on the Sine Qua Non wine club list.

"It's potentially dangerous," he said. "But can someone do it? Yes. It's a very unique situation. It's not an issue of morality or willpower. It's being hypervigilant and always keeping in mind the fear of not wanting to go back to what it was before, that you're just a drink or two away."

Though Hanni doesn't drink, he wants others to feel empowered with their wine choices, even if it's the much-maligned white zinfandel. He says the wine is fine, especially for someone who's a "hypersensitive" taster. A bottle of Petrus, though one of the ultimate red wines from Bordeaux, might normally make someone with a pronounced sweet tooth wince.

"If you're truly a supertaster in the highest sense, you will not like cabernet, you will not like pinot noir or sauvignon blanc," said Hanni. "You will genetically only be able to drink low-alcohol sweet wines. The true supertasters are drinking moscato and white zin."

So break the rules. Decide what tastes best to you. It's a message Hanni's hoping other wine educators will embrace.

"We need to be more responsible about the information, the expectations and false judgments we put on people," he said. "I've had successes and I've had failures, but ultimately I have a mission: To simply make wine enjoyable to more people, and not operate on any preconceived notions anymore."

Kids These Days

By Sara Deseran

From *San Francisco Magazine*

We all know them, don't we?—and it's no surprise that they abound in the Bay Area's rarified food culture. *San Francisco Magazine* editor-at-large Sara Deseran, who's also a co-owner of the restaurants Tacolicious and Chino, is a savvy observer of the foodie kid phenomenon, with three children of her own.

My nine-year-old son, Moss, has been exhibiting signs of food snobbery for a while now. The other day, he refused some Jell-O chocolate pudding as if it were beneath him. He lobbied for months to eat at the "real" Delfina—not just the pizzeria. And he asked me to buy him a foam charger after watching David Chang wield one on *The Mind of a Chef*. "What the heck are you going to do with a foam charger?" I asked. "Make Ferran Adrià's microwave cake," he replied.

And then there was the time that I took him to the Divisadero Popeyes, whose rumored closing had sparked in me a nostalgic desire for one last taste of deliciously fried commodity chicken. I assumed that my boys would find it exhilarating to be allowed a normally ver-boten lunch of fast food. But instead of getting high fives, I got judged. While his 13-year-old brother, Silas, gingerly nibbled on a drumstick, Moss flat-out refused to ingest even a biscuit crumb. "I don't want to get diabetes," he said staunchly, on the brink of calling child services. "Who told you about diabetes?" was the only response I could muster. It's a strange feeling to see the values that you've been attempting to instill in your child come back to bite you. It makes me wonder: Have I created a wunderkind or a monster?

The boys' father, a juice-cleansing chiropractor, might be responsible for their overt health consciousness, and I, a professional food writer, and their stepdad, a restaurateur, are probably to blame for Moss's culinary effeteness. But we are far from the only culprits. The Bay Area as a whole is a fertile breeding ground for juvenile foodies who are abnormally nutrition-minded. Inspired in part by the Edible Schoolyard Project, public and private schools alike proudly trot out garden programs intended to educate kids about the glories of freshly harvested chicories and undervalued root vegetables. The San Francisco Unified School District Wellness Policy forbids schools from selling junk food in their cafeterias and vending machines—not to mention serving soda and potato chips at class parties.

On the epicurean side of things, our shores boast at least a dozen cooking programs for kids (Junior Chef Stars, based on the Peninsula, starts teaching kids knife safety at age three). And then there's TV: On Fox's *MasterChef Junior*, 8- to 13-year-olds compete for $100,000; the Food Network, not to be trumped, launched *Kids Baking Championship*. The underage foodie obsession has spread to higher-brow realms, too: The cover of the *New York Times Magazine*'s 2014 food issue featured Flynn McGarry, a 16-year-old, home-schooled fine-dining "chef" who conjures dishes like seawater-brined uni with carrots and coffee. In January he presented a $160 nine-course pop-up at San Francisco's Michelin-starred Atelier Crenn. It sold out.

Moss, meanwhile, is transfixed by *MasterChef Junior*—to the point of referring to our kitchen counter as his "station." Ever since Gordon Ramsay submitted the young chefs to a fried egg challenge, Moss has been practicing making flawless eggs every morning before school. He's also starting to define himself by his palate, serving as my companion for Korean barbecue and Indian thali. At the sushi bar, he's the weird child kneeling on his stool so that he can peek over the glass to watch the chefs make nigiri.

Yes, Moss can be a bit insufferable (if cute). But given that we live in a city where good food is often conflated with existential enlightenment, I have to ask myself: What, exactly, is the problem? What's so off-putting about a pint-size epicure?

Perhaps it's an issue of privilege and perspective. I like to think that my obsession with good eating is the kind that stems from a relatively deprived upbringing backed by years of culinary bootstrapping. I grew up in Baton Rouge in the '70s, well before grocery stores started selling lemongrass and gorgonzola. Gumbo aside, my hometown was an average place to eat, and while my parents were great cooks, we didn't bat an eye at having Popeyes for a treat. The most worldly restaurant exposure I had before the age of nine was eating a strip mall lunch of Lebanese shawarma.

But Moss is growing up in a horn of plenty, a city where farmers' markets abound, restaurants sling everything from $2 tacos to $42 steak frites, and city government is a vocal proponent of good nutrition. Many Bay Area kids, it's true, don't have access to sufficient food, healthy or otherwise—but for those fortunates whose parents are able and willing to make eating well a priority, good food is here for the taking. And take I have, creating in the process this heirloom tomato-sniffing child. So it's incumbent upon me to keep him grounded—to make sure that he has an appreciation for the incredible privilege he enjoys, but also some humility. And in that, I fear, I'm failing.

Daniel Duane, the Bernal Heights author of *How to Cook Like a Man*—and an obsessive eater since his birth in Berkeley—shares my anxieties. He and his wife have two daughters, one of whom has taken to cooking out of the El Bulli staff-meal cookbook. "I started thinking about this when my eldest, Hannah, was really little," Duane says. "I'd take her to the farmers' market, and she'd scream, 'They have channies!' which meant chanterelles, and I'd find myself feeling this mixture of pride and profound embarrassment."

Of course, you don't need to be a food writer to raise this kind of kid. My friends Julia and Charlie work in law and tech, respectively, and their son, Zach, now 13, has simply followed in their food-loving footsteps. "We went to our friend's house, and they made mac and cheese for the kids and quiche for the adults," Julia says. "Zach asked for quiche, and the adults were like, 'Whoa, we've never seen a kid who will eat quiche.'" While Julia delights in Zach's tastes, she is also keen that he not be rude to kids who don't share them. "It's super fun and exciting when you have a child who's open to trying different food," she says. "But it's also important that he be sensitive to the politics of it."

For some perspective, I turned to Karen Rogers, the founder of Sprouts Cooking Club, a kids' cooking school that's been around since 2005. I figured that she'd seen it all, and she has: from the disadvantaged kids to whom Sprouts provides scholarships—some have never heard of an eggplant—to the, well, less disadvantaged. "We were doing a market cooking class at Oliveto in Oakland," Rogers comments, "and a kid comes up to me and says, 'I'm training for *MasterChef*.' And we said, 'When are tryouts?' And he said, 'Two years.'"

When I tell Rogers of my anxieties about Moss turning into some kind of pompous braggart, it's clear that she thinks I'm overreacting. "It's such a beautiful movement," she says of the increasing number of children interested in cooking. "We're empowering kids to preserve their health. I think it's awesome that we're so focused on the next generation, even if it's a trend that we're seeing largely with parents who have the means and knowledge to take the time to teach their kids."

For my part, I've started a program for Moss that I'm calling Unlearning Food Snobbism (named after the Unlearning Racism workshop that I was required to take at UC Santa Cruz). Its edicts: No criticizing another person's cooking; no snubbing your friend's Lunchables; and, most of all, no showing off. Suffice it to say, it's a learning process. The other night, I dined at Ichi Sushi with my sons, Julia, Charlie, and Zach. Within seconds of the menu's presentation, Zach exclaimed, "Okonomiyaki! I love that!" Moss, of course, echoed his enthusiasm for the Japanese pancake. Meanwhile, Silas took a look at the menu and paused for a second, his eyebrows scrunching in honest confusion. "What's sake?" he said, rhyming it with "cake." Zach and Moss looked at him, slightly appalled, while I noted that when it comes to nature versus nurture, the jury is still out. As part of his unlearning, Moss was told to cool it. "Silas," Zach said. "It's *saké*. Not sake."

At that moment, though, I was delighted with both of my kids: Silas for being unwittingly, and refreshingly, normal—a kid who appreciates food as just food, not something to be intellectually consumed by. And Moss for knowing what sake is, 12 years before he can legally drink it. For a parent, balance is everything.

How to Get People to Cook More? Get Eaters to Complain Less.

By Tamar Haspel

From the *Washington Post*

In her monthly *Washington Post* column "Unearthed," Tamar Haspel writes about the intertwined issues of food policy, health, and the environment with a lively, funny, pull-no-punches style. She's equally plain-spoken here, on the vexed issue of why Americans don't cook more.

We're being told to cook. The benefits attributed to home cooking and its corollary, the family dinner, include lower weight, better diet quality and decreased risk for kids' smoking, drinking and using drugs. When health authorities tick off the factors leading to our obesity epidemic, the decline of home cooking is generally on the list.

Does that mean home-cooked family dinners make those good things happen? Or could it be that they're just markers for well-functioning families that succeed in other ways? We don't have enough research to know for sure, but even if a home-cooked dinner doesn't transform family life, there's still one strong reason to cook: If you're looking for an affordable, healthful meal, home cooking is your best, and sometimes your only, option. Every expert I spoke with agreed that home-cooked meals tend to be more nutritious and less calorie-dense than takeout, fast-food and restaurant meals.

Perhaps it's that health halo that imbues the act of cooking with a kind of mystique. It's not just the result, but also the process, that matters. In his book *Cooked: A Natural History of Transformation*, Michael

Pollan asks, "How many of us still do the kind of work that engages us in a dialogue with the material world that concludes ... with such a gratifying and delicious sense of closure?" In his kitchen, "even the most ordinary dish follows a satisfying arc of transformation, magically becoming something more than the sum of its ordinary parts."

In other people's kitchens, the magic isn't always apparent. A recent study of home cooking, published in the journal *Contexts*, had researchers from North Carolina State University interview the mothers in 150 middle- and low-income households and sit in on 40 of their family dinners. Their paper, "The Joy of Cooking?" painted a picture of harried women trying to shoehorn dinner into tight days and budgets. "I just hate the kitchen," says Samantha, a single mother of three. "Having to come up with a meal and put it together. I know I can cook, but it's the planning of the meal, and seeing if they're going to like it, and the mess that you make. And then, the mess afterwards. . . . If it was up to me, I wouldn't cook."

I suspect that most of us who cook sometimes feel like Pollan and sometimes feel like Samantha, but studies of family mealtime dynamics find a lot more Samanthas. Which leads the scientists, doctors and public health officials trying to improve the way Americans eat to focus on identifying, and then lowering, the barriers that stand between busy working parents and healthful home-cooked meals.

The focus has been on the cook. She (and it's almost always a she) doesn't have time, she doesn't have skills, she doesn't have access to fresh ingredients. But one line in "The Joy of Cooking?" jumped out at me. In all of the meals they watched, the researchers wrote, "we rarely observed a meal in which at least one family member didn't complain about the food." And that's when there's an observer in the room! If you're one of those fortunate cooks who takes pleasure in putting dinner on the table for your family every day, ask yourself how long you would last if someone complained about the food at almost every meal. Me, I'd throw in the kitchen towel before the week was out.

Why doesn't some of the research on the barriers to home cooking take a look at the ingrates who are doing the eating, rather than the hard-working women doing the cooking? The book that describes the state of American home cooking isn't *Cooked*. It's Russell Hoban's 1966 children's classic, *The Little Brute Family*: "In the morning, Mama cooked a sand and gravel porridge, and the family snarled and grimaced as they spooned it up. No one said 'Please.' No one said 'Thank you,' and no one said 'How delicious,' because it was not delicious. . . . In the evening Mama served a stew of sticks and stones, and the family ate it with growls and grumbling."

There's not a whole lot of data on why people complain at meals, but there are two trends that might be taking a toll on the dinnertime dynamic. The first is "kid food."

According to Barbara Fiese, director of the Family Resiliency Center at the University of Illinois at Urbana-Champaign, many versions of foods, often sweet and calorie-dense, have been developed specifically for, and marketed specifically to, children. The industry recognizes kids' "pester power," and its goal is to get the kids to persuade the parents— sometimes by the time-tested tantrum method—to buy the food. "Although there's not much data on how often kids get separate meals at the table," says Fiese, "more parents are reporting that they feel pressure to prepare kids' meals."

Sales data for kid food—the snacks, drinks, cereals and meals targeted at children—back Fiese up. In the United States, the category is estimated at $23.2 billion annually and is growing faster than the market as a whole. That's more than $500 for every kid under 10.

Kids have been taught that there is special food just for them, and Fiese says that 10 percent of kids will throw a tantrum if they don't get the food they want. It's easy to see how peace is sometimes more important than broccoli.

The second trend is like kid food, only for grown-ups: It's the processed, sweet, salty, calorie-dense adult foods that are convenient, inexpensive and ubiquitous. "It's so easy to get extremely palatable food that's been perfectly concocted to be absolutely delicious," says Julie Lumeng, an associate professor at the University of Michigan Center for Human Growth and Development. And that makes it hard for a home-cooked meal to compete. "The expectation of how tasty dinner is going to be is out of control," she says.

Prepared and processed foods are made by people whose job it is to formulate delicious dishes. In some cases, they devote vast resources to irresistibility. (Michael Moss's *Salt, Sugar, Fat* is an eye-opening chronicle of the process.) They don't care whether you eat your vegetables or whether you're getting fat. Their job is to make you like what they cook. So the hard, cold fact of it is, as Lumeng says, "the food you cook at home is often not as tasty." No one says "how delicious" because it is not delicious.

Of course, that's not always true. Some skilled home cooks turn out deliciousness night after night. And if you can do that, it's sometimes difficult to see how other people can't. As with anything else, once you get the hang of it, it's not that hard. But it's easy for those of us who do food for a living—by growing it, cooking it or writing about it—to lose track of how tough it is for people who do other things for a living to master home cooking.

And so, for too many people too much of the time, that home-cooked meal will not please those it has been cooked for, who go into it with expectations set by the many diabolically palatable meals they have under their belt. And those people complain. And the cook loses any inclination she might have had to spend yet more time in the kitchen to get better at this, and the dinner dynamic spirals downward.

How can we reverse the trend? Jayne Fulkerson, director of the University of Minnesota's Center for Child and Family Health Promotion Research, has a suggestion: Get those ingrates, particularly the kids, into the kitchen, because "kids are more likely to accept a meal they've had a role in preparing." She's working on a project that gets children involved in cooking and has found that "you can get the kids engaged in thinking of what they want to make, and pulling it off, and looking in wonder at what they just created."

Hey, wait a minute! That sounds a lot like Michael Pollan's description. He gets criticized for being tone-deaf to the real-life constraints of working parents, but I think it's important to keep his version of cooking in our sights. On a good day, there is wonder in transforming humdrum ingredients into a satisfying, good-tasting meal; if kids see the magic, it's not just a manifestation of elite privilege.

Would that strategy work for adults? Fulkerson says "parents can be as picky as kids," and she thinks the same principle applies. So, if you're an adult or a kid over about the age of 10 and you're guilty of complaining, grab an apron and see whether you can't do better.

I asked Daniel Post Senning, co-author of the 18th edition of *Emily Post's Etiquette* (and great-great-grandson of that etiquette icon), about complaining at the table, a practice so brazenly discourteous that mention of its prevalence left him "slack-jawed." When he recovered his wits, he had several suggestions for changing the family dinner dynamic. First, he seconded Fulkerson's strategy: "If you're not participating in the process, you don't always have standing to offer a critique," he says. "Offer to participate in a meaningful way: planning and shopping, if not cooking."

And even then, be careful. "The compliment sandwich—praise, critique, praise—would be appropriate. There's always something you can thank someone for when they've worked on your behalf." Also, "have a solution." Don't care for creamed spinach? Volunteer to try roasting cauliflower.

What you don't do when someone—probably someone you love—has made a meal for you is gripe about the food at the table. Just don't.

The Little Brute Family stumbles through a grim and joyless life eating sticks and stones until, one day, Baby Brute finds a daisy, and the daisy gives him a good feeling. That evening, at supper, "when his bowl was filled with stew he said, 'Thank you.'" From that moment, the good feeling catches on. "When Papa Brute went out for sticks and stones the next day, he found wild berries, salad greens, and honey, and he brought them home instead. At supper, everyone said 'How delicious!' because it was delicious."

Okay, *The Little Brute Family* is a fable, and decreeing that, from this day forth, no one shall complain about dinner won't magically turn the home-cooking trend around. But, unlike most interventions, it doesn't cost us anything. And if home cooking is something worth encouraging, and I think it is, we all need to take a tip from Baby Brute. When someone cooks a meal for you, whether or not you found your daisy, here's an appropriate thing to say: Thank you.

Cooking's Not for Everyone

By Molly Watson

From *Edible San Francisco*

Bay Area food writer and recipe developer Molly Watson (check out her delightful blog TheDinnerFiles.com) offers another real-world perspective on America's vanishing kitchen skills—reminding us what the high-minded foodie elite always seems to forget.

We are bombarded with this truth: Family dinner is a magical and yet endangered institution. What was once commonplace—lo, quotidian!—for people who lived in the same house is, because of dual-income households and yoga classes and Lego workshops and screens of all sizes and Hot Pockets, going the way of whalebone corsetry.

Sure, it exists, but more as a fetish object than something you pull out and put on everyday.

We must fight for its survival, we are told. Not only is it an insanely effective way to stay connected as a family, but it's even better at getting the kids into Harvard than mission trips to Guatemala and it can coax elves to dance with unicorns in our backyards.

And here's the latest promise coming directly from the better-food movement: It will de-industrialize our food system. That last bit only happens, though, if someone in the house cooks this magical meal. And herein lies the problem.

When people who write about food for a living tell everyone else how easy it is to make dinner (and I'm including myself here), a suspicious eyebrow should be raised and the obvious question asked: Isn't that like an accountant saying that doing your own taxes is easy?

Look, I'm all about family dinner. We all have to eat. My mom cooked family dinner most nights. So do I. I like to cook—it's part of the reason I write about food instead of, say, the competitive pétanque circuit or the kinship relations of a tribe in Papua New Guinea.

If I'd only ever put dinner on the table while working as a freelance writer, I'd probably still be beating on the "everyone cook" drum kit I used to have. But for awhile there I had a staff job that required a commute. If I left before 7 and drove like my mother, I could make it door-to-door in 27 minutes. When I let up on the lead foot, it took at least 45 minutes, and I quickly saw the problem with family dinner.

It's a beast. A beast that needs to be fed. Every single night. Whether it's easy or not.

I could no longer honestly concur, as I once had, with Laurie David's assessment that "To not be cooking in your own home is to be missing one of the best parts of the day."

It was a humbling glimpse into the lives of people who don't like to cook, because the lack of time and the fact that as a food writer and recipe developer I'd already spent most of the day cooking turned me into someone who no longer looked forward to making dinner.

Suddenly I understood in a visceral way the trajectory of humanity—the minute people get any money they tend to pay people to do three things: clean their house, watch their kids and cook their dinner. As my husband and I checked in to confirm who was picking up the kid and what dinner might be, I came to understand why so many housewives used to have a "pork chops on Tuesday" weekly rotation: at least the menu didn't need to be reinvented every night.

What had once been a real creative and satisfyingly productive outlet during my day became a dirge. I saw why feminists used to commonly lump cooking in with the rest of housework as mind-numbing, endlessly repetitive labor, the fruits of which were tied primarily to other people's appreciation of it. "The validity of the cook's work is to be found only in the mouths of those at her table," Simone de Beauvoir wrote. "She needs their approbation, demands that they appreciate her dishes and call for second helpings; she is upset if they are not hungry, to the point that one wonders whether the fried potatoes are for her husband or her husband for the fried potatoes."

So where I once stood out front twirling a baton in a the-world-would-be-a-better-place-if-everyone-cooked parade, I stopped telling people they should at least try cooking. I no longer pontificated about how easy it was to make a homemade dinner on a regular basis. I started to see the call to whisks and the homage paid to homemade bread that have become part-and-parcel of the food movement as what they are for anyone who doesn't feel like cooking: oppressive bullshit.

First, it's worth noting the obvious: Responsibility for getting dinner on the table still falls disproportionately on women's shoulders. It's changing, for sure, and I know plenty of men who cook for their families. But at this moment in time, calling for people to cook more for their families, without specifically calling out dudes, is asking women to do it.

Equally important, when you tell grown-ups who have a decent sense of what they like and don't like that they have to do the latter, they tend to do one of two things: the healthy tune out, the neurotic feel guilty. Neither of those outcomes gets people to engage more deeply with their food, to know where it comes from, to ask how it's produced.

Don't get me wrong, I believe everyone should know how to cook, at least some basics, but not because learning to cook is "the most important thing an ordinary person can do to help reform the American food system," as Michael Pollan claims, but because it's a basic life skill. Everyone should also know how to sew on a button, use a drill, change a tire and perform CPR. I no more believe there is some larger good in cooking than I think anyone who doesn't want to should sew their wedding outfit or build their houses or never call AAA or 911.

There is tremendous arrogance, I now see, in the assumption that if people would just give cooking a try, they'd like it enough to become more interested in food instead of getting pissed off that they're wasting so much time doing something they don't like. For many people cooking is like gardening for me: something they're only glad to have done and which they fantasize about paying someone else to take on. Wouldn't it be awesome, they think, to hire a personal chef?

About the connection between everyone cooking and a more sustainable food system—it's bunk. I don't see how it matters whether the locally grown organic kale salad with a lemon dressing was made by someone in my house or not. That fried foods are easier to produce on a large-scale level than fresh tossed salads (and fresh tossed salads easier to produce on a small-scale, home kitchen level) is a hurdle to people who want to feed their families healthful food without cooking, but it's not a roadblock. That it is a hurdle is something systemic that needs fixing, but everyone cooking their own food isn't a realistic solution. There would be a whole lot less labor abuses in the garment industry if we all sewed our own clothes, but can anyone imagine suggesting more home sewing as a first step towards changing that system, much less present it as a key component of a long-term workable solution?

Home cooking is good for the food system because it leads to or involves other things. People who cook tend to have healthier diets because of what they are cooking; there's no magic fairy dust released during the cooking process that makes the food better (and if there is, I'm pretty sure it doesn't happen when the cook is bitter about stirring the pot).

People who cook are more likely to pay attention to the quality of the ingredients they use, the thinking goes, so there's a greater chance they're going to shop at a farmers market or buy organically grown foods or, at the very least, buy whole food ingredients instead of processed foods.

Yet, it's easy to imagine how the environmental good of more communally produced food might be greater than more home cooking. A more efficient use of resources is certainly possible, both on the raw material side—25% to 30% of food that makes its way into U.S. homes is simply tossed out—and the auxiliary elements like water and power. Baking bread, for example, can be a satisfying activity for those who like it, but there's a reason bakeries took off. It takes a lot of sustained heat to bake bread, if nothing else. Having one reliably hot oven per community makes some good wood-cutting sense. Then having an oven where people can place their pots to cook up their stew or casseroles, after the bread is baked but the oven is still hot, while they tend to other things, as used to be common practice in plenty of rural villages, seems like a decently sustainable practice to the modern eye.

Somehow the food movement's "how can we make people who don't cook care as much as people who do" became "we should try to get more people to cook." And I know how that happened: People who write about food, in general, like to cook. If you like to cook, it's easy to say it's easy. It's easy to say everyone else should do this thing that I like to do; less easy to see why people who don't do it don't even want to do it. I know because that used to be me saying it. I have changed my tune.

Along with providing resources for those who want to cook or cook more, those of us who care about the food system should create ways to make family dinner truly easier, more enjoyable, more healthful and more delicious for everyone, even those people who don't want to cook it. That realism, more than all the chiding in the world, would raise food consciousness and make sure everyone cares as much about the quality of that food and how it's produced as we do.

When told we must cook the family dinner to harness all of its power, we need to push back, de Beauvoir style: Is the food system for our cooking or our cooking for the food system?

There is no moral good or bad in cooking. I am always struck by the language people—or, to be exact, women—use when commenting on the amount of cooking I do. They say that I am "good." It is often followed by a confession about how they are "bad" because they hardly ever cook. It's the culinary Madonna-whore dichotomy.

People who are passionate about quality food and a more sustainable food system shouldn't be out encouraging such nonsense. We shouldn't be proselytizing cooking and fetishizing the homemade. We need to debunk those ideals and get the focus back on making all food—whether homecooked, convenience, order-in or just plain fast—good food.

Me, I would like a better food system for the sake of my cooking. But also so that, when no one in the house feels like lighting the stove, we know whatever food we choose to eat will be as healthful and sustainably produced as possible. No one should have to cook to make that happen.

The Restaurant Biz

Dinner Lab Hopes to Build the World's First Data-Driven Restaurant. But Is That a Good Thing?

By Besha Rodell

From *LA Weekly*

LA Weekly's restaurant critic since 2012, Australian-born Besha Rodell is still a reporter at heart, continually taking the pulse of Southern California's food culture. In a city where image is everything, it's no wonder that restaurateurs would convene focus groups for new dishes and dining concepts.

The dinner takes place in a Studio City storefront, one that used to be a yoga studio but now feels as barren as any gutted store-front waiting for its next inhabitant. Tables are set up in long rows, a makeshift kitchen in back, a makeshift bar in the corner.

We're well into the meal, and only slightly past the social awkward-ness that comes with dining alongside strangers, when the waitress deftly delivers our third course. A hush comes over the table as all 12 diners pick up tiny spoons and dig into what she's given us. Held in small glass pots, a warm, duck egg custard comes topped with a jellied, tart, black pepper jus, studded with halved red grapes. The grapes burst in our mouths, providing fresh contrast to the silken custard.

The diners around me spend a few noiseless minutes tasting, star-ing intently at their own hands and spoons and food as they eat. Then utensils drop, quickly replaced by pencils. We scribble furiously on the white comment card before us. It's at this point that we begin to hear some opinions, though they're slightly guarded; the outpouring of honesty is going on paper. You wouldn't want someone to steal your thoughts.

"The temperature just weirded me out," one woman says to her companion.

"The texture is an issue," another diner offers.

"This is one of the coolest things I've eaten in a long time," I think, apparently alone in my opinion.

Welcome to Dinner Lab, the country's most sprawling series of pop-up dinners. Begun in 2012 and now in cities all over the country, Dinner Lab holds up to 19 events weekly, from L.A. to Atlanta to Chicago. It's much like any pop-up experience—odd spaces, prix fixe offerings, chefs trying out new ideas that perhaps wouldn't make it onto a restaurant menu . . . not quite yet, at least.

The difference with Dinner Lab, aside from the sheer scope of the operation, is the feedback component. Each guest is asked to fill out a comment card addressing almost everything about the meal: each course, the wine pairing with that course, the taste and creativity of each plate of food. And that's only what you're asked at an actual dinner. When you sign up for Dinner Lab, many more questions are part of the process, including your relationship status, your drink of preference and how you "rate yourself as a foodie." (I choose "Early Adopter: I tell people where to eat" from five potential choices.)

This mountain of feedback and personal information from thousands of diners over hundreds of dinners adds up to what Brian Bordainick, Dinner Lab's founder and CEO, believes to be a gold mine. And he plans to use it to open the world's first data-driven restaurant.

"We're going to reverse-engineer a restaurant," Bordainick explains. "We're going to use our data to open the world's first entirely open-sourced restaurant. A programmable restaurant, if you will."

How does he plan to do this? Over the course of the summer, Dinner Lab has nine chefs traveling throughout the country. Each chef is cooking at least one dinner in 10 different cities—that's 90 dinners, minimum. At the end, Dinner Lab will gather the data collected, select a chef and pick a city, mainly based on customer feedback. Then they'll open a restaurant. The who, where and how of this, supposedly, will be based almost entirely on data.

All of this poses a number of questions, the most obvious of which—will it work?—is perhaps the least important. But the questions that spring from that initial "will it work?" conundrum are integral to the way we eat and the business of restaurants going forward.

Can you use data to determine trends that have yet to fully emerge? Can you use data to outsmart the restaurant gods and build a business that's less likely to fail?

Are the people who go to pop-ups inclined to have insight that leads to a successful brick-and-mortar restaurant? What's the difference between this and trying to build a restaurant based on an overview of Yelp reviews?

Do people even know what they want? And, in an era in which diners are increasingly opting for unique food events and pop-ups, isn't Dinner Lab's undertaking akin to using the information gathered from a successful personal-computer business to start a typewriter company?

D inner Lab began as a New Orleans experiment, one driven by the fact that there isn't much to eat late at night in that city, apart from bad pizza sold out of the all-night daiquiri houses on Bourbon Street. While New Orleans is a food city, that food has been mainly limited to just a few genres. "New Orleans has a lot of Creole and Southern contemporary cuisine," Bordainick says, "but there's a huge dearth of variety." So in August 2012, he began setting up pop-up dinners with different chefs. The dinners started at midnight.

"It was a terrible idea," Bordainick says. "People showed up already hammered. It was not a very good decision-making process on our behalf." But the foundation had been laid for a pop-up business, with Bordainick's startup collaborating with different chefs for one-off events.

After figuring out that regular pop-ups were "a pain in the ass, and don't make very much money," Bordainick came up with the model Dinner Lab has been using ever since: a subscription-based, membership format. Customers pay for an annual membership and then gain access to ticketed dinners, for which they also pay. Memberships cost between $100 and $200, depending on your city (in Los Angeles, it's $175). The price of dinners varies but is comparable to other dinner events—around $80 per person, including booze and service.

This model worked. It worked well enough that eventually Bordainick and Dinner Lab were able to expand from New Orleans to other cities. First Austin, Texas; then Nashville, Tennessee; then New York; and then, in September of last year, Los Angeles.

Dinner Lab now is in 19 cities and has about 50 employees.

Despite the membership fee, which effectively adds a big surcharge to the cost of dining out, people have signed up all over the country after hearing about it through word-of-mouth or local media. Most of the L.A. members I ask first heard of its launch through Daily Candy, the now defunct lifestyle email newsletter.

Bordainick now spends most of his time on fundraising. He has raised $2.1 million to date, much of it from one of the original founders of Whole Foods, even as new investors are being brought on board all the time.

Bordainick himself is very much in the model of startup dudes. Young (28), tall (6 foot 3 inches), white, with a vocabulary that swerves easily into corporate-speak (he talks a lot about being "in that space" when discussing the directions the business might take), he relishes his role as an entrepreneur. When I first met him to discuss this story, he said he'd be wearing "a green hoodie and shorts—typical entrepreneur garb." If he weren't into food, he could be a character on *Silicon Valley*.

A native of New York's Hudson Valley, Bordainick moved to New Orleans right after Hurricane Katrina to work for Teach for America. After that, he went to work in the mayor's office. Then he worked in education technology, where he was immersed in a culture that thought data could save the world.

Now he's trying to use data to save dinner.

Bordainick says the feedback component of Dinner Lab first was requested by the chefs working the pop-ups—often, they were trying out new ideas at Dinner Lab, dishes they thought were too experimental for the restaurants that employed them. A system was put in place, in which every dish at every dinner was rated. As the company expanded and the volume turned the feedback into data, Bordainick became aware of how valuable that much market research might be.

"It got to the point where we could predict trends before they happened. The fact that octopus is a huge ingredient now, that everyone's using it? We knew that way before it happened," he says.

How? In part because octopus dishes score particularly high at Dinner Lab dinners but also because, when people sign up for a dinner, they're asked why they bought tickets to that particular event. "We saw people saying they came for the octopus, for instance."

I find this hard to believe. People are choosing a night out, spending hundreds of dollars, based on one dish? But when I ask my fellow diners at the meal with the warm custard (which also has an octopus dish on the set menu) why they are at that particular meal, three different people say to me, "Because of the octopus."

Restaurants typically are viewed as risk-filled business ventures. They have a reputation for high failure rates and low profitability, with ingredients for success that are never easy to predict. Studies show that restaurant failure rates aren't that different from other small businesses, but lenders still see them as much more precarious: It's practically impossible to get a bank loan to start a restaurant. Hence the need for individual investors.

And overnight success doesn't always mean a place lasts. While there's little definitive national data on restaurant failure rates, various local studies indicate the rate is somewhere between 23 and 60 percent as you go from the first to the fifth year of operation.

The most extensive research, done about 10 years ago by Ohio State University's Hospitality Management program, showed that about one in four restaurants closes or is sold within the first year of business. At three years in, three in five restaurants are closed or change hands.

It's this riddle that Bordainick hopes to solve with Dinner Lab—to create a restaurant that's guaranteed to succeed.

It's easy to dismiss the very concept of Dinner Lab and the tour as slick gimmickry, but once you drill down past the "data-driven" sales pitch, Bordainick starts to make a lot of sense. The "winning" chef from the tour will be chosen based on his score with diners, and also his ability to stick to a budget, keep food costs reasonable and work well with others. After each dinner, the support crew is asked to rate the chef on leadership, execution and how easy it was to work with him. "If someone is a dick, we don't want to work with them," Bordainick says.

And so, at the end of the tour, that leaves a chef who has consistently cooked food that the public has enjoyed, who has had national exposure, and who also can manage a budget and be a good boss. That's a hard thing to find in any field.

The chefs are mostly sous chefs and chefs de cuisine from the country's best restaurants. When you look through their bios, names such as Eleven Madison Park, Momofuku and Per Se litter the blurbs. They're exactly the types who are on the verge of becoming executive chefs but don't have an easy path to get there.

The regular route to becoming an executive chef can take years of networking and/or fundraising. With culinary schools turning out more graduates every year, even having a pedigreed restaurant on your résumé doesn't guarantee a job running your own kitchen, and first-time executive chefs hardly ever get a gig where they're allowed to execute their own vision.

Dinner Lab is offering these chefs a way to bypass the hard route of applying for job after job, or finding their own angel investors. They just have to uproot their lives, take to the road, and then beat out eight other highly qualified applicants.

Aaron Grosskopf, the chef who made the duck egg custard, is a Napa-based private chef looking to find his way back into the restaurant world. He says he had to turn his life upside down to accommodate the logistics of the tour, but he has a job to come back to if needed.

For him, it's about road testing his ideas and getting back into the swing of restaurant life. Private cheffing is solitary. Grosskopf knows it would be silly to participate in Dinner Lab just in the hopes of winning.

When I ask him how it would work if he won, we talk about the fact that the restaurant likely will be in the city where a chef's food scored highest. "So if I did best in Denver, that might be where the restaurant would be," he says, "which would suck, because I don't want to move to Denver."

But the chefs I speak to all say that the feedback component has helped them. Kwame Onwuachi, a New York chef who gave up his position at Eleven Madison Park to go on the tour, says the feedback is "very helpful," though he does take it with a grain of salt. "One diner said my beef Bourguignon needed coconut in it, which is obviously outrageous. But some suggestions are really helpful."

When pressed, Onwuachi acknowledges it can sometimes be tough. "I think food is objective. And it can be hard to get the feedback. It's like an artist making an elaborate painting and, when it's done, someone coming in and saying, 'I think it could use a little more green.' But in the end, we're in the hospitality industry, and what people have to say does matter."

All the chefs on the tour are men, but when I asked Bordainick if he's worried about diversity, he thinks I mean diversity in the food. He also says this is only the first in what he hopes will become an endless series of tours, an ongoing platform to find and develop talent.

"We are constantly looking for chefs," he says. "Next time we'll do better. Next time, hopefully, we'll have some women on tour. This is just the beginning."

The one question that keeps nagging at me, though, was whether the public should really have that much of a say in how, and what, is cooked in a restaurant. Bordainick talks a lot about "bringing people into contact with new ideas in food," but that food must have populist appeal, by definition, to make it in this system.

I'm also not convinced that the type of people who relish the idea of dining at a pop-up where they get to play critic are the same people who would support a regular restaurant night after night. In fact, many of the guests I speak to at Dinner Lab dinners admit that they *aren't* those customers—they are people who seek out one-off experiences, the very opposite of return customers. One couple has sworn off restaurant meals altogether in favor of pop-ups. These diners might love the trendiness of octopus, but are their tastes representative of what sustains a neighborhood restaurant?

Which brings us back to the computer/typewriter quandary. The way people are eating is changing. Special dinners can sell out in minutes, even at restaurants that usually are half empty. Food festivals are more and more popular. Noma and the Fat Duck, two of the world's most lauded restaurants, are taking their show on the road in the coming year, popping up for extended stays in countries outside their own. I wouldn't be at all surprised to see traveling food circuses within the next few years. But restaurants? They continue to thrive or fail at a fairly steady rate.

If Dinner Lab manages to open a successful restaurant that has longevity, it will be because the company found a very good chef who runs a tight ship. Just like anyone else.

The fact that Bordainick has feedback from hundreds of diners in 10 different cities is sure to help convince investors. But does that make it a data-driven restaurant, or just the most elaborate market-testing scheme ever?

And is that market feedback always a good thing? Bordainick says that, even after the Dinner Lab restaurant opens, the feedback component will remain, allowing chefs to tweak and adjust the food they're serving, just as they're doing now on the tour. "Feedback will always be a part of anything Dinner Lab does," he says.

Sitting at Dinner Lab's dinners feels to me like sinking into Yelp soup, being surrounded by people picking every dish apart and gleefully scribbling criticism. It seems the opposite of what a meal out ought to be, the antithesis of the relaxing experience of being swept up in the joy of dining, of letting pleasure find you, of not thinking too hard about it.

As a full-time restaurant critic, I realize that distaste for enthusiastic dinnertime analysis might sound strange. But no matter what's going on in my head as I do my job, I try never to let the parsing and negativity seep into the experience itself. Perhaps, with Yelp and blogs and the constant flow of pop-ups, this is just the direction dining is taking in general. All food will be rated and parsed; all cooking will be a competition.

Dinner Lab may have hit on a formula that allows restaurants constant feedback, but what's lost is the ritual of uncomplicated hospitality.

I'm also not convinced that feedback always yields the greatest results. The greatest chefs show us something we didn't know we wanted in the first place, and make us question our preconceived notions of what is good and what isn't.

Aaron Grosskopf's duck egg custard, for instance, was close to brilliant when I ate it. The people around me disagreed, but, when pressed, their reasons seemed superficial. One woman, when questioned about her reasoning, admitted that, really, she just doesn't like grapes.

Grosskopf tells me the duck egg custard was one of the dishes where the feedback element has helped him the most. In fact, he has now tweaked the recipe, and its scores have risen considerably as a result.

But the way in which Grosskopf has achieved that success will not surprise anyone who has spent time deeply mired in the world of food trends, or hung out with epicures whose enthusiasm trumps their palate. "Now," he says, "I put bacon on it."

At Your Service?

By Oliver Strand

From *Fool*

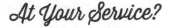

Oliver Strand's coffee-culture writings for the *New York Times* and other publications have made him a hero to java geeks. But he's also a shrewd observer of restaurant culture—and in this essay for the Sweden-based magazine *Fool,* he reminds us of the difference that one crucial dining element can make.

Two years ago, the chef of a small, ambitious Stockholm restaurant that had recently been named one of the World's 50 Best Restaurants sent out the following tweet: "Seriously?! 7 tables and 7 Different allergies or special diets . . . Come on . . . " He posted a photo of a reservation printout that listed everybody's names (redacted here), and everybody's needs. You can still find it on the internet, and see that somebody at H's table was lactose intolerant but could handle a little butter, that somebody at D's table was allergic to shellfish. P, party of two, didn't have any dietary restrictions, but it was their wedding day, and they asked for a private table. Seriously?! Come on. I wasn't surprised that the chef publicly shamed his guests because their allergies—or, in the case of the newly married couple, their happiness—might mess up his flow, and throw off what could otherwise be a flawless night for the kitchen. I had been crushed by his perfectionism a few weeks earlier, when my wife and I ate at the restaurant. We went for a 21-course tasting menu that lasted more than three hours and started 40 minutes late. We arrived on time and took our seats at the counter, but the chef wouldn't feed us because it would spoil the meal of the two strangers who reserved the places to our left, and who were delayed for reasons never explained to us—he didn't want them to see what they were going to eat. Instead, my wife and I sat opposite the chef, watching him expedite dishes, and saw what we were going to eat. Our obvious discomfort didn't seem to matter to him. He stood over us, as unsmiling as Marina Abramović, refusing us bread (which was considered a course), or any other food (that might fill us up). When he wasn't looking, my wife snacked on almonds she found in the bottom of her purse.

A few months earlier, I was sitting at the counter of Ishikawa, a small, serene Tokyo restaurant first awarded three stars by the *Michelin Guide* in 2009. I arrived 20 minutes late. Tokyo is a famously difficult city to navigate, even for taxi drivers—my hotel gave me a map to hand the driver, but he missed one turn, then another, and after shutting off the meter and apologizing for his mistakes, he made a few anxious calls to the restaurant. We finally found the street, where a woman in a kimono standing in front of the restaurant was waiting for me. Inside, I took my seat at the counter across from Hideki Ishikawa, the chef and owner, who was using a knife the size of a sword to slice a radish into tissue-thin sheets. I tried to apologize, but he just smiled and he welcomed me as if he knew me, using his careful English to ask me what I wanted to drink.

Setting aside the obvious geographical differences, these two restaurants have much in common: they are intimate, modern, fastidious. Both are expensive, and only serve intricate tasting menus that aim to challenge and seduce you. If you were to chart all of the restaurants of the world on a scatter plot, these two would be crowded together over on the farthest end, the two dots so close as to be indistinguishable. Yet one of them served me one of the most memorable meals in my life, and the other one of the most miserable. The single, greatest factor setting the two apart? The service.

Ishikawa was practising what in Japan is called *omotenashi*, a term that is usually translated as "hospitality," which is a little like saying that Hermès sells bags—it's a bland word for something so exquisite and refined that it's a source of obsession among some. Hospitality is regarded as an extra, a bonus, a bit of pleasantry that is enjoyable, but in the end, superfluous to the transaction at hand. It isn't essential, especially in a restaurant: service is a footnote to the food and the room. *Omotenashi* describes a comprehensive approach to human interaction that values courtesy and helpfulness, and that integrates professionalism and how one conducts oneself—grace and attentiveness are respected as much as skill and technique. In a restaurant, *omotenashi* isn't on the periphery, it's central: service is as important as the food and the room. To put it another way, it's illogical to say that a meal was fantastic even though the food was disgusting, because the food is the meal; once you understand *omotenashi*, it's just as nonsensical to say that a meal was fantastic even through the staff was rude, because the experience is the meal.

Omotenashi is complemented by *omoiyari*, which is often translated as "empathy" but refers to a sensitivity so acute that you can anticipate the needs and desires of others. It's not enough to be kind and polite, you should also be attuned to what that particular person wants. Ishikawa not only welcomed me into his restaurant, ignoring that I was late, but when he saw that I was flustered he sincerely wanted me to relax, have a drink, and start eating only when I was ready to enjoy it. I was always a little buzzed on *omotenashi* and *omoiyari* when I was in Tokyo, but I didn't realize it at the time. I just thought it was wonderful and strange to wander around the largest city in the world and feel so good about myself. Almost every interaction was a pleasure, every transaction a delight. It was true not only in the expensive establishments where you might expect to find it, but even at the places where the prices were more modest: the yakatori stall under the train tracks by Ueno Station, the Omotesando Koffee bar on the ground floor of a private home on a quiet side street. Once, I rented a bicycle from an elderly gentleman who meticulously checked every gear and cable with me before he walked me to the street, bowed deeply and wished me well. The rate: $2.50 for three days.

After I left, I talked with Merry White, author of *Coffee Life in Japan* and professor of anthropology at Boston University, who explained *omotenashi* and *omoiyari* and put terms to what I experienced. The words also gave me a vocabulary to describe what is sometimes missing. That restaurant in Stockholm might have had a sense of purpose, but there was little *omotenashi*, and absolutely no *omoiyari*. Sitting there at the counter that night, I was watching a chef so focused on getting the food exactly right he didn't see how much else he was getting wrong.

In 1975, the keyboardist Gary Wright released the single *Dream Weaver*. It was his biggest solo hit. Wright played on George Harrison's album *All Things Must Pass*, and the two artists followed a similar spiritual path—*Dream Weaver* is about cosmic enlightenment, or maybe drugs, or a night of really good sex, or a combination of the three. You might not be able to conjure up the song from memory, but if you were to hear it you would recognize the tune when Wright's tenor takes up the chorus:

> *Oh Dream Weaver, I believe you can get me through the night.*
> *Oh Dream Weaver, I believe we can reach the morning light.*

One afternoon this summer, Will Guidara, one of the owners of Eleven Madison Park in New York, sang those words to me, searching my face to see if I could place the melody. "Still nothing?" he asked.

Not exactly. I knew the song, but Guidara's serenade didn't answer my question: what does a Dream Weaver do? I was sitting in on a conference in which he and Daniel Humm, the chef and co-owner of Eleven Madison Park, met with the restaurant's two top managers and two head chefs to discuss what they called Strategic Planning, but what seemed more like an unusually enthusiastic response to the employee suggestion box. Several weeks earlier, every member of the staff had been asked how the restaurant could be improved, fine-tuned or completely rethought; the submissions were consolidated into a six-page, single-spaced document with 136 items. Guidara and Humm took it seriously. That day, they made it as far as #23.

Suggestion #16 was a "curveball" course to be served to a few randomly selected tables every night, an unexpected gift from the kitchen. Guidara didn't like it. "I feel that's what the Dream Weaver does," he said. "A course isn't necessarily food. I want to talk about that at premeal tonight."

When I asked what, in fact, the Dream Weaver does, Guidara broke into song.

The Dream Weaver, I learned after a long and example-filled discussion, is a combination of concierge, prop stylist, research assistant and artist-in-residence. The Dream Weaver responds to whatever it is a guest might want or need. Sometimes, those wants and needs are practical: directions, ibuprofen, a couple of minutes with a needle and thread to repair a dress.

Sometimes, those wants and needs invite more creative endeavors. During a winter storm, a couple from Spain mentioned that their children, who were back at the hotel, had never seen so much snow; the Dream Weaver went to an all-night hardware store, picked up two sleds, painted the four-leaf logo of Eleven Madison Park down the middle, and gave them to the couple so that the children could go sledding in Central Park in the morning. Another time, a couple joked that New York's urban wildlife was always rustling underfoot; the Dream Weaver stitched together a small squirrel. When someone wants to keep a wine label too fragile to be removed, the Dream Weaver will paint a watercolor of the bottle on thick paper. The more tipsy the conversation, the more fluid the response. One couple joked about loving the pizza from a particular uptown slice joint; the Dream Weaver jumped in a taxi— the slices of pizza were presented as if a part of the tasting menu.

The Dream Weaver is a position usually filled by Christine McGrath, who studied fashion at art school and minored in architecture. She keeps a set of paints at the restaurant, along with a sewing kit and an engraver. She is in charge of the Warby Parker reading glasses loaned to diners having trouble making out the wine list, and the late-night tickets to the Empire State Building observation deck given to moony couples. She manages the "plus-one" documents that form part of the restaurant's institutional memory—if a guest asks about the history of the building, or the distinctions between different rums, or where to get a drink later that night, or the best place to go for a run in Manhattan, or where to buy maternity clothes, or which New Orleans hotels are comfortable and not too rowdy, the waiter will return with a reply printed on heavy-stock paper. At latest count, there were more than 800 plus-ones in the system.

Not all of what the Dream Weaver does is improvised. After you make a reservation, a captain will call to confirm the time and number of people, and to see if it is a special occasion such as a birthday or anniversary. Sometimes, the meal is the special occasion, or the reason for a trip to New York. All of this information is fed into the Guest Notes, a database that lists the particular habits, preferences and pleasures of every person who has been to the restaurant. There's not much to go on for first-time visitors, but if you return your entry starts to fill up. Every week Guidara and Humm will look at reservations flagged by the captains. Then, before each meal, the captains and sommeliers will go over the Guest Notes, distributing a 15-page document filled with astonishing detail. The night I was there, they discussed every table, all 107 covers. For a couple coming in for a last meal before moving to Toronto, they batted around ideas that might make the night more special. *Poutine?* That's Montreal. Something jokey about Mayor Robert Ford? Too off-color. They decided to put together a guide to Toronto restaurants and bars. The Dream Weaver would be tasked with getting in touch with the chefs, mixologists and journalists the restaurant trusts, formatting their recommendations into a bound book, and painting a red maple leaf on the cover. It was an extra course that wasn't food.

Which was the point that Guidara made later that afternoon at pre-meal, the briefing he gives before service starts to the more than 40 staff members working on the floor. After going over a short version of the Guest Notes, Guidara brought up the suggestions discussed in the meeting earlier that day. "There was an idea in there that we should have a curveball course that just a handful of guests get to eat. The idea is to make a few tables feel special. I hated that idea, and I want to tell you why not to make whoever came up with that idea feel badly, but because I want to talk about what we want to accomplish at the restaurant," he said.

"I feel it's lazy to expect the kitchen to come up with an extra course that we can use to make the diner feel special. If we're going to call somebody out, and make them feel loved, let's come up with something that's unique to them. Is lobster prepared in a certain way going to make them feel more special? It's not spontaneous, so it's not authentic," Guidara said. "I really want to make this point super clear. We use Christine to come up with special things to do for the tables. That's what the curveball should be. Rather than just hope for another dish from the kitchen, we should be finding opportunities for her to do her work."

Guidara let his statement settle over the room. In the end, he agreed to suggestion #16, but on different terms. Yes, a random table should be thrown a curveball that could transform the evening, but it should be generated by the floor staff, not the kitchen. In the calculus of Eleven Madison Park, another delicious mouthful of something is too easy; if you want to make somebody's night extraordinary—and create a memory—you practice *omoiyari*, and use your intuition to figure out what will make that person happy. Then you talk to the Dream Weaver.

When Guidara and Humm were brought in to take over Eleven Madison Park in 2006 by Danny Meyer, who owned the restaurant at the time, they were asked to turn what was at that point a successful brasserie into one of New York's temples of fine dining. The restaurant already had a strong sense of *omotenashi* (Meyer's book *Setting the Table* is a bible for the hospitality industries), which they further cultivated. By the time they bought the restaurant from Meyer in 2011, the collaboration between the two partners had evolved. The service wasn't just effusive, it was seamless. Both the front of house and back of house shared the belief that hospitality was as important as the food, and that Vidal Sassoon was right: if you don't look good, we don't look good.

"Our service is possible because of him and our relationship, because he believes in it as much as I do," Guidara said of Humm, as the three of us sat in a windowless office next to the kitchen. "There are chef-driven restaurants, and restaurateur-driven restaurants, and I don't think either can be as good as a restaurant that's chef-driven and restaurateur-driven. There are decisions made in the kitchen that give the dining staff the opportunity to shine. He could easily do it differently, and in another environment I could never challenge it."

"Trust is important. I trust that if he has an idea, that it's the right idea. I might challenge it, but if something is really important to him, I have to trust it's the right thing," Humm said. "It's so much more fun, too."

The chef seems awed and amused by Guidara's consuming need to tinker with what happens on the floor so that service is both more pure (there are no visible signs of technology in the dining room, nothing that will beep or vibrate or strobe and remind you that you are in the 21st century—even the checks are copied by hand on to creamy paper), and more playful (depending on the weather, your final course might be served on the sidewalk outside, where a hot dog vendor will hand you an ice pop—strawberries and cream in the summer, apple and caramel in the fall). When Humm develops a dish, he isn't just concerned with the balance of flavor, texture and composition. He consults with Guidara to discuss how it will be incorporated into the service.

In turn, Guidara has a deep admiration for Humm's cooking, which has become more confident and fluent in recent years. It's stripped-down: if fine dining sometimes feels overdecorated, Humm's food is a well-lit room with tastefully high ceilings and just the right chair. The restaurant now only serves a tasting menu, a 16-course meal that lasts three hours.

That seems like a long time to keep your own company, but one night I saw a distinguished gentleman in a bow tie alone at a table. He was a regular—according to the Guest Notes, it was his 41st visit. His entry took up more than one page: he likes one table in particular and sparkling water; he doesn't like chicken, mustard or braised beef. He hated the carrot tartare (one of Humm's signature dishes, no longer on the menu), and the Baked Alaska (another signature dish, which was still on the menu). He loves lamb, and a specific brand of gin. He hates oaky wine. When served a meat course, his table is set with a knife engraved with his name.

Most come to Eleven Madison Park for a culinary journey, and to cede control to the kitchen. The restaurant has three stars from the *Michelin Guide* and four stars from *The New York Times*; last year, it climbed to #4 on the list of the World's 50 Best Restaurants. If it seemed strange to me that somebody would sign up for such a specific and expensive experience only to strike through parts of it as if it were a first draft, the captain on the floor that night told me the guest was quite popular with the staff.

"He's the best," he said with sincerity. "Always alone, always likes things a certain way, always served by the same team. We love him."

That night there were 40 tables, and 20 different allergies or special diets: a vegetarian, a pescatarian, a person who hates beets. The brother of a heavyweight politician was there with his lithe girlfriend. They sat not far away from a Danish couple with a young daughter who spent the first ten minutes at the table squeezing her hands together with nerves. The waiters modulated how they interacted with each table, leaving the famous alone, lavishing attention on those who might never spend so much on dinner again. The restaurant purred like a Mercedes S-Class, the powerful engine so quiet you couldn't tell when it was running at top speed, and when it was coasting downhill.

That's what happens when you over prepare. Guidara and Humm have worked so hard to thread hospitality and intuition through the fabric of Eleven Madison Park that every meal is a performance of material already mastered, and not a struggle to get it right. As dinner service picks up, the staff is relaxed and responsive. "We try so hard to achieve something, sometimes you need to stand away for a second," Humm told me at the end of the night. "You have to let it go. If you don't force it so much you have greater results."

Coding and Decoding Dinner

By Todd Kliman

From the *Oxford American*

Veteran dining editor of the monthly *Washingtonian* magazine,
Todd Kliman—a former English professor at Howard
University—addresses the elephant in the room: A racial blind
spot in American restaurant culture, which manifests itself in so
many unacknowledged, insidious ways.

S outhern hospitality is more than what we call "etiquette." It's a sen-
sibility. A way of being in the world. A philosophy. A spirit. You
don't just open your doors to a stranger; you lavish that stranger with
kindness, attention, and care. Nor are you simply accepting someone
you don't know into your home. In the purest sense, you are accepting
that stranger as an extension of yourself.

This is what is known as "welcome" in the South. And there is no
thinking of it except in the purest sense. "Welcome" is an almost mythic
conceit, one bound up with the very ways the region chooses to think
of itself—sun-dappled land of kindness, grace, and mercy.

But if we choose to see the South as it really is, and as it once was—
and if we are honest in admitting that in many ways what *is* is not so very
different from what *was*—then we find ourselves with a messier, more
authentic picture of welcome.

Last year, on the fiftieth anniversary of restaurant desegregation, we
celebrated a signifying moment in the long march toward full and equal
citizenship for black Americans. But we delude ourselves if we don't

acknowledge that there is a difference between being admitted and being welcomed.

The court order that ended desegregation stipulated that every cafe, tavern, Waffle House, and roadside joint must open its doors to all. It did not, could not, stipulate that whites in the South must also open their hearts and minds to all. Welcome was, and is, the final barrier to racial parity.

We have witnessed remarkable progress over the past five decades, yes, and we should acknowledge this, too. What seemed fanciful, even utopian, a generation ago is now so commonplace as to not bear any comment at all. We have come to expect and accept black and white in the workplace, on the playing field, in politics, in the military, and we congratulate ourselves on our steady march to racial harmony. But our neighborhoods and our restaurants do not look much different today than they did fifty years ago. That Kingly vision of sitting down at the same table together and breaking bread is as smudgy as it's ever been.

I have a day job in Washington, D.C., as a food critic. I've done it for ten years. During that time, the city has become bigger and more cosmopolitan, the restaurant scene has evolved from that of a steak & potatoes town to that of a vibrant metropolis, and people now talk excitedly about going out to eat. But what no one talks about is the almost total absence of black faces in that scene.

I count faces, I have to confess. It's a habit. Something I began doing when I was teaching at Howard University, when I was made to see myself as white in the world—whiteness not as neutral, as baseline, but as an idea, a construct. I began to keep a tally, each night, of the non-whites in the room. I eat out, on average, ten times a week in restaurants that span the gamut from ambitious fine-dining to so-called ethnic mom & pops. So let's do the math. That's 40 restaurant visits a month for 4 months, or 160 restaurant visits. Only 8 times—8 times out of 160—did I see more than 10 black folks in the room during any one lunch or dinner. On more than 90 of those restaurant visits, I did not see any faces other than white faces.

We're not talking about Provo, Utah. Or Johannesburg, South Africa. We're talking about a town enshrined in song, four decades ago, as Chocolate City.

Yes, the black majority may be a thing of the past—the recent census shows that whites now make up a paper-thin majority—but blacks remain a force in local politics. They are heavily represented in both the government bureaucracy and the workplace. And Prince George's County, where I live, is home to the largest black middle class in the country.

So why aren't they coming to dinner? It's a question I've been asking for almost as long as I've been a restaurant critic. And—not that I'm surprised—no one seems interested in answering it. Or even addressing it.

I've tried, for almost ten years now, to get a publication interested in a piece that would go in search of an answer. That's dynamite, one editor told me—and then he immediately sought to make me understand how fraught such a piece would be. I was white, he said, and that meant simply taking on a subject like this, in a candid and honest way, would invite attack or censure. And, he reminded me, most whites would not care.

This was meant, I suppose, to dissuade me from wading too deeply into choppy waters. From wasting my time. But my fascination with the question has not gone away, and, if anything, as the years have gone on, I am more interested in finding the answer or answers, not less.

I mentioned that I've lately been keeping a tally. Well, for the past five years, I've also been making notes and interviewing restaurateurs and industry observers for a piece I thought might never reach an audience. None I have spoken with over the years has been willing to go on the record and put a name and title to the observations and insights they've shared with me. So you'll have to take it on faith when I say that the things they've told me are true.

Most of those folks are white; the men who make decisions in the restaurant world—they are almost unfailingly men—are almost unfailingly white. The common denominator of my honest but off-the-record conversations with these white insiders—the one thing they all spoke to me about—was something I've taken to calling the 60–40 line, a line they live in fear of crossing.

Sixty-forty: that's a dining room that's 60 percent white and 40 percent black. Forty percent is the tipping point, they all said. More than

40 percent black, and suddenly, they said, the numbers don't just flip. More than 40 percent, and—said one—the whites scurry to their holes like mice. Soon, he said, you're looking at a restaurant where the clientele is predominantly black.

I said I thought that might be just a tad paranoid. This one restaurateur, a good, well-meaning man—they were all good, well-meaning men, the men I spoke with—looked at me and said that you could never be too careful when it came to running a business where every day you essentially began from scratch. But 60–40 would seem to me to be a problem to think about only if you have a 40 percent black audience. And there aren't more than a handful of restaurants in the city that can say that.

The black folks in the industry I've spoken with have been similarly reluctant to go on the record, mostly for fear of reprisal; they don't want to be seen as angry or unhappy or ungrateful. One, a former general manager who now manages an underground supper club, told me that it was important to remember that it hasn't been that long, historically. Yes, he said, blacks today have a mobility their grandparents lacked. But that's not to say that they've been exposed to the experiences many whites have. This explains, he said, the glaring absence of blacks from most Indian, Vietnamese, Bolivian, Afghan, Thai, and sushi restaurants in the D.C. area.

When I pointed out that I myself have only been eating sushi for twenty years, he said, "But see, you were exposed to other kinds of food earlier. And that probably prepared you for sushi."

What about younger blacks who are growing up in a world in which sushi can be found in grocery stores? I asked. And yet you still don't see them in the restaurants.

"Because their parents didn't grow up eating sushi," he said.

"Well, neither did mine."

"But your parents grew up eating—I'm guessing—grew up eating all kinds of different foods, right? And you grew up, I'm guessing again, in a world that was not a segregated world. Most black folks, they grew up in black neighborhoods and went to black schools. So: exposure."

And what about the non-so-called ethnic restaurants?

That's a matter of exposure, too, he said. "To know the protocol. To interact with a sommelier. Whites—not all whites, but more whites—have been doing it for longer. They tend to know these things. Going out to dinner isn't just about the food. It's a whole system you have to learn. And an etiquette. It's not as simple as just showing up."

There was a Yogi-ism in here, I said. There are no blacks in the dining rooms, because—there are no blacks in the dining rooms?

"I mean, don't laugh," he said. "Seeing black faces out front—the GM, the chef, that would go a long way. But we don't have a lot of black chefs or GMs. Having black staff—you know, a third black, for example—that surely would help. But again, you don't see much of that."

Those who were most outspoken feared reprisal from two directions, from whites and blacks. These, to me, were the most interesting—people whose ideas were likely to disturb folks on both sides.

I shared the former GM's exposure theory with a woman who has been in the food world in Washington for more than twenty-five years, as a cook and a consultant. She said, "Well, exposure, sure. But also the fact that, I'm sorry—black folks are just plain ol' conservative in their tastes. Nobody wants to hear that, but it's true. So you take a fish restaurant, or a fish and seafood restaurant, or a barbecue place, and you're gonna see black folks. Guaranteed. These are the foods we know. These are our comfort foods. Now, you take unusual foods, and in a setting that doesn't feel familiar, and with lots of white folks in the room? Uh-uh. Remember, why do we gather to eat? For most of us—black and white—it's to feel good. To feel a sense of well-being. Of home."

I thought about her comments recently when the office of the Prince George's county executive invited me to lunch to solicit my ideas for attracting a name restaurant. I said that I thought the right kind of restaurant would be a crossover restaurant, a place that would appeal equally to black and white. Ideally, I said, a fish and seafood spot of such high quality and freshness that diners from all over the region would be persuaded to make the trip. One of the CE's staff members, a woman, nodded her head enthusiastically in agreement.

And then I began talking about the hypothetical menu. Stews teeming with langoustines, mussels, and cuttlefish. Oysters on the half shell and other items from the raw bar. Crudo.

"Crudo?" she wrinkled up her nose. "What's that?"

I told her.

"Raw fish? Uh-uh. Nope. Not gonna work." She suggested instead a fried fish restaurant—"you know, something like the Neelys on TV would do"—and began describing the kind of place that, even new, would feel like a relic. A place, in other words, that is unlikely to generate broad excitement.

So much of what I was hearing, on both sides, came down to fear. The 60–40 was about fear. About not taking chances, and not risking a good thing. The exposure theory, the remark about culinary conservatism—these, too, were about fear. Not venturing beyond safe harbor. Sticking with the known, with what's easy. Needing reassurance.

It is no wonder we talk so much about comfort foods, I thought. Food: it's where we run to for safety. It's what we hide behind.

It was a man named Andy Shallal who helped me to understand the possibilities for a better, more integrated future while also reinforcing the manifold problems of the present. Shallal made me understand that no one ever need say, "keep out." That a message is embedded in the room, in the menu, in the plates and silverware, in the music, in the color scheme. That a restaurant is a network of codes. It's a phrase that, yes, has all sorts of overtones and undertones, still, in the South. I'm using it, here, in the semiotic sense—the communication by signs and symbols and patterns.

I don't see coding as inherently malicious. But we need to remember that restaurants have long existed to perpetuate a class of insiders and a class of outsiders, the better to cultivate an air of desirability. Tablecloths, waiters in jackets and ties, soft music—these are all forms of code. They all send a very specific, clear message. That is, they communicate without words (and so without incurring a legal risk or inviting criticism or censure from the public) the policy, the philosophy, the aim of the establishment.

Today, there are many more forms of code than the old codes of the aristocracy. Bass-thumping music. Cement floors and lights dangling from the ceiling. Tattooed cooks. But these are still forms of code. They simultaneously send an unmistakable signal to the target audience and repel all those who fall outside that desired group.

I spoke to a restaurateur not long ago who told me, "I don't engage in coding." I responded that I begged to differ. We code even when we're not aware that we're coding. He may not have been trying overtly to exclude—I know he would never do such a thing—but his restaurant speaks a very particular language. It has a microbrewery on the premises—and, according to the Madison Beer Review, only three percent of craft beer drinkers in the U.S. are black. Its staff is almost exclusively white. Attached to the restaurant is a general store selling penny candy, knickknacks, and other nostalgic oddities that take browsers back to the Fifties—hardly a time that most black Americans want to relive.

When Shallal opened the first location of Busboys and Poets, near U Street in Washington, D.C., he told me that he wanted to create a restaurant that would knit together black and white. He was not the first D.C. restaurateur to make the attempt. Gillian Clark's Colorado Kitchen, now shuttered, was the kind of homey, self-effacing place you see much more of in the South than in the North. I once described it as the most integrated restaurant in the city, which was, in retrospect, a regrettable bit of sloppiness. Yes, blacks and whites came together to break bread, but allow me now to adjust the image that is no doubt taking root in your mind. From the time it opened until about seven o'clock, the room was predominantly black. From seven until closing, it was predominantly white. In the sweet spot of about 6:45, the dining room was, yes, the fulfillment of King's vision. Clark told me that it bothered her to see this division, and that she tried hard to integrate the room. To little avail.

Shallal decided to try harder. U Street was a kind of hallowed ground for black Washingtonians, the heart of their nightlife during the benighted period of Jim Crow, where Duke Ellington, Ella Fitzgerald, Cab Calloway, and others played nightly to packed houses. It was destroyed in the 1968 riots and was slowly groping its way back to life. His hope, Shallal told me, was to create a space that would show what the new U Street could look like. He felt uniquely qualified for the task, given that he was Iraqi and had for years brought together Jews and Arabs in the Peace Cafe dinner discussions he hosted after performances at the Washington, D.C., Jewish Community Center. Shallal was well aware of the 60–40 principle, and as much as he intended the restaurant to be a place of racial harmony, he was careful not to cross certain lines. Sitting down with me one day to talk about his vision a few weeks after opening, he told me that 60–40 guided many of his early decisions.

The restaurant was a kind of multiplex, which, in addition to serving food, would serve as a coffeehouse, a bookstore, and a performance space. There were nightly events, sometimes two or three plays or performances or readings in a single night. He spoke to me at length, and also with great angst, about how important it was to not schedule too many events in any given night that would attract a predominantly black crowd. If the restaurant scheduled no events that attracted a black audience—if its programming was regarded as appealing much more to whites than blacks—then that was just as bad. Busboys and Poets could be a spectacular financial success, but he said he would consider it a failure if the mix tipped too far in one direction or the other. His menu, I understood that day, was written in code.

"I have field greens on the menu," he said. "Only I don't call them field greens. I say—lettuce. I have chorizo on my pizza. Only I don't call it chorizo—I call it pepperoni."

On the tables he would not put out just salt and pepper, he would also include tiny bottles of hot sauce. And that was not the end of it. He commissioned an artist to paint murals on the walls—murals that included images of Martin Luther King, Malcolm X, Gandhi, and others.

Shallal knew that what he was doing was, at some level, a form of pandering. And that some, like my more waggishly cynical black friends, would see his restaurant not as a symbol of hope, but as an emblem of condescension. At lunch one day not long after Busboys and Poets had opened, one of those friends of mine nodded toward the mural along one wall, with its images of King, Malcolm X, and Gandhi, and its inspirational quotations, and smirked and said, "I feel like I'm walking down the halls in junior high."

Shallal and I spoke for five hours that day, and as the afternoon light receded and the house lights came up, I told him that he had gone to lengths that no other restaurateur in the city had gone to. He looked at me across the table and said, "I have to. If I don't go to these lengths, it just won't work." In other words, if he didn't make a very conscious— even self-conscious—attempt at reaching a black audience.

It's impossible to know whether people came because of his concerted efforts, or whether they would have come anyway, because Busboys and Poets is such an interesting and irresistible mix of elements. But almost from the start the restaurant drew throngs of customers, black and white (and Asian and Latino), old and young, hipster and square, and emerged as a new symbol of U Street—that magical third place we all seem to want so desperately in our neighborhoods and towns.

The first Busboys and Poets opened ten years ago. I was hopeful, then, that its success and the exciting vision it portended might inspire a new generation. There's a contagiously progressive spirit in the air right now, and some young D.C. restaurateurs speak earnestly and excitedly of blurring the old divisions. The city is witness to some fascinating experiments in high-low, in rusticity and refinement, as chefs draw inspiration from old truths to create new ideas, new techniques, new flavors.

But black and white are still largely separate. Shallal was interventionist in coding this restaurant, flagrantly and unapologetically so. He made explicit, sometimes straining overtures to a long-neglected audience, while being careful to limit their numbers in the building. He purposely framed his cuisine so as to not exclude anyone, underselling the quality of his ingredients for what he perceived to be the greater good. Yet Busboys and Poets has inspired no followers, other than Shallal himself, who promptly opened three more locations, with another on the way (there are now six locations along the East Coast).

Is it that everyone is too fearful to take a chance? Or is it that there is only one Andy Shallal? Or both?

Or is it that this kind of social engineering in the context of dining out feels, even to some progressive ears, not just intrusive, but somehow also contrary to the very spirit of breaking bread, of the table?

Food is intimate. We take it into our bodies. When we gather at the table with friends and family, we're gathering to affirm something. When we gather for business, we're gathering to cement something. The table, the notion of breaking bread—this is meant to establish an intimacy and gesture toward trust.

What Andy Shallal has proven—indisputably proven—is that it's possible. It's possible to bring black and white together under one roof. It's possible to do it both peaceably and profitably. But not without enormous work. And not without conscious and even self-conscious outreach. And not without a daily, even hourly, tending of the delicate mix.

Waste Not, Want Not (and Pass the Fish Skin)

By Pete Wells

From the *New York Times*

As the *New York Times's** chief dining critic since 2011, Pete Wells is tasked with judging restaurants at their finest. But sometimes, it's not only about awarding stars. Here he enjoys a special event that goes beyond farm-to-table or even nose-to-tail dining—tapping into a growing concern about food waste.

On Monday, I chopped a week's worth of food scraps. It took most of an hour in my kitchen to reduce carrot leaves, cauliflower stems, onion butts and scallion greens to small bits that I hoped would make an appetizing lunch for the molds, mini-bugs and earthworms in the backyard compost bin.

The next night, I had a meal that made me wonder if my time would have been better spent tossing everything with a good vinaigrette and eating it myself.

The setting was Dan Barber's Greenwich Village restaurant, normally known as Blue Hill. For three weeks in March, he has converted it into a pop-up called wastED where he and his cooks sell fish bones, bruised and misshapen vegetables, stale bread and other items not commonly thought of as food for $15 a plate. The pop-up presents a creative challenge to the kitchen crew (how can we make this stuff taste good?) and an intellectual challenge to the diner (why do we assume it won't?). It was a night of thoughtful, creative, entertaining and surprisingly tasty agitprop.

Chefs with an eye on the bottom line try to avoid kitchen waste. In a memorable scene in Bill Buford's book "Heat," Mario Batali berates Babbo's cooks for throwing out vegetable scraps that could make perfectly good ravioli fillings while he roots around in a trash can like a bear cub at a campground. In their search for overlooked ingredients, Mr. Barber and his crew did more than that. They went out on a crosstown refuse hunt.

From Baldor Specialty Foods, a restaurant supplier in the Bronx, came bruised outer leaves from heads of bok choy and peelings from fennel, kohlrabi and apples for the "Dumpster dive vegetable salad" that persuaded me to reconsider my compost habits. To be painstakingly accurate, most of the persuasion was done by a buttery vinaigrette of ground pistachios, a swipe of tarragon sauce and a heap of white froth made by draining the liquid from chickpea cans and whisking it.

Smashed pulp from Liquiteria's juice presses was dyed to a reasonably convincing beef color by beet juice, shaped into burgers and slapped on buns made from "repurposed" bread. From Raffetto's, the shop on Houston Street, they picked up remnant noodles that ran from the pasta rollers between batches of dough. These were boiled together, so they ranged from floppy to taut, and were dressed with a mildly fishy sauce made from monkfish tripe and smoked fish heads.

The kitchen staff members took turns dropping off plates. One showed pictures of Baldor's bagged, peeled produce on an iPod and another pantomimed how he had scraped skate wings until his arms hurt. The night's guest chef, Philippe Bertineau from Alain Ducasse's bistro in Midtown, Benoit, appeared with head cheese, a pig foot croquette, stewed offal and tongue layered with foie gras, a reminder that French country cooking has a long tradition of turning scraps into treats.

Halfway through dinner, Mr. Barber came to the table with a sheet of wax paper holding a fish skeleton as long as a baguette. "I grew up on this stuff," he said. He didn't mean the bones, which used to belong to a black cod, but the shiny white flesh sold in appetizing shops as sable. When sable is filleted, some meat sticks to the carcass. I unstuck it with a sauce spoon. Sable is always a treat, and this came with a bonus: the gooey, soft bits hugging the spine. Between mouthfuls, I crunched on some crisp carrot tops with fried fish skin. The skin, the bones, and the heads in the salad dressing came from Acme, the Brooklyn facility that gives New York some of its finest smoked fish.

The restaurant was packed to the gills, one part of the fish that was left off the menu. A long row of high tables had been shoehorned into the center of the dining room. These were not just any tables, either.

"The tables were grown—yes, grown—during the second half of February with compostable materials and mycelium," read a note on the back of the menu. The walls, meanwhile, were covered by a white fabric draped over crop rows to keep out frost and aphids. They were backlit, which gave the restaurant the feel of a wedding tent.

"A wedding tent, that's nice," Mr. Barber's brother and partner in Blue Hill, David, said when he stopped by my table. "Most people say it looks like a meth lab."

Breaking with protocol, I had asked Dan Barber for a reservation. This, of course, gave him the chance to set aside the choicest carrot tops and fish heads. Let the reader beware. I dropped the fake-name routine because seats have been scarce, my deadline was zooming in, and I am not trying to write a restaurant review.

Still, the forewarned reader may wonder what I thought of the meal. I had one of the best times I've enjoyed in a restaurant in the last year. The food was great, full of the surprises that happen when cooks run into inspiration at full creative tilt. Almost every bite was delicious, with a few exceptions.

"Repurposed" buns did not knock Martin's potato rolls from their place in my heart. I had trouble getting at the fried monkfish wings, which were shaped like a V, with most of the good stuff jammed down in the crevice. If I were going to enjoy them on a regular basis, I'd need to grow a snout. Also, the crackers served alongside an intense and rich bowl of broth made from desiccated dry-aged beef trimmings had almost no flavor. They were made from field corn, the commodity crop that goes into high-fructose corn syrup, cattle troughs and ethanol. It accounts for 99 percent of the nation's cornfields, and it is the only ingredient used at wastED that I'm convinced humans have no business eating.

This was Mr. Barber's point, of course. The meal was gently and consistently seasoned with a protest against the grotesque way Americans waste food while millions of us go hungry. Lack of money and other resources forced members of 6.8 million households in the United States to eat less than they normally would at times during 2013, the latest year for which government statistics are available. At the same time, 133 billion pounds of the food that is available to consumers goes into the garbage annually. The facts and numbers could go on, but I feel ashamed already.

Our food is produced and consumed in a bogglingly complex web. It can't easily be changed, certainly not by a three-week stunt in an expensive Manhattan restaurant.

Perceptions do change, though, and quickly. Sliced white bread was a prestigious item in 1960. Many find it worthless today. For years our restaurant culture has placed supreme value in pristine, high-priced ingredients. What if everybody who could afford restaurants like Blue Hill learned instead to prize bruised vegetables because they had been transformed by a chef's skill and ingenuity? What might we do with the ingredients that any hack could cook? It's a provocative, appealingly subversive idea.

For now, whenever one of my children complains about dinner, I'll silence him by saying that I once ate garbage, and liked it.

The Last Supper

By Tom Junod

From *Esquire*

Esquire staff writer Tom Junod has covered a host of topics since he joined the magazine in 1998. In this elegy to New York City's acclaimed restaurant WD-40, he widens the scope beyond chef Wylie Dufresne's culinary innovations, digging into how WD-40 redefined dining culture.

"Who are you calling a pussy?" Wylie Dufresne asked. We were at a booth in the back of his restaurant, wd-50, next to the entrance to the kitchen. The kitchen did not have a door but rather a garage-doorsized opening that afforded people eating dinner an unimpeded view of—and, if they asked, unimpeded access to—the people making it for them. That Dufresne, known as the great trickster of American cuisine and its chief practitioner of molecular gastronomy, insisted on absolute transparency was one of the paradoxes he engineered into the experience of eating at wd-50, his way of saying *There are no tricks.* The wizard might fry mayonnaise, but he never hid behind the curtain.

For the 11 years Dufresne cooked at wd-50, diners watched him cooking. He often stood at the entrance of his kitchen and watched them dining. What I didn't know until my last supper at wd-50 is that he also listened.

Now, it was true that a gentleman at our table had called American chefs "a bunch of pussies." But then he had also said the same thing about American writers. And he was calling American chefs and American writers a bunch of pussies only to contrast them with Wylie Dufresne. Indeed, there were five of us, and we had come to the vinous consensus that everybody involved in the production of American culture was a pussy *but* Wylie because everybody but Wylie had compromised.

Of course, we often hear of "uncompromising chefs"—chefs fanatical about the quality of their ingredients. But Dufresne was uncompromising about his *ideas*, about his refusal to use an ingredient that hadn't been reinvented or at least recontextualized. He wasn't just an artist with food; he was an artist with *hunger* who had confronted diners with the question of just how much artistry they found appetizing. He had no ambitions for empire, no designs on wd-50s in Vegas and Dubai. His struggle to keep wd-50 open even in the face of a dining room often half filled was no more and no less than a struggle to keep cooking the way he wanted to cook until someone stopped him.

And now someone had stopped him. His landlord had sold the building, and the new owner intended to build something in its place. The official line was that wd-50 was a victim of progress, not of taste. But it was still closing, and the five of us, like many others, had come there to mark its demise after not having eaten there in years. We told ourselves that we were celebrating Dufresne's achievement, and it was not until he came to our table that we understood the sadness of the occasion. He had always been the essence of modesty and congeniality in a business that lavishly rewards egomaniacs and assholes. He still looked the same, with his unstained chef's whites and his pinstriped black apron, his owlish eyeglasses and his long straight hair parted on the side, his fine patrician nose and his quick smile, which flashed both amusement and forbearance. But his pride was all the more apparent for its having been wounded, and when he came out of the kitchen there was something I had never seen in him before—a proprietary and almost imperious sense of solitude. He had never been anything less than determined. And now he was determined to see wd-50 through to its end, and he walked through the restaurant sharp-eyed and sharp-eared, as though on patrol.

This is not to say he was unhappy when he visited us. We were four dishes into his tasting menu. We had eaten oysters in edible shells. We had eaten cuttlefish with a square of "schmaltz"—the rendered chicken fat once so ubiquitous in the delis of the Lower East Side that it became

synonymous with Jewish sentimentality was now so thoroughly al-
chemized that it dissolved on the roof of the mouth like a communion
wafer. We had eaten ropes of raw tuna tied into knots that presented not
just culinary but also mathematical conundrums. He wanted us—he
wanted everybody—to be delighted and we were, even when he enthusiastically explained that he had used a "bonding agent" on the tuna.
"Mmmm, nothing makes me hungry like the words 'bonding agent,'"
said the gentleman who had first gotten Dufresne's attention by casti-
gating the conservatism of American chefs . . . all right, by calling all
American chefs a bunch of pussies.

Five minutes later, Dufresne returned with the next course, a scrawl
of liquefied chicken liver "hit with a blowtorch" and flanked by intricate mounds of mousse-like honeydew melon compressed with yuzu
juice. Four of us couldn't read the script on our plates because Dufresne
had invented a language that didn't include words. But one of us could.
Dufresne personally delivered his plate after writing in charred chicken
liver the word *pussy,* curved along the bottom of the plate like a smile.

O f course there was music playing. There always was, not in the
restaurant but rather in the kitchen, so loud that the people eating
in the restaurant could hear it. Dufresne was a music fan, devoted to
classic rock and the Grateful Dead. He had put a list of wd-50 favorites
on the menu under the moniker "From the Vault," in honor of the series of live albums that the Dead had made from unearthed tapes, and
he told us that Phil Lesh was scheduled to come by and eat when he
came to New York the following week. But what was striking about Dufresne's food was not just its rock 'n' roll spirit; it was also the tension
between its rock 'n' roll spirit and the rigor of its preparation. The Dead
were famous for feats of improvisation; Dufresne was famous—or almost famous—for feats of control, for molecular gastronomy Diony-
sian in effect but ruthlessly Apollonian in execution. He wanted to be
Garcia; he had turned out to be Owsley, the band's chemist, creating
dishes almost pharmaceutical in their precision. He made tiny time
capsules of food that delivered not only novel combinations of flavor
but also novel combinations of flavor designed to be experienced in the
order Dufresne intended. He served us plates of lamb bacon meant to
answer the persistent criticism that his food wasn't "delicious" enough,

but what lingered was the taste of the dried black chickpeas scattered on the plate like crumbs. He described them as "blackchickpea hummus," but sampled alone they tasted like nothing at all—postmodern parsley, a throwaway element that functioned only to interrupt the void of the vast white plate. Tasted in conjunction with the lamb, however, they became intensely peppery and made the slippery lamb almost crunchy in texture. They appeared, disappeared, and reappeared, and, like all of Dufresne's best inventions, they kept doing his will in the staging area he made of your mouth.

The kitchen was playing "When the Levee Breaks"—the Led Zeppelin song that sounds as though John Bonham is playing with cinder blocks instead of drumsticks—when Dufresne came to the table with the lamb bacon. And the juxtaposition of what he served and what they played raised a question: "Hey, Wylie, in the years you've been running wd-50, food has surpassed music as the thing people talk about, at least in New York City. But do you think that food can ever be as good as music? Do you think it can deliver the same experience as 'When the Levee Breaks'?"

"Do I think that food can be as *heavy* as 'When the Levee Breaks' or 'Achilles Last Stand'?"

"Yes."

"Well, I don't know. Those songs are pretty heavy. But it's a good question. Let me think about that one for a while."

But he didn't leave. He didn't go back to the kitchen, because he had tried to make art out of food, and he wanted to tell us what he'd found out. "It's been a struggle to get people to come eat for fun," he said. "You know, the way they listen to music. You can do all kinds of things with music. But food—it's something people *need*, and that changes everything. You start playing with it, people have all sorts of reactions."

He was a pioneer who wanted to start a movement and now had to be satisfied remaining a pioneer. "When I first opened, I thought there would be 15 people in the city doing what I do. Instead, Copenhagen has more of these kinds of restaurants than New York City does. The small town of *San Sebastián* has more of these kinds of restaurants than New York City does.

"I don't know," he said. "I just never thought I'd be the only one."

I wanted to tell him that rock 'n' roll was dying, too. But as Dufresne scanned the room from his place alongside our table, he did not look like the musician he styled himself to be. He looked like an astronaut who still can't believe that humans would never return to the moon.

The last course before the desserts was described on the menu as "Wagyu Flatiron, Watermelon, Fermented Black Bean." This was typical of wd-50—the seemingly discordant list of ingredients stated without elaboration, the provocation of a simultaneously mild-mannered and supremely self-confident man. But the last course before the dessert—the meat dish—had always been the course that revealed the weakness of wd-50, and we did not know what to expect of it. The meat dish is supposed to be the climax of the meal, at least in America, and Dufresne had never done anything to dampen anyone's sense of expectation. Indeed, by orchestrating and calibrating every aspect of the menu leading to the meat dish, he only sharpened the hunger for a final transcendent gesture, for meat that had been somehow re-invented. But meat turns out to be as hard to reinvent as the wheel. It's not that the beef and pork and chicken that Dufresne served weren't delicious; it's that people eating beef and pork and chicken are looking for pleasures *outside* deliciousness, and Dufresne was often loath to provide them. He often cooked meat with water as much as fire, with the perfectly controlled and calibrated technique known as sous vide. He often served meat not only without blood but also without smell, and it made the wide-open atelier of his kitchen seem suddenly as antiseptic as an operating room.

But Dufresne was *cooking* on this night, in every sense of the word. I do not remember anything about the watermelon or the fermented black bean that accompanied the lobe of Wagyu beef. But I remember the meat. It was red without being bloody, all the way to the lightly charred margin, and though it lacked smell, it looked like a heart, with a strange kind of life preserved in its density of flavor. Ah, we agreed, with our presumed sophistication, *this* is the kind of meat for which sous vide was created. The molecular had at last found expression in the elemental, so we moved on to the desserts feeling freed of the spectre of disappointment. And it was here that we confronted Dufresne's willingness to experiment with what he called "the undelicious," in the form of the final dessert, a nod to the gin and tonic in the form of a sorghum parfait, with a cake made of quinine and the taste of tonic replicated in tiny heaps of clear jelly.

It wasn't the invention of Dufresne but rather of his pastry chef, Malcolm Livingston II, but in a way it was what we were all waiting for—the risk that did not pay off and, in not paying off, confirmed that we were in the hands of a kitchen genuinely willing to take risks. How do we know that Wylie Dufresne is an artist and not just a gifted and daring chef? Because he sometimes does the impossible. How do we know he does the impossible? Because he sometimes fails to do the impossible. And it was that whiff of failure that hung on the night of our last supper at wd-50 and confronted us just as surely as quinine cake. Dufresne's experiment—a truly experimental restaurant—was closing. Did that mean it had failed? Did that mean *he* had failed? Or was the failure our own?

He did not accompany us to the door when we were leaving. He showed up when we were waiting outside and invited us back in for cake at the bar. It was late, yet wd-50 was more crowded than it had been in the flush of many an evening before Dufresne had announced its end. Now he looked at the people at his tables and listened to their clamor with the same look of vigilance that had crossed his face when he thought we were calling him names. "It's great," he said, "and it's really gratifying. But where were they two months ago? Where were they last year and the year before that?"

He didn't know what he was going to do next. He was obsessed with two things as a chef: the food of the Lower East Side as it existed before restaurants like wd-50 started moving in and the excellence of the egg. Hell, what most people didn't understand was he was obsessed with *cooking*, so maybe he would open a restaurant where he could work as a short-order cook, frying and scrambling eggs without feeling the need to transform them, like Picasso returning to sketch work just to show that he could draw.

"That's why I'm really proud of what we did here," he said over his cup of sake. "I'm proud of the big things, but I'm also proud of the little things we routinely did well. Do you know what made me most proud in the meal I served you? The Wagyu beef. It was *perfectly* cooked."

"The advantage of sous vide," someone said.

"But it wasn't sous vide!" Dufresne said. "That's the thing. It was cooked in a pan. And it had no *gray* on it! Do you know how hard that is? Do you know how much work that takes? Turning the beef every seven or eight seconds . . . And so that question you asked me before, about food and music—that's my answer: a perfect piece of Wagyu beef cooked in a pan that comes out without any gray on it. It might not be 'When the Levee Breaks,' but it's definitely 'Achilles Last Stand.'"

Someone's in the Kitchen

No Chef in America Cooks Dinner Quite Like Phillip Foss

By Ryan Sutton

From Eater

As the website Eater.com has re-energized long-form food writing, so has its iconoclastic food critic Ryan Sutton, who also blogs for Bloomberg.com (*The Price Hike, The Bad Deal*). When he anoints a Chicago chef as the cutting-edge guy to watch, sit up and take notice.

I've never done blow, but many of my ex-girlfriends have, and so when Phillip Foss hands me a mirror, a razor, and a gram of white powder, I know what to do. Sort of.

I'm sitting at a table at EL Ideas, Foss's restaurant in a warehouse-filled corner of Chicago's near south side. Against a backdrop of an empty basketball court, a juvenile detention center, a shuttered animal shelter in a condemned building, a freight train yard, a bar that serves strong drinks to strong train yard workers, and a gas station convenience store whose clerk sits behind bulletproof glass, a tasting-menu-only restaurant with a Michelin star stands out. But this isn't your ordinary tasting-menu-only restaurant. For starters, there's the cocaine course.

"Of course, it's culinary cocaine," clarifies Akiko Moorman, the restaurant's director of operations. "So it goes in your mouth and not up your nose."

I pick up the tiny straw that accompanies the dish and use it to orally inhale the powder, which turns out to be a mixture of dehydrated coconut and lime. The taste is clean and clear. It evokes a high-end riff on

Pixy Stix, the powdered sugar candy that my rough-and-tumble friends and I would eat (and occasionally snort) before high school track meets in the mid '90s.

As I use the razor to separate the powder into narrow lines, Moorman nods her head toward an adjacent table, where a pair of diners—a young man with a black mohawk, and a woman who I recognize as a manager at one of Chicago's most heralded restaurants—are making sharp, studied, chopping motions with their razors.

"That's how you know they're experts," Moorman jokes, explaining that the practice grinds out any lumps in more potent versions of the powder. The cocaine course reveals a lot about people. "We actually just had an incident," Moorman says. "A guy came here who had been to rehab not too long ago. When the cocaine course came out, he briefly left the restaurant to call his sponsor."

EL Ideas—the name begs to be pronounced with a Spanish accent, but don't: "EL" refers to Chicago's elevated public transit system—is an atypical restaurant in an atypical location. It's officially in an area called Douglas Park, tucked into an industrial corner that feels miles away from everything, but to consider it a neighborhood restaurant, one must take an expansive view of the word "neighborhood."

At EL Ideas, sometimes one must also take an expansive view of utensils. Sure, there's a fancy scallop course with arugula puree, and a lamb course with olive sauce, both consumed traditionally, with knives and forks. But then there's that inhaled coconut-lime powder. On some occasions, there's a "Twix Bar": a chicken liver-topped crouton dipped in chocolate that's eaten with the hands. On other nights, there's a raw milk course served in a baby bottle. "Foss was going through this infantile stage," Moorman recalls. "I've never seen so many uncomfortable men! Foss told everyone to pinch the nipple, shake it, and suck."

On the night I'm there, patrons aren't asked to suck anything, but they are asked to lift a small, clear glass bowl to their faces and lick a caviar-topped, solid-state White Russian off of it. Why a glass dish? "So you can see a person licking in front of you," Foss says. "And who doesn't enjoy that?" Indeed, a roomful of diners ingesting the dish is so collectively suggestive that the performance wouldn't be out of place on Cinemax After Dark. Is it the best way to appreciate good caviar? Not necessarily. But it loosens you up for the cocaine to come.

It's not quite what you'd expect from a forty-five-year-old Milwaukee native who speaks with a proper Midwest accent and a mouthful of curses. Foss is five-foot ten. He's dirty blond. During service he wears a blue button-down whose design has more in common with an auto mechanic's uniform than it does with traditional chefs' whites. His cooking has been exuberantly praised by the Chicago *Tribune*, but you won't find his spot on a national or global best-restaurants list, nor will you read much about it in national publications run by out-of-town food writers or gastronauts. For all its brilliance, EL Ideas is still very much under the radar, still very much undersold.

This may be because Foss is very good at underselling. "I'm not going to kid myself; this will never be a three Michelin-star restaurant, ever," he tells me before dinner service. Guests are starting to fill up the room; it's warmly lit with lots of exposed brick, roughly divided into dining room and kitchen by a waist-high wall. "We're so far outside the box. We play loud hip-hop. We do not give a fuck."

Except he very much does give a fuck. He lives with Moorman in the apartment above the restaurant (the two have been a couple since 2012). He produces intelligent, whimsically modernist food that's studied enough to earn EL Ideas one Michelin star, if not yet three. He talks about the expansion of his empire with more circumspection than some policy analysts lend to prognostications of nuclear war. He admits to being very stressed about my presence in the dining room. He hasn't left the country since EL Ideas opened, has barely left the city. Chicago is one of the world's most important food cities, and he's one of Chicago's most important chefs.

More than any other city, Chicago is the heart of America's experimental dining movement. A progressive, inventive philosophy underscores many of its best restaurants, one that isn't found with the same intensity or focus elsewhere.

To be sure, other major cities have their own culinary stories. The tasting menu spots dotting the San Francisco Bay area, from Manresa to Saison to Meadowood, fit into the region's ethos—celebrations of Pacific seafood and odes to vegetables—as befits both a region that is (current drought notwithstanding) the country's largest supplier of agriculture, and a contemporary restaurant lineage that stretches back to Alice Waters' mission to teach diners to value their beets as much as their beef. In New York, fine dining has long been driven by the city's financial titans, whose risky market behavior doesn't always extend to their eating habits; for the most part, the Big Apple palate remains neo-classical, inoffensive, and indulgent, anchored on restaurants like Le Bernardin, Daniel, Jean-Georges, and Del Posto. Despite the city's recent trend towards lighter, longer, let's-have-a-slice-of-pizza-afterward set menus, New York generally plays to the center, rather than pushing the envelope too hard.

In Chicago, all bets are off. Think: helium-filled taffy balloons at Alinea, edible menus at Moto, ice-encased old-fashioneds that you crack open with a slingshot at Aviary, psychedelic king crab terrariums at Grace, spruce juice-filled test tubes at Elizabeth, and at EL Ideas, spearmint ice cream that's nitro-frozen to such an intensely frozen hardness that it mimics the texture of a candy cane. "I do think Chicago is the food capital of America," says Moorman. "It has the most interesting food. The most soulful food. The most thoughtful food."

But it takes more than soul and thought to run an experimental restaurant—Chicago's plentiful and relatively affordable real estate (paired with a good number of affluent, open-minded diners) seals the city's position as the *avant*-avant-garde. "The rent is the biggest factor," Moorman explains. "Coming here from New York, it's like traveling to a country with a favorable exchange rate. You don't have to put a burger on your menu to be successful here. You don't have to pay back $1.4 million dollars that you borrowed to open your restaurant. There are truly chef-owners here, in a way that nobody in New York can say they are. In New York, they're slaves to their investors."

Indeed. Foss doesn't rely on a single dime of outside capital at EL Ideas. Thanks to the restaurant's out-of-the-way location, he can afford to be the business's sole owner. He doesn't carry any real debt on the restaurant's equipment; paying off all of any major purchases within the month, from the immersion circulators to the high-tech Pacojet that makes sorbets so clean and stable you can go out for a mid-course smoke and your dessert still won't have melted by the time you come back inside.

All of this enables Foss to take risks he couldn't elsewhere. But the other advantage of being experimental in Chicago is that the city is used to it. "You have a dinership that is forgiving and incredibly adventurous,"

Moorman says. The proof is on the books: Nearly four years after opening, tables at EL Ideas are still mostly all booked up two months out.

Foss seems surprised by his own success: "It was never meant to be sustainable on its own," he says of the restaurant. "I was always just expecting this place to be a stipend, financially, to the food truck." He ran that food truck, a mobile protein purveyor called MeatyBalls, from 2010 to 2011, regularly attracting lines two dozen deep. But his career didn't necessarily point to a career selling *Saturday Night Live*–inspired lamb-and-pork "Schweddy balls" out of a service window on wheels.

After graduating from the Culinary Institute of America in 1991, Foss accrued a serious lineup of fine dining merit badges on his resume, including stints at New York's Quilted Giraffe and Oceana in the early 1990s, a five-year tenure at Le Cirque that same decade, as well as some time at seminal Chicago-modernist restaurant Tru in 2000. But then things get muddy: Foss, rather than staging at Ivy League restaurants like Noma or Mugaritz, spent many of his pre–EL Ideas years at hotel restaurants that weren't exactly known as incubators of promising gastronomic talent. He put in two years at the Four Seasons in Maui. He logged ten months at The King David in Jerusalem (Foss, a non-observant Jew, speaks Hebrew). He bounced around Brazil ("best time of my life") and Bermuda (where he unhappily cooked old-school French fare).

"I thought my dreams of being a respectable chef who would ever have a nice restaurant were drifting," he says of that period. He came back to Chicago in 2008 to run the show at Lockwood, the fine-dining restaurant inside the Palmer House Hilton, where he pulled in critical raves but was fired two years later after making a lighthearted pot joke on Twitter. Now, he makes cocaine jokes on your plate.

The story Foss tells is that EL Ideas happened by accident. The building that now houses the restaurant was being used as a commissary for his meatball truck; the twist that transformed it into a sit-down dining room was the result of, of all things, a health department inspection. During a routine check, Foss recalls, the inspector said, "I'm not really sure what type of license to give you, but you have a dining space over here, and so I'll give you a restaurant license." That was all it took. Says Foss: "That was the epiphany. And two months later we were open."

At first, Foss ran EL Ideas and MeatyBalls simultaneously. The early days were rocky. A week after EL Ideas opened, Foss and his wife separated. (His two daughters, six and eight years old, stay with him on Sundays and Mondays.) Six months later, the restaurant was on the verge of closing, an outcome Foss averted by taking on a zero-interest loan from an angel investor (which he has since paid back in full). Shortly after that investment, Foss found out an office manager had siphoned off around $30,000 in funds to pay for her wedding.

So he closed the food truck and focused all his energy on EL. The extortion "turned out to be quite a blessing in disguise," Foss says. Running two businesses at once was taking its toll: "I was getting up at four a.m., I wasn't coming home until after midnight." Shutting the lights off on the meatball business "gave me my sanity and energy back."

With nothing else competing for his culinary attention, Foss was able to double down on those elevated ideas that give his restaurant its name. Given all the culinary boundary pushing that happens in this corner of Douglas Park, you'd be forgiven for thinking that Foss is positioning himself to become the next Grant Achatz or Heston Blumenthal. But then you watch a staffer dressed up as the Dude from *The Big Lebowski* stroll through the dining room, the entertainment portion of the White Russian caviar course. Foss explains that the preparation was inspired by a regular who took advantage of the restaurant's BYO policy to mix up the namesake cocktail for himself during dinner service.

Nope, EL Ideas is definitely not the Fat Duck. And Foss is not Blumenthal. Nor is he Achatz. Nor—his suggestive coconut-lime intermezzo notwithstanding—is he your standard coke-addled cook, despite the drug's ubiquity in the hospitality industry. ("I never understood chefs who do cocaine," he says. "It numbs your mouth. You can't taste anything.") And while the easy answer would be to say he's his own man, offering his own wacky take on the avant-garde, Foss's brilliant-slacker approach to fine dining is in fact the product of a thread that started in Chicago's restaurant community back in 2005.

If really you want to understand Phillip Foss, you have to understand Michael Carlson. The famously mercurial chef, proprietor of Chicago's famous (or perhaps infamous) restaurant Schwa, can arguably be credited more than any other figure for influencing what EL Ideas—not to mention the city's entire laid-back approach to high-minded cooking—has become. If Alinea is the flagship for Chicago's culinary avant-gardism, Schwa is the restaurant that, in Foss's words, helped "take the stuffiness out of fine dining," launching a new generation of more affordable, more low-key tasting menu establishments. "We all certainly owe a tip of the cap to Schwa," Foss says. "They really are the beginning of the genre."

And if you want to eat at Schwa, you need to learn the rules. First: call often, as the phones are not answered on a terribly regular basis, and Carlson has a history of closing the restaurant entirely—for a night or two occasionally; one time for a whole six months—with no warning. Second: come bearing gifts. "Should I bring a bottle of booze?" I ask Foss before I head to the restaurant. The booze isn't for me; it's a gift for the cooks. "It never hurts," he replies. "You may find yourself with a little more attention." And so I show up to Schwa, located in a three-story building so unremarkable I'm half certain I'm really walking into a Knights of Columbus hall, with a bottle of Elijah Craig twelve-year as a welcome gift. The kitchen accepts it graciously.

Now here's the thing: America's best-reviewed and most expensive tasting menus tend to go hand-in-hand with the country's most expensive wine lists. The conventional wisdom is that restaurants want to offer a beverage experience that's as *haute* as its culinary counterpart. You wouldn't want to drink boxed wine with your multi-hundred-dollar dinner even though you might chug it at home in your sweatpants, so you get the multi-hundred-dollar wine pairing.

But that's a generous way of looking at things. The larger truth is that the razor-thin margins that accompany high food and labor costs mean that restaurants often rely on pricey beverage options to turn a profit—selling a dozen tasting menus won't make a restaurant nearly as much money as would selling hundreds of pizzas. Wine, which commands markups often measured in multipliers rather than percentages, helps offset that imbalance. If a tasting-menu restaurant has no liquor license, it means it can't get one. No normal restaurant would turn that revenue stream down.

But Schwa isn't a normal restaurant. A liquor license isn't that hard to obtain in Chicago, yet there's no sign that Carlson has any plans to obtain one. Instead, he lures entry-level diners (and wine buffs attracted by his next-to-nothing corkage fee of $2.50) to an off-the-beaten-track block where a small staff (there are no servers; the cooks run the food to diners) and low rents allow him to stay in business despite the lack of alcohol (and despite running a reported sixty percent food cost). Whether Carlson actually makes any money is a different question, but the Schwa model paved the way for other affordable(-ish) tasting-menu-only venues with BYO policies to open in other un-frilly neighborhoods. Among them, the Michelin-starred Goosefoot in Lincoln Square, the two-Michelin-starred 42 grams in Uptown, and of course, EL Ideas.

"I always thought we wanted to be like Schwa," Foss says of his restaurant. "But just with a little more attention to the front of the house, and the service aspect, and not to be *so* punk rock." He pauses to consider. "Maybe we're a bit more rock-and-roll."

Maybe. Walking into Schwa feels like stepping into the studio apartment of a bunch of guys who play a lot of *Grand Theft Auto*, eat a lot of Lucky Charms, and smoke a formidable quantity of expertly rolled blunts. The restaurant is staffed by laconic, heavily bearded men dressed in aprons and sweatshirts; they're the cooks, but also the servers, delivering plates of food to the bare-walled dining room at irregular intervals. EL Ideas, by contrast, is a light, bright, dinner party of a restaurant, with a dedicated front-of-house manager helping the courses land on time. The seating plan, like at Schwa, is table-only, which is somewhat retro-revolutionary by modern fine dining standards, where chef's counter seating is increasingly the norm. EL Ideas books in seatings— all guests dine at once—and Foss addresses the room before each course. A teacher, an announcer, a preacher.

Foss's explanations and segues are illuminating, informal, and, when appropriate, concise. As a roomful of diners faces down a one-bite course of dark chicken meat filled with blue cheese mousse, a side of hot sauce, and a shot of Pabst Blue Ribbon beer, Foss introduces it by saying "This time of year is all about football. And football is all about cheap beer and wings."

A few minutes later, Foss invites all dozen or so of that night's guests into the kitchen half of the space. We gather around a long silver prep table that runs the length of the cooking area, ready to sample what Foss later describes as a "French onion soup ball"—it's beef stock encased in a crouton, topped with gruyere. Once we're all done slurping it up, Foss keeps the party moving. "Okay guys, that's the end of this course," he says. "So you can pretty much get the fuck out of the kitchen."

Up next is a bite-sized square of Miyazaki Wagyu wrapped in matsutake mushroom leather, an edible napkin of sorts, which comes with neither knife nor fork. The result is that you end up eating one of the world's most exalted pieces of beef with your hands, as you would an hors d'oeuvre at a cocktail party.

If you didn't know what was in them, none of these unassuming-looking courses would appear out of place at an Applebee's—or inside a cardboard box in the freezer section of your local supermarket. But when you experience their clarity of flavor—the concentrated poultry punch, the airy assertiveness of the blue cheese, the fattiness of the Wagyu— you know you're at a restaurant where serious things are happening.

Yes, Foss is a product of the Chicago avant-garde movement, and he's an upstanding and popular member of the set-menu BYO scene. But what defines him as a chef, most of all, are not his techniques or his liquor policies, but rather his allegiance to both ennobling and subverting the everyday American dining experience, without deconstructing things to the point where they're unrecognizable. (To underscore this point, the French onion soup ball is presented as a surprise: patrons are handed the bite-sized sphere without explanation, and asked to guess what they're eating. It tasted so purely, exquisitely like the bistro staple that I guessed in about two seconds.)

Foss isn't the only one reimagining the American fast food and casual dining palate through a sophisticated lens: Christina Tosi draws on similar references at the Milk Bar bakery chain, with her cereal milk ice creams, Thanksgiving croissants, and birthday cake truffles, and every other fancy chef has a elevated riff on the creamsicle these days. But no one except Foss is so consistently fusing the nostalgic and the innovative in a high-end sitting—and with such aplomb and accessibility.

Pack that all in with the Big Lebowski guy and the baby bottles and you've got yourself a proper dose of interactive performance art, or as Moorman calls it, "dining-tainment." In the past, that phrase has evoked hokey theme restaurants geared toward little kids or bad first dates. In the modern era of dinner as theater, however, such frivolities are a more seamless (if not subtle) part of the evening. Think of the card tricks at New York's Eleven Madison Park, or watching smoke come out of a fellow diner's nose after the nitro-lime mousse at The Fat Duck. At EL

Ideas, the playfulness is built into the foundation. I haven't had a more entertaining dinner in years.

The best course I try at EL Ideas is one Foss tells me is inspired by his daughters, who have cottoned on to the classic Wendy's off-menu pairing of dipping french fries in a chocolate Frosty. In his homage, Foss pours liquid nitrogen–chilled vanilla ice cream over a classic potato-leek soup, turning the vichyssoise into a creamy slush for a split second, before the heat of thrice-fried yukon gold nuggets at the bottom of the bowl melts everything back to liquid. The changing textures and flavors paint a culinary sine wave, starting at one place, rising up, and falling back down again. Ferran Adrià would wish he thought of this. But I bet Adrià never wished his beloved El Bulli, in its picturesque stone farmhouse on Spain's beautiful Costa Brava, was situated here, in a rundown part of Chicago.

Wander south of the restaurant, and you'll pass anonymous buildings with faded signs and indistinct names like Midwest Folding Products, Midland Warehouses, and Top of the Line Total Auto Repair. Walk to the northwest and you'll eventually hit the Cook County Juvenile Temporary Detention Center. There's little residential housing over here. Pedestrians are rare too, but cars are not—there are plenty driving through, they just don't stop. "We're in a vortex of Chicago," Foss tells me. "More like a black hole," Moorman adds, joking that there's no reason to come to the neighborhood "unless your child is in jail."

Strolling the streets around EL Ideas evokes stories my father used to tell me about working in the Brooklyn neighborhood of Bushwick in the 1980s, back when that part of town was an industrial area full of warehouses and the junkies who'd squat in them. Now, thirty-five years later, Bushwick's warehouses have been turned into desirable (and increasingly costly) loft apartments, and the neighborhood is full of young, artsy types. This is thanks in part to the anchoring effect of a single groundbreaking restaurant: in 2009, a place called Roberta's started wooing in residents from Manhattan and other parts of Brooklyn with ambitious, Italian-accented small plates and some of the city's best Neapolitan pizzas, all served in a cool, quirky, stripped-down setting. It turned out to be the type of restaurant you could build a neighborhood around.

It's not clear if EL Ideas is cut from the same cloth. For all its friendliness and inviting appeal, a tasting menu–only format doesn't create the same kind of vibe as Roberta's expansive fiefdom, which started with pizza but now—behind just one door—includes a hip pizza shop, an outdoor tiki garden, a shipping-container indie radio station, and a high-end chefs' counter tucked away in the very back, where a handful of lucky diners each night get to have one of New York's most acclaimed tasting menus. Nearly four years into EL Ideas' run, there are few new businesses nearby, and no new residential housing. The closest a la carte eateries are a Burger King and a dive called Watering Hole, whose website boasts "Our pizzas aren't frozen!"

But Foss has plans. He says he's toying with the idea of opening a barbecue joint in a shipping container across the street, and a cocktail den in the same building as the restaurant. To his mind, the key to any expansion would be proximity to EL. "I couldn't do something on the north side of Chicago," he says. This is because he is, to use his phrase, a control freak: "If I don't have control, I wind up not being happy." He also believes in his neighborhood, placing his faith in a *Field of Dreams*–style determinism. "This place is a little freak of nature," he explains of the success of EL Ideas. "I call it the Costner project: 'If you build it, they will come.'"

The real heart of Foss's strategy isn't necessarily what he plans on doing, but how he plans to do it: with his own money. And while the chef is relaxed on the issue of financing, Akiko Moorman is not. "I've been a very strong advocate of getting others to understand that need to start self-funding in this industry," she says. "Letting outside investors control what the chef does, where the chef cooks, what goes on the menu—really, that's one of the industry's biggest downfalls. And until we have enough successful chefs who are willing to give back and start funding younger chefs with an angel investment group, we are not going to see what this industry can do. We're not going to see artists really flourish, because they'll still have a money man saying 'I want a TV in the bar, and I want a loaded baked potato on the menu.'"

Moorman walks the talk: a former bookkeeper and line cook, she manages the restaurant's payroll, as well as the entire restaurant's finances. This gives her less of an urgent eye towards profit, and more room to understand how to help the restaurant grow organically. "Most of the time, investors are money men or real estate guys," she points out. "At the end of the day, they don't give a shit. They want their money. And that could be the death of a restaurant."

It's hard to imagine an investor approving of Foss's wacky "Tastes like Teen Spirit" dinner series, during which he collaborated with other local chefs on 1990s inspired dishes (the late Homaro Cantu, of Moto, made a Clintonian Cuban "cigar" sandwich course, served in an ashtray). I also wonder what a backer might think of Foss doing shots of bourbon (poured from a bottle bestowed by a guest) in the kitchen with a crowd of diners, as he does at the end of our dinner service. No one's doing that with Joshua Skenes at Saison, I'd guess. Foss knocks back his drink quickly, Schwa style. And this is when Foss tells me a bit more about his wonderful culinary cocaine.

"We had a state rep in from Illinois recently," he tells me, a few steps away from the crowd. "And she saw the cocaine back here, where we keep it in a jar, and she just put a little bit in her nose. And I'm like, 'No, don't do that, don't do that! You put it in your mouth!' And so she goes to put it in her mouth, and she's rubbing the cocaine on her gums."

He pauses for dramatic effect. "A fucking state representative!" He's thrilled, delighted, a little disbelieving—exactly how I feel after a night spent eating the man's food. Foss turns back to the crowd of adoring diners, says his goodbyes, and heads upstairs to his apartment.

Author's Note: It's impossible to talk about avant-gardism in Chicago without talking about Homaro Cantu, the Moto chef who pushed boundaries (scientific, culinary, and more) like no one else. On April 13, after I reported, wrote, and filed this story, Cantu committed suicide. It turned out that the '90s dinner on which Foss and Cantu collaborated happened to take place on the same day that Cantu was hit with a lawsuit by one of his investors. I called Foss shortly after I heard the news. "I half expected him not to show up," Foss recalled of their dinner. But show up he did, and the evening was a wild success. Upon learning of Cantu's death, Foss told me that he had all his cooks come to the front of the house before service, and raise a glass to the chef's memory.

The Meat Prophet of Peru

By Nicholas Gill

From Roads & Kingdoms

A fork illustration

Based in both Brooklyn, New York, and Lima, Peru, travel writer/
photographer Nicholas Gill fits in well with the globe-roaming
adventurers writing for online magazine RoadsandKingdoms.com.
Here he reminds us that culinary visionaries can be found
anywhere—even in the back room of a suburban butcher shop.

The most interesting things being done with meat in South America at this very moment aren't happening in the beef temples of Buenos Aires. They're not happening in the open pit asados of Mendoza or Salta or the parrillas of Uruguay or the churrascarías of Brazil. They're happening in Peru, the country with the lowest meat-eating index in all of Latin America.

Specifically, they're happening around a large table in a back room at Osso, a butcher shop on the outskirts of Lima, inland across the traffic clogged artery of Avenida Javier Prado and beyond the dusty brown hills in the residential district of La Molina. This is where butcher Renzo Garibaldi is doing things with meat that no one here or anywhere has ever seen or thought to do.

Six foot two with a shaggy goatee and a Paul Bunyan build, Garibaldi, the son of textile entrepreneurs, took a job at Sushi Samba while studying international business in Miami. When he moved back to Lima he enrolled in a culinary school and later took a job slicing fish at Costanera 700. He moved to the US to be a part of Gastón Acurio's team at La Mar in San Francisco and while there, he took a class with master butcher Ryan Farr of 4505 Meats. Everything changed. He fell in love with meat. He became fascinated with the art of the cut and the anatomy of cows and pigs. He soon quit La Mar, landed an apprenticeship with Farr and immersed himself with some of the world's best butchers. He moved to La Granja Baradieu in Gascogne, France, for a stint with the Chapolard brothers to master charcuterie and pig butchery, then to New York to work with Joshua Applestone at Fleisher's. Wanting to bring a touch of that meat culture home, he and his wife moved back to Lima and opened Osso in the upscale suburb in mid-2013.

The primary operations here are the same as any other butcher shop. Glass cases are filled with different cuts of meat. There is an entire rack of house-made chorizos, with uniquely Peruvian flavors like anticuchero or rocoto pepper marmalade and ají limo. There are smoked porterhouses, pastrami, Duroc pork belly bacon, and pre-made burgers, plus a blackboard list of offerings for barrel ovens and caja chinas, like pancetta and pork shoulder. There's also Kurobuta fat, Peruvian craft beers, bags of pork rinds, and even Kobe beef-infused treats for dogs.

Garibaldi and his team can often be seen behind the glass counter breaking down entire carcasses. Behind them another temperature controlled case stores the finer cuts, like the NY Strips of marbled wagyu from Snake River Farms, which he imports from Idaho, plus bone in rib-eyes and cowboy steaks. Then there is the meat locker full of large carcasses hung from the ceiling, all in different stages of decomposition.

But it's what's happening in the back of Osso that has been capturing everyone's attention. This is where for the past year Garibaldi has been holding clandestine dinners around a single large wooden table for no more than eight guests at a time.

As I enter the back room with a few friends, the table is already set with trays of charcuterie: duck rillete, roast beef, and salami. Behind the table is a wood-fired grill. It's as raw and crude of a space for a tasting menu as I have ever seen. There's not even silverware. Everything is eaten with your hands here.

Soon out comes a bowl of lardo, a soft mound of cured pork fat, which we scoop on to crackers. Next come chorizos, one of ají amarillo with huacatay, classic Peruvian flavors, and another made with maple syrup. Then sliders made with 30-day-aged beef and topped with gruyere. Ten minutes later Garibaldi wheels out a stand with a wooden bowl with a pile of chopped beef. He cracks open an egg and starts mixing this crude tartar tableside with onion, chives, and salt. An assistant of his scoops out servings into our hands right from the bowl.

All of this makes for a rousing start, but the real magic occurs when the meal moves to the grill. Cooking over live fire is irregular. Controlling the heat with the consistency he does is something few can do. Cut after perfectly cooked cut comes to us right off of a cutting board. The Wagyu short rib, seasoned with soy sauce and panela, is probably the best short rib I've ever tasted—the perfect combination of sugar, salt, fat, and smoke.

He follows with a porterhouse, an axe-handle rib eye, and a string of other imposing cuts that he's carefully aged at Osso. This is where Garibaldi is moving the traditional grill master role into unchartered territory. They start at 30 days, then increase to 45 and 60. You can taste the collagen breaking down a little bit more with each cut, resulting in more nuanced flavors. Each is muskier and funkier than the last. He finishes some by holding them directly over the flames. Others he sits right in the charcoal and covers in ash. He moves on to a steak aged 120 days, and then, for the grand finale, a 160-day-old piece of Wagyu. Over the course of nearly six months of aging, natural enzymes in the protein break down and the carbohydrates are converted into sugar, so the flavors are richer and more concentrated. The sizzling beef smells like buttered popcorn. Every bite tastes of pure umami.

It wasn't supposed to be like this. Osso was just supposed to be a butcher shop. He liked the idea of resurrecting serious butchery—a once dying art that just a decade ago was left for dead in most corners of the culinary world—in Peru in the way it was being done in Brooklyn and San Francisco. He'd follow the path of this emerging movement of sustainable, hormone-free meats and find ways to use every part of the animal. There would be six of them working, including his wife, Andrea, who handles all of the administration. They had the back room built and added the grill so he could just invite friends over to hang out. "I thought the meat I had that I didn't sell beyond 21 days we would eat and maybe have a few beers."

He casually mentioned he would do this to a few friends. Two of them were Gastón Acurio, the iconic Peruvian chef, and Mitsuharu

Tsumara, of Nikkei restaurant Maido, and they took him seriously. Suddenly, three weeks after opening the shop, they began getting calls for reservations. They said they must have the wrong number. The calls kept coming. They would say, "But Gastón and Micha said you have this amazing place in back, no?" Finally they said they would put something together.

"We didn't understand exactly what was happening and we weren't prepared, but when someone like Gastón pushes you in this direction you have the responsibility to try," he said.

They didn't have silverware, so they decided diners would just eat with their hands. They didn't have glasses so they borrowed some from his parent's house. There was no intention of opening a restaurant.

Now there is a staff of 30 and they've done 230 dinners over the past year. Sometimes two per day. Curious eaters make the pilgrimage from all over of the world. A cast of Chilean soap opera stars flew here for one day just to eat in the back room. A group from Spain came after they overheard a waiter from El Cellar de Can Roca talking about it while they were eating there. The Peruvian cardinal even came. They are sold out at least two months in advance and that list keeps growing longer every day.

This brings us to Osso phase two, where things get even more interesting. Next door to the butcher shop, where the café Eggo used to stand, the butcher shop is being extended into a full-blown restaurant. The one table in the back of the butcher shop is still the heart of the operation, though they'll now have 38 seats and a kitchen designed for zero waste, so everything that he butchers will be used.

They added the restaurant so they can accept walk-ins and serve a standard menu with some plates coming off the tasting menu, like the tartar or an asado de tira, or short rib, that has been smoked for four hours, cooked sous vide for 30 hours, and then finished by holding it directly over the flame.

He won't be using much charcoal, mostly eucalyptus, which has been growing in abundance in Peru since Franciscan friars planted it in the Andes in the 19th century. There's also sustainably managed applewood, orange wood, and pasapailo, a native wood his supplier turned him on to.

Garibaldi takes Osso's eco footprint seriously, but he also takes pleasure in less earnest aspects of the meat business. His favorite part of the restaurant is a picture of a sausage in the men's bathroom. "So you're peeing and you look up on the wall and it says 'nice sausage.'"

A few days after opening the new restaurant, I meet up with Garibaldi. We drink beers and talk about the future of Osso. Another degustation is about to happen over on the other side in the back room and we join the guests waiting for the rest of their party to arrive. It's BYOB in the back so one brought a bottle of wine and Garibaldi tells someone on the staff to put it in a fridge at 15 degrees Celsius. Another brings a cooler filled with bottles of beer and champagne.

Garibaldi starts talking to them about golf, which he recently picked up. He says he goes to the course still wearing his flannel shirts and that the other golfers are probably afraid of him. He doesn't give a shit. "I'm like a lumberjack golfer," he says.

He has picked up other habits, too, and his natural curiosity pushes him to extremes. He mostly drank beer when the restaurant opened, but he has also gotten into wine lately because all of the guests keep bringing different bottles and insist he has a glass. "I've been getting into Super Tuscans. One day someone brought in an 86 Chateau Palmer."

He's careful not to make Osso a fine dining experience though. Even if someone brings in a $2,000 bottle of wine he wants it to still be food you eat with your hands.

The heart of the dining experience, the cuts of hyper-aged meats, is another part of the happy-accident narrative that defines Osso and Garibaldi. He didn't learn anything about this from the Chapolard brothers or Applestone or other experimental butchers. It all happened here.

"After we opened we realized I was bad at handling inventories," he tells me. "I thought I was going to sell 21-day-old meat and that was it."

At times he over bought, so instead of throwing it out he just kept it in the coolers to see what happened. "People started to get excited about things that were 50 days old. I didn't really think about the numbers then."

Now he is thinking about the numbers. The longer this lower quality national meat isn't eaten, the more the connective tissue is broken down and becomes something else.

"With meat that has been aged for 21 to 60 days there is a change, but it won't blow you away," he tells me. "At 150 days old it's another story. At 200 days old it's like the difference between a boxed wine and a 30-year-old Bordeaux. It's so complex, so elegant to analyze."

In the back other cuts are still waiting their right time. As is the cattle business here as a whole.

Beef has never been Peru's strong point. There's not a culture of eating prime cuts and most of the higher quality beef is imported, therefore expensive. Despite the country's biodiversity, the barren coast and arid Andes lack the grasslands and the water to support large scale grazing. Therefore national cattle are of rather low quality compared with Peru's more carnivorous neighbors like Chile and Argentina. Yet, within the various microclimates artisanal ranchers have potential to carve out a niche.

"Peru needs another one or two more years and the meat industry will explode," he says. "We'll start having people investing in long term cattle projects."

Things are already happening. Most of them have some sort of Osso connection. In the jungle, there's zebu, the hump-backed tropical cow from Southeast Asia that some ranchers are trying to develop. They need some help from the government to be able to move their product to the coast, but it should happen eventually. In another part of the jungle another group is breeding a cattle that eats the upper part of sugarcane plants, which are usually just tossed out. "The fat has a lot of character. A lot of flavor," he tells me. "It's intense. Aggressive. Very cool. Salty."

They need about another year and a half before he'll be able to get the meat regularly.

What's so encouraging about Garibaldi's future, and the country's potential with meat in general, is how much Peruvians have already done with meat for so long with so little. No scrap has gone to waste. Slaves working on coastal plantations took the leftover bits from a butchered cow, such as the heart, and seasoned them, skewered them and continually marinated them so they taste as tender as a filet mignon. Anticuchos are now a favorite Peruvian snack. Cow's foot? Toss it in a soup until it's rich and gelatinous. Guinea pig? Roast it, grill it, fry it, or turn it into a terrine. Throw out chicken blood? Fuck no. Season it and cook it and you'll have sangrecita.

The country's biodiversity seems to always be the topic of conversation here when it comes to food. You have tree resins that can be turned into gels and more naturally occurring fruits and freshwater fish than anywhere else on earth, but there's a spirit of culinary innovation here too. It has existed for as long as humans have walked the Andes, from the Incas finding ways to freeze dry potatoes to expand their empire to Japanese chefs in the '70s tweaking how long citric acid should be doused over raw fish for ceviche. Osso isn't just a butcher shop or a carnivore's paradise. It's another part of that story.

In Search of the Perfect Taco

By Jeff Gordinier

From the *New York Times T Magazine*

Wide-ranging curiosity and enthusiasm enliven Jeff Gordinier's food and culture writing for the *New York Times.** Those qualities make him a perfect guide for this gastronomic road trip: cruising around Mexico with star chefs René Redzepi (Noma) and Danny Bowien (Mission Chinese).

"Closing my eyes
I open them inside your eyes."
     —*Octavio Paz, "Across"*

I t happens on a Thursday morning in Oaxaca, and everyone at the table can see it. René Redzepi takes a bite of a breakfast dish that has been placed in front of him, and something passes across his face like a wave of light. Over the years there have been pilgrims who have traveled to Mexico to experience mind alteration with buttons of peyote, but for Redzepi, a man who is often referred to as the greatest chef in the world, transcendence comes in the form of enfrijoladas.

Admittedly, it doesn't look like the food of the gods. Enfrijoladas consist of little more than soft handmade corn tortillas that have been blanketed with a sauce made out of pulverized black beans. It's classic peasant food—simple and satisfying, with an aesthetic that suggests a big smudge on a plate. But what ferries Redzepi through the portals of illumination is a leaf. The trailblazing Oaxacan chef Alejandro Ruiz, who is beaming at the head of the table at his Casa Oaxaca Café with his wife and son, has spiked this black-bean sauce with a hidden depth charge of flavor: patches of foliage from a local avocado tree. The leaves electrify the sauce with an unexpected thrum of black licorice. Suddenly it's clear that simplicity is only what we see on the surface. With one bite, layers begin to reveal themselves.

"You think you know what it's going to taste like," Redzepi says. "This to me is the best mouthful I've had in Mexico. I can't believe the flavor of this leaf. Wow. I'm getting chills."

"I never take pictures of food, but I have to," mutters Danny Bowien, an American chef who has come along for the ride. "I have to, man."

Redzepi has traveled to Oaxaca on something of a crusade. People who know about the chef's cooking at Noma, in Copenhagen, might be surprised to learn that the man who is cast as the charismatic godfather of the New Nordic movement that has transformed the global restaurant landscape has a gastronomic infatuation that's as far from the forests and fjords of Scandinavia as you can get. Redzepi is truly, madly, deeply in love with Mexico.

I learned about this one cold afternoon when I met the 36-year-old Dane at a coffee shop in downtown Manhattan. I figured we'd spend an hour or so murmuring in solemn Ingmar Bergmanish tones about the chilly wonders of the wind-blasted Scandinavian shore. Much to my surprise, Redzepi carried himself with a bright, self-effacing, surfer-like casualness. He seemed practically Californian. After a few minutes, he stopped talking about the New Nordic thing altogether. Instead, he drifted into a trance state about the flavors of Mexico and the great, game-changing chefs he had befriended all over the country. He mentioned Ruiz, Enrique Olvera, Roberto Solís. He got a faraway look in his eyes. He assured me that Mexico was the Next Place in the evolution of global gastronomy—a "sleeping giant" about to wake up with a roar.

He liked to say that for decades—centuries, really—the indigenous spirit of Mexican cooking had been muffled, like the ruins of a Mayan temple buried beneath a Catholic church put up by Spanish conquerors: "For many years in fine dining in Mexico, you had the cathedral on top of the pyramid. With chefs like Enrique Olvera, the pyramid starts to become visible again." After the innovations of Ferran Adrià's experimental cuisine in Spain and the New Nordic movement in Scandinavia, gastronomes have been amping up their interest in Mexico and Central and South America. In the United States, chefs like Roy Choi, April Bloomfield, Alex Stupak, Jean-Georges Vongerichten, Wesley Avila and Bowien are finding ways to reinterpret the taco, and around the world there's a burgeoning sense that the culinary spotlight might be shifting to Mexico. Cloudberries and lumpfish roe? What Redzepi was really craving was a taco.

And so, for nearly a week, he planned to eat, talk and swoon his way through Mexico City, Oaxaca, Tulum and Mérida. The most influential chef on the planet was about to embark on the ultimate taco quest.

These days Noma occupies the top spot on the most attention-getting international ranking of elite kitchens: the annual list of the World's 50 Best Restaurants. It first landed there in 2010, propelled by Redzepi's aptitude for wresting deliciousness and color from the austerity of the surrounding landscape. Noma's cookbooks overflow with a bounty of nourishments that many of us didn't even know we could eat: musk ox and milk skin, sea buckthorn and beach mustard, bulrushes and birch sorbet, ramson leaves and rowan shoots, Cladonia lichen and Icelandic dulse, pig's blood and ants and hay. Somehow Redzepi brings out the stark beauty in his foraged, fermented, smoked and salvaged ingredients, and, perhaps even more impressively, he makes you want to pick them up with your fingers and place them on your tongue. He comes across as a man with a mission, and his overriding manifesto might boil down to this: Look more deeply. There is so much around us to relish.

On the surface, the cuisine of Mexico might seem like the New Nordic movement's chile-peppered antithesis. You don't find a lot of jalapeños in Denmark. What you do find there is the same thing you can scarf down in college towns around the United States: fat, bland burritos, watery salsa made with half-white tomatoes and cheap, cheese-gooey nachos that are about as far from the true flavor of Mexican food as Speedy Gonzales is from Emiliano Zapata. For most of his life, that's what Redzepi assumed Mexican food was. "I'll be honest with you," he says. "Back then, my idea of Mexican food was what we have in Europe, which is like a bastardized version of Tex-Mex. Everything's terrible. It's grease, it's fat, it's big portions. That was my impression."

But in the summer of 2006, Solís, a cook who had interned in the kitchen at Noma, invited his former boss to the Yucatán Peninsula for a few days of cooking at Nectar, his pioneering restaurant in the sleepily mesmerizing city of Mérida. Redzepi soon found himself on a draining daisy chain of flights from Copenhagen to Mexico. "It was one of those stupid trips," he remembers. "I was just so tired and bummed out." He arrived in Mérida in a sour, foggy mood, and much to his annoyance, Solís immediately escorted him to Los Taquitos de PM, an open-air taco stand on a desolate thoroughfare. This is what Redzepi found: "Coca-Cola. Plastic chairs everywhere. Mexican music out of a loud-speaker." Not exactly the French Laundry. Solís ordered three plates of tacos al pastor. In the dish, chunks of pork, stained scarlet after first being bathed in a chile sauce with achiote and other spices, are shaved off a spinning vertical skewer and placed on a bed of corn tortillas with strips of pineapple on top. It is said that Lebanese immigrants helped create the dish when they brought shawarma to Mexico, which means that tacos al pastor qualifies as a weird example of Mayan-Caribbean-Middle-Eastern fusion. But all you need to know is that when the gods find themselves hunting for drunk food after a bender on Mount Olympus, these tacos are what they want. They're that satisfying.

Redzepi had never seen such tacos before. He winced. Pineapple? he thought. Like on a bad pizza? Then he took a bite and his worldview trembled and reeled. "That first mouthful," he says. "Soft. Tasty. Acidic. Spicy. It's like when you have sushi and it's great for the first time. I couldn't believe it. My virginity was taken. In the best possible way."

From then on, Redzepi couldn't stop himself. It was as though he was caught up in an intoxicating affair. Even as he polished and per-fected the New Nordic cuisine that would make him famous, he started slipping away for pilgrimages to Mexico. Back in Denmark he had to uproot flavor by yanking at tufts of sea grass and burrowing his fingers into the dirt, but here, in the massive open-air markets of Oaxaca and Mexico City, the bounty overwhelmed him. Walking through these markets was like spinning through an aromatic fun house.

Look more deeply, the country seemed to say to him. There is so much around us to relish. In street carts as well as in high-end restaurants, Mexicans were cooking with ant eggs and fried grasshoppers and seeds and sprigs and pods and powders and more varieties of chiles than he could count. Every village and roadside stall felt like a new world. Redzepi might try to make enfrijoladas outside of Mexico, but even he would probably fail. "You have to have an avocado leaf," he says. "From that little tree. On a hill. Near Oaxaca."

"It's like a whole new energy enters your body when you come out to these parts," says Eric Werner, the chef and co-owner of the Tulum restaurant Hartwood. As he says this, that energy is being delivered in the form of thunderous jolts to the spinal column. We're in a Jeep heading into the humid thickets of the Yucatán jungle, and the red-dirt road is turning into a thumping riot of dips and jags.

"This is where it gets worse," Werner says.

"This is where it flips over," Redzepi says.

The vehicle keeps tossing back and forth like a dinosaur's plaything. Redzepi is holding a Ziploc bag with an aloe vera leaf jutting out of it. Yesterday, on the beach in Tulum, he fell asleep on a lounge chair and ended up with a stinging sunburn. Every now and then he squeezes the spiny leaf and applies a dab of fresh goop to his face. The aloe fills the Jeep with a gamey scent. Flanking the road are thousands of teeming anthills. Redzepi starts wondering whether the ants are edible. Werner, a 36-year-old with the tangly beard and piercingly bright eyes of an Old Testament prophet, is an American, but in 2009 he and his wife, Mya Henry, uprooted their lives in a gentrifying New York City and headed for the shaggy-drifty refuge of Tulum. A year later, they opened Hartwood, which has quickly gained a reputation for the elemental beauty and purity of its food. Many of Hartwood's chief ingredients come straight from a milpa, a rural organic farm a couple of hours away from Tulum where the "crops" seem to sprout straight out of the surrounding wilderness.

It's that milpa that we're bouncing into now. When we get there, Redzepi enters another state of rapture. He darts around the rocky, weedy expanse with Werner and Antonio May Balan, the 54-year-old father of 10 whose family has tended this land for many years. (Balan and his wife, who come here a couple days per week, sleep in hammocks that hang from the ceiling of a tin-roofed shed in the middle of the milpa; they speak to each other not in Spanish but in a Mayan language.) Redzepi approaches this land and its produce with the same voracious curiosity that he might bring to a sylvan glade back in Scandinavia, except that for him, being here is akin to being on Mars. There are dwarfish lime trees. There are pineapples that seem to be popping up from the ground like "Invasion of the Body Snatchers" pods. There are chiles the size of Tic Tacs that, when plucked from a branch and placed on your tongue, unleash an instant conflagration of capsaicin. "I burrow into the rare ingredients," Werner says. "I try to find what's most rare."

"And how excited does that make a chef?" Redzepi says. "It's like a present. A new flavor."

After a tour of the milpa and lunch in the shed, Werner presents Redzepi with a gift: a machete. "Look, I'm walking out of the jungle with a bag of mangoes and a machete," Redzepi says. As we steel ourselves for the ride back out, Redzepi spots a long, green, Seussian fruit dangling from the branch of a tree. "This is the weirdest fruit I've seen," he says. "This is like something from a Tim Burton movie." Werner says he doesn't even know what to call it. Redzepi suggests "torpedo fruit." (I later learn that it is bonete, which is papaya-ish and native to the region.)

If Redzepi were to shimmy up the trunk of the tree and lop off the torpedo fruit with his newfound blade, none of us would be the least bit surprised. His hunger for those new flavors borders on the pathological. On the way back to Tulum, we drop into a market and take a whiff of a sphere of flora that appears to be some kind of evolutionary prank: On the outside it looks like a pumpkin, but when you smell it, you realize it's as sweet as a cantaloupe. (Werner refers to it as a melón de milpa.) When top chefs get hold of these ingredients, the results can be consciousness-shifting.

In Mexico City we sit for a tasting-menu feast at Pujol, the Enrique Olvera atelier that some gastronomes consider the best restaurant in the country. (Olvera has been gearing up to open Cosme, his first restaurant in New York.) At Pujol, what tips Redzepi over into euphoria is mole. A lot of Americans assume that mole is a sauce made with chocolate, but there are scores of moles around Mexico, many conjured up with marathon lists of ingredients. Olvera does something unusual with his mole: He keeps feeding it. For months. "When I tried it the first time, I had goose bumps," Redzepi says as Olvera sidles up to our table. "Enrique, how old is the mole?"

"Three hundred and seventy days," Olvera says.

Like a sourdough starter, Olvera's mole has been steeping in its own funky lagoon of flavor for, yes, over a year. But Olvera does another bold thing with his mole: He serves it by itself, on a plate, spooned into a mahogany circle. On top of that year-old mole is a smaller circle of rust-colored mole. That's it. There's no chicken or fish underneath the two moles. All you get is sauce on a plate, accompanied by a basket of warm tortillas for sopping it all up. When the mole arrives, Redzepi gazes at it, rapt, and compares it to the Eye of Sauron. "There isn't a Danish designer from the '50s who wouldn't have an orgasm looking at this," he says.

Everyone moves in for a taste. The table falls silent. "Guys, let's think of what's happening here," Redzepi finally says. "You're taking a pancake. And you're dipping it into a sauce. If you went to Per Se and you dipped a pancake into a sauce? There's something going on here."

Two days later, in Oaxaca, with Ruiz as his guide and Bowien as his sidekick, Redzepi steps into a market that seems to stretch on for miles. He plows through it like Bugs Bunny on a carrot bender, nibbling into tacos and plums and tamarinds and densely fatty corozo nuts, spitting out seeds and shells as he walks. He picks up a sheaf of green leaves and gasps. "Look at the quality of this epazote," he says.

We meet two women standing next to a vat of liquid. "You have to try this," Ruiz says. The drink is tejate, a pre-Columbian elixir that is made with corn, fermented cacao, the pit of the mamey fruit and a tree-borne flower known as rosita de cacao. Its gray-brown hue calls to mind the bubbling runoff from a storm drain. Crowning the drink is a beige froth that hovers ethereally, like the meringue in île flottante, the French dessert. We buy a few scoopfuls of it and take deep slurps. It tastes like primeval Yoo-hoo. "Wow, it's amazing," Bowien says. "The stuff on the top is like cream."

Redzepi and Bowien make a fascinating duo. Redzepi is the New Nordic pioneer who is not entirely Nordic: His father, of Albanian heritage, moved to Denmark after growing up in Macedonia. Bowien has specialized in giving a souped-up vroom to Sichuan and Mexican cuisine, but he was raised on neither: He was born in South Korea but adopted by a white couple in Oklahoma. Both chefs carry themselves with the confidence and wariness of the perpetual outsider. And both of them had a lousy go of it last year: Bowien saw his molten-hot Manhattan flagship, Mission Chinese Food, shut down because of violations of the city's health code, while 63 diners at Noma came down with norovirus just a couple of months before the restaurant temporarily lost its top spot on the World's 50 Best list.

Because of all this, perhaps, they've bonded—and Redzepi appears to have taken Bowien under his wing. As we amble and devour our way through Oaxaca, Bowien starts to fret about whether he's going to be able to come along for the Tulum leg of the journey. His wife and their new baby son are stuck back in Mexico City. He feels guilty being apart from them. Redzepi, whose own wife is due to give birth to his third child in a matter of weeks, shifts into life-coach mode.

"Tell your wife," he says. "You're coming to Tulum."

"I could go, yeah," Bowien says. "That would be insane, though."

"Chef, this is your future here we're talking about," Redzepi argues. "You have a Mexican restaurant." Although Bowien gained fame with his psychotropic spin on Sichuan cuisine in San Francisco and New York, his latest enterprise is a Lower East Side taco-and-burrito shop called Mission Cantina.

"See if you can get there by three," Redzepi goes on. "You'll have a swim in the Caribbean sea. That's better than 15,000 Xanax."

"I just had a baby," Bowien protests.

But resistance is futile; he's already faltering. Bowien materializes in Tulum the next afternoon. He looks simultaneously fired up and dazed. As the sun goes down, he joins us as we wander up the road to get a taste of Werner's cooking. Hartwood, at night, glows in the coastal blackness. Torches flicker. A hot orange light radiates from the wood-fired oven. "Look at that heat in that kitchen—heat and smoke," Redzepi says, admiringly. The place has a kind of wild, primitive elegance: If Keith McNally had existed back in the Stone Age, this is the restaurant he would have dreamed up. Werner and his team take local proteins—octopus, grouper collar, pork ribs slathered in jungle honey—and roast them to a point of breathtaking tenderness and char. With each platter that comes to the table, Redzepi and Bowien pretty much wilt with pleasure.

Everyone is full, everyone is exhausted. But Redzepi has one last command. "One thing we have to do?" he says. "We have to go to the beach. We have to go look at the stars now."

Moments later we're huddled silently on the shore, scanning the Mexican night sky and scouting out the rim of the waves for sea turtles. Naturally, it is Redzepi who sees the racing flare that the rest of us manage to miss. "Did you see that shooting star?" he asks. "It was like the brightest I've ever seen."

Shepherd's Tacos (Tacos al Pastor)

Margarita Carrillo Arronte

35 minutes

Serves: 6

Ingredients

5 guajillo chiles, membranes and seeds removed
5 tablespoons apple cider vinegar
3 cloves garlic, peeled
Pinch of ground cumin
2 cloves
1 pork leg or rump, thinly sliced
2 to 3 tablespoons corn oil
1 large onion, thinly sliced
Sea salt

To serve

12 small tortillas
½ pineapple, peeled, quartered, cored and sliced
1 small onion, finely chopped
4 tablespoons finely chopped cilantro (coriander)
Salsa
Pineapple juice

Preparation

1. Put the chiles into a saucepan, add the vinegar and simmer for 15 minutes, until the chiles are soft. Add the garlic, cumin and cloves, then transfer the mixture to a food processor or blender and process to a paste. Add more vinegar, if necessary, and pineapple juice, if using, and strain.

2. Transfer the paste to a saucepan and cook over low heat for 10 minutes, stirring constantly to prevent it from sticking. Remove from the heat and let cool.

3. Spread a thin layer of chili paste over the slices of meat. Stack them on a plate, cover them with plastic wrap (cling film), and let marinate in the refrigerator for 5 hours or overnight.

4. Heat the oil in a frying pan or skillet. Add the pork slices and cook for 2 minutes, turn them over, and cook for an additional 2 minutes, until partially cooked.

5. Remove from the pan, cut into small pieces, and return to the pan. Add the onion and cook for another 3 minutes. Transfer the meat to a serving plate.

6. Put the tortillas, one at a time, into the pan and cook for 20 to 30 seconds on both sides. Remove from the pan and drain on paper towels.

7. Divide the pork among the tortillas, sprinkle with pineapple juice, onion and cilantro, and top with salsa. Serve immediately.

Table Lessons

By Allison Alsup

From *Edible New Orleans*

In *The French Quarter Drinking Companion,* New Orleans–based fiction writer Allison Alsup and her co-writers share the inside stories of 100 bars in their hometown. There's a mini-novel here, too, in this thoughtful portrait of the groundbreaking 91-year-old chef of a landmark New Orleans restaurant.

L eah Chase stands at the center of a long prep island. The back kitchen at Dooky Chase's is a windowless space bred for function—wide burners, industrial sinks and metal counters. In contrast, Chase wears a pink baseball cap and an immaculate fuchsia chef's jacket with her name stitched in white script.

She's been cooking a fall feast since yesterday, some six to seven courses of wild game: duck, rabbit, Cornish game hen, venison, quail, alligator and what she calls "critter gumbo"—a studded combination of land and seafood that's as much solid as liquid—as well as sides of diced turnips and cooked greens, wild rice, jalapeño cornbread and puréed sweet potatoes dotted with marshmallows and scooped like ice cream into hollowed orange halves.

Barely visible is the walker that braces Chase's round hips. At 91, the Queen of Creole Cooking still works full time in the Treme landmark restaurant she's run since World War II. She vaguely alludes to the day the younger generations of her family will take over the kitchen; it's unclear if this transition will happen months or years from now or even if she wholly welcomes the idea.

But at the moment, talk is just talk, and Chase still runs the show. Though she is quick to flash her iconic smile, her focus remains as hard as the steel counter in front of her. Right now her concern is plating and presentation.

"Sliced orange. Sliced," she orders Cleo, her kitchen assistant and niece.

Light-skinned with short hair, Cleo is a tall, substantial woman who moves in the narrow lanes with a grace honed by her former years as a basketball player. After working alongside Chase for 30 years, Cleo knows what will be asked for, some 10 seconds before the chef speaks. Cleo is Chase's right hand woman, now that Chase's own fingers do not bend as easily they once did.

Cleo holds out more garnish: a sprig of parsley.

"Pinch," she tells Chase. "Thumb to forefinger."

"I can't pinch."

"Pinch."

Chase manages to get the garnish between her fingers and tucks it into a meaty crevice. A paper towel holding duck cracklings makes its way around the group, and Cleo's raised eyebrow says, You want this. There's no need to chew; the fat melts as soon as it lands on the tongue. Chase uses the rest for lagniappe—golden nuggets flanking the duck.

"I'm always thinking about the details," Chase tells me. "I wake up and think about food. Now I'm thinking how to plate each of these. Not this one," she says, pointing at the oval dish on the counter. "Round."

With each successive display, the hues of fall emerge: ambers, pale oranges and smoky, woody browns. Indeed Chase explains the inspiration for today's menu comes from a Dooky Chase's autumn tradition: cooking wild game caught by New Orleans's first African American mayor, Dutch Morial, and his friends. Over the years, the meals grew from 40 ducks and a small group to three-day endurance cooking events that fed hundreds of men and rivaled a king's banquet.

"I don't know how I did it," Chase says. "And Dutch wouldn't have paper or plastic. Water glasses. Wine glasses. Cutlery."

Chase doesn't let her mind wander for more than a few moments before she's back on task.

"Give me two cherry tomatoes. I love color. I say if it doesn't look good, it won't taste good."

There is no danger of anything not looking good. As Chase tilts the array of glittering skins for the camera, the loaded plates shake slightly. But Chase doesn't complain about her joints or cease to smile, revealing teeth as perfect as a row of white corn.

Chase's staff helps her navigate the walker into the restaurant's dining room. With the demands of preparation over, Chase settles at the head of table, surrounded by walls painted her favorite red and covered with the explosive colors of her lauded African American art collection.

A plate is put before her, but Chase doesn't eat. Chase presides. More specifically Chase talks, slipping from one story to the next with the kind of cyclical breathing a jazz singer would envy. She has nine decades of experience to draw from, and it's obvious she remembers all of them. It's a ticker-tape mind.

As we eat, Chase manages to cover an astonishing number of subjects: Dutch Morial, Harry Lee, Edwin Edwards.

"I'm a fan of good old-fashioned politicians," she says. "They knew what they could get away with."

Kudos also go to Hilary Clinton and Eleanor Roosevelt, whom Chase once heard speak. "She said the only person who can hurt you is yourself!"

Not so much admiration is offered for former Mayor Ray Nagin or anyone from the excuse-maker class. She weaves her way through children. Grandchildren. Great-grandchildren. Cell phones. Spanking. Education. NASA. Art. Work. Rifles. Women.

"Men are born dumb. I'm used to that. But women? I can't stand a dumb woman. Young women today need to know their power."

On the subject of "nice stuff," she grips the arm of her chair and explains that as a young woman she used to covet these very chairs as she passed by the window of a segregated restaurant on her way to work in the French Quarter.

"Of course, I could never have sat in them then," but for her, the traditional lines and richly colored wood represented elegance itself. Later, when the restaurant closed, she was able to buy the lot for Dooky Chase's. She smiles, still clearly satisfied that they are hers.

It's hard not to be overwhelmed by Chase, not because she lords over her accomplishments or her status as a living legend, though she has every right to. Still one can't help but be aware of her stunning accomplishments and experience. It's also why it's tough to write about her; the general tendency is to fill the page with a list of honorary degrees, awards, recognitions and positions that encompass women's and civil rights, arts and education.

And then there is, of course, the cooking itself. In addition to publishing three cookbooks, Chase has fed two Presidents, the Jackson Five, Jesse Jackson, James Baldwin, Duke Ellington and Ray Charles, among thousands of others. It's a list that would go to the end of this article. Suffice it to say Chase has fed a significant portion of the significant people in this world.

However, one recent honor allows us a more intimate glimpse of Chase, one that asks us to see not the phenomenon but the fellow mortal. In 2012, Gustave Blache III's portrait of Chase, "Cutting Squash," was chosen to hang in the National Portrait Gallery, earning a spot alongside images of this country's most august citizens.

Blache's small, realistic painting captures an unposed Chase at work in her prep kitchen. The clearly aged Chef wears a baseball cap and slices a yellow squash. Both the vegetable and the act of chopping couldn't be more ordinary; still, the canvas suggests complexity, even vulnerability within Chase's tough exterior. Blache's portrait, like Chase herself, is a study in contrasts. Her eyes may be fixed on her knife, but the viewer suspects her mind may be in more than one place, remembering something someone said, people she's known.

We pass plates, slicing and sampling, grateful not to be rushed. Chase's preparations are not overly fussy and let the flavor of the game come through. While she's known for her Gumbo Z'Herbes, her Critter Gumbo deserves its own reputation with a savory, rib-sticking taste that may be best described as deep brown goodness.

With fall on the table and tongue, family and food flavor the conversation. While the wild game feasts she cooked for Dutch Morial served as inspiration for today's meal, Chase reveals that much of what's on the table goes back much further to her own beginnings. Her father hunted many of the same animals on our table today: duck, venison, rabbit and quail, whose days were numbered the moment they entered the family's strawberry patch.

Chase explains her mother cooked the birds with government "commodity" butter, one of the free staples her family relied upon. With a limited pantry, her mother, Hortensia Lange, added flavor with stewed plum sauces made from the fruit of the tree that shaded their home. Chase acknowledges she still borrows from her mother's plum sauces when she cooks wild game.

"This is country food," she says with obvious satisfaction, and adds she makes a mean squirrel pie.

Chef is now four generations removed from her 1923 birth in the small town of Madisonville, Louisiana. Her parents had elementary-level educations, Jim Crow–era segregation prevented more and while they were determined their daughter would finish high school, circumstances required that Chase knew work and responsibility from a very young age. Her eldest sister died as a toddler from a tragic burn accident; as a result, Chase was raised as the oldest of 12 girls. (Her parents eventually had two sons.)

As a young girl, Leah and her sisters rose at 4 am to walk to the strawberry fields three miles away, work for a few hours, then walk back and head to school.

"I grew up hard, I guess," she says.

But what Chase shares is not a litany of difficulties or even injustices. Indeed what she seems to emphasize is not what lacked but what received: steadfast and powerful lessons about work, morality and family, lessons often imparted around food. For instance, Chase believes she was given something that most city kids won't ever know—a connection to the natural world, the changing of the seasons, the names of trees and a knowledge of "which plants you could pick, which ones you couldn't."

For some, farm to table may seem like a recent hot trend; for Chase, it was a way of life born from necessity. In addition to what her father hunted, the family vegetable garden helped to fill the plate. She smiles as she tells us how her mother once sent her out to pick wild purslane when they had run out of greens in their garden. Young Leah was to be secret about it.

"She was proud," Chase says of her mother, "and didn't want anyone to know we were so poor we had to eat weeds."

Decades later, Chase sat down to dinner in an upscale California restaurant only to open the menu and find purslane named among the pricey appetizers.

"We always came to table," Chase says of her childhood meals. Mondays through Saturdays, the table was laid with practical oil cloth; but come Sunday, this Catholic family sat at a table dressed with good dishes and a pressed tablecloth her mother sewed from flour sacks. It was from her mother that Chase learned what she calls "an appreciation for the finer things," an aesthetic she would bring to her own white-linen restaurant.

Chase says she has always believed in the power of beauty to inspire individuals to strive for better circumstances. Her mother also trained her daughter to be aware of appearances, especially in the face of guests. It's an attitude Chase has retained with her own staff who are instructed that customers are to be treated "like company."

When she expresses concern for children who grow up eating a corner store stock in front of a television, it's clear that, for Chase, her family table offered more than food or future recipes. Indeed food, as important as it is to her, is not what she most speaks about. What she most speaks about is people.

As a girl, she learned an important connection between meals and humanity: The table was a place to build consensus, not opposition. Her parents would not tolerate arguments and infractions were met with the razor strop.

Years later, amid the full tensions of the civil rights era, Chase would use the upstairs dining room of Dooky Chase's to build the boldest sort of consensus of the day. Defying segregation laws, Chase used her tables as a meeting point between black and white.

Of all seasons, autumn's food is most about memory. As the leaves turn and the days shorten, we find ourselves craving hearty fare and local ingredients, longing for family recipes and traditions of exactly the kind Chase has served in full today. And so I ask Chase, herself a tradition and now deep into the autumn of her own life, if there are particular foods that continue to compel and resonate with her emotionally.

"Oh, yes," she replies without hesitation. "Gumbo, stuffed mirliton and peppers."

Her loyalty to what she calls the cuisine of Creoles of color clearly runs deep on the Dooky Chase's menu. She says she's proud to have run a restaurant where patrons can sample authentic preparations after they've tried "the other Creole" restaurants like Commander's Palace and Galatoire's.

"Go back to what you know," she advises. "Go back to what you know."

After 91 years, what Leah Chase knows is more than most of us ever will. Outside the kitchen, Chase is known as a staunch advocate for social progress, but today she's been a model of another era and its table lessons. And if there is a commonality between those lessons, it's dignity: the dignity of the land, of good food, of the table, of fine things, of choice and, above all, of work and action.

What comes through Leah Chase the talker is Leah Chase the worker. Such lasting values explain why, when others would have considered retiring 30 years ago and simply let the accolades roll in, Chase continues to rise early to come to Dooky Chase's.

"I wasn't raised on kisses and hugs," Chase says. "We kissed twice a year, Christmas and New Year's." She admits she could be more generous with her shows of affection. In the several hours we've spent talking, it's the closest she's come to voicing regret. "But we did learn that family was there for you. No matter what."

"You see, I have to be able to do this for people," she says, pointing to the dishes between us. After some two hours at table, the birds have been picked over, and the gumbo bowls sit empty. She instructs her staff to bring out the peach cobbler, a final country food finish. The sliced fruit and crumbles are neither too tart or sweet.

"I do. That is who I am," Chase proclaims. "This is how I show my love."

Kitchen Diplomacy

By Nic Brown

From *Garden & Gun*

Novelist Nic Brown (*In Every Way, Doubles*), who also teaches at South Carolina's Clemson University, traveled north to the other Carolina to profile chef Bill Smith, leading light of the Southern food renaissance. What Brown discovered was that it's not just his cooking that made Smith a pioneer.

B
ill Smith is a big deal. This is something he would never, ever tell you. And you probably wouldn't guess it either, not from just looking at him. Today, for example, he's wearing a T-shirt with the word LARD on it, a baseball cap, very worn jeans, and incongruously shiny loafers. He just got off his bicycle, which, incidentally, is his only means of transport, and the radio in his restaurant kitchen—*loud*—is tuned to La Ley 101.1, the local Mexican station.

"This is the whole show," he says, gesturing around him.

On the counter is a plastic container labeled HAM JUICE. It holds the drippings from a ham cooked in Coke. A small mountain of bacon sizzles in a skillet the size of a stop sign. Sebastian Lopez-Leon, a cook from Mexico in his thirties, slices tomatoes at the prep station with a sly grin on his face that seems poised to burst into laughter.

It all feels more like the diner where your college buddies used to work than it does "sacred ground for Southern foodies," which is what the *New York Times* has called it. But don't be fooled. This is sacred ground. This is Crook's Corner—Chapel Hill, North Carolina's revered corner of cuisine—one of the birthplaces of the modern renaissance in

Southern cooking. Smith's humble demeanor belies the fact that he's the one who's kept this kitchen at the center of that movement for the past twenty-one years, a feat he's achieved by serving food that's at once sophisticated and simple, elegant and playful, and so down-home good that I, for one, have at times been known to dream about it.

With Smith at the helm, Crook's Corner has been named a James Beard America's Classic Restaurant. Twice he's been a finalist for the organization's prestigious Best Chef: Southeast award. He's written a lauded cookbook, *Seasoned in the South*, and he has a new one, *Crabs & Oysters*, due out later this year. If you ask him when he started thinking of himself as a chef, though, he says, "I don't know if I do, even now. I never set out to be a chef. It never crossed my mind."

Originally from historic New Bern, North Carolina, Smith, who is sixty-six, moved to Chapel Hill to go to college but was soon headed to New York City with the Red Clay Ramblers as a dancer in the successful 1975 off-Broadway run of the show *Diamond Studs*. When he returned, he got a job clearing tables at La Résidence, a local French restaurant owned and operated by Bill Neal and his wife, Moreton. The atmosphere seemed to suit Smith.

"I liked the idea of making dinner an event," Smith says, and he was excited by the effort "to make good food and gather people around you." After all, he says, "it was like what I was used to growing up. My great-grandmother entertained the family every day."

Nothing inspires Smith's cooking more than family. In New Bern he was surrounded by a large extended family of cooks. It was his great-grandmother, though, who ruled the roost. Look on the menu at Crook's Corner on any given night, and odds are you'll find at least one of her dishes there—maybe the crab stew or her corned ham, a recipe Smith recently shared with fellow North Carolina chef Vivian Howard on the Christmas episode of her PBS series *A Chef's Life*. Other classic Smith dishes, such as Aunt Hi's oyster stew, steak with bourbon sauce, and honeysuckle sorbet (which started from blossoms he picked while riding his bike), speak to both his home state and the large family roots that have grown here.

"It informs everything we do," Smith says. "The longer we've been here, the more I've gone back to North Carolina as a source."

But North Carolina is a complicated source. Smith, who is gay and came out in his twenties, was raised in a small conservative town that, in a classic Bill Smith understatement, he describes as "being *very* unlike Chapel Hill," long one of the more progressive zip codes in the state. And while the city isn't as much of an outlier as it once was, North Carolina as a whole still struggles with acceptance. The state's recent passage of Amendment One, banning same-sex marriage (since struck down in federal court), is a prime indicator to many, Smith included, that equality is not yet at hand. Even if he's quiet about it, which he usually is, Smith has long campaigned for a variety of human rights causes. This past June he participated in the Big Gay Mississippi Welcome Table, an event held in New York City to protest Mississippi's Religious Freedom Restoration Act, which many fear will facilitate discrimination against gays and lesbians.

Another issue close to Smith's heart these days is the integration of the South's growing immigrant community. North Carolina doesn't look like it did when Smith was a child. The region has long felt the increasing influence of Hispanic culture, and today, the Latino population in North Carolina stands at 9 percent—a number that surely rises if you peek into the kitchens of its restaurants. Crook's Corner is no exception. Most of Smith's excellent cooks hail originally from Mexico.

It takes only a few minutes in the kitchen to see that these staff members are not only the faces of the new North Carolina—they're also the newest additions to Smith's family. He speaks and jokes with them in playful Spanish. They spend time with one another outside of work. Smith has loaned Lopez-Leon money to help with his child's schooling. He visits Mexico with his staff at least once a year, if not more. He's sponsored two of his cooks' families for citizenship. And just like his large New Bern family, these new brothers and sisters exert a profound influence on his cooking.

It's an openness that Smith is well known for.

"Bill's dishes aren't just an expression of North Carolina ingredients, but also the people he loves," says Andrea Reusing, the celebrated chef-owner at Lantern, another one of Chapel Hill's best restaurants. Frank Stitt, the award-winning chef at Highlands Bar and Grill in Birmingham, Alabama, says, "He's a leader in recognizing the incredible contribution that our Latin community makes to our businesses and to our culture."

Today Smith is making tamales from a recipe given to him by the wife of one of his kitchen staff. These savory dough packets recently brought down the house at the annual Southern Foodways Symposium in Oxford, Mississippi, where Smith cooked a Nuevo North Carolina Supper—just a little family dinner for four hundred, with dishes all inspired by his Latino coworkers. He opens a small plastic bag filled with different peppers—jalapeño, habanero, and tiny ones called chile pequin—given to him by one of his cook's uncles. A deliveryman drops off some produce, and within a minute he's pulled out a necklace and is comparing it with the one Smith is wearing. They're both scapulars—Catholic tokens often given by women in Mexico to men in the family. Smith received this one from Lopez-Leon's wife.

Lopez-Leon stops slicing tomatoes and comes over, wrapping both arms around Smith. "He's like my *padrino*," he says.

"I am not!" Smith says. "*Padrino*— that means godfather. I am not your godfather." Smith shakes him off, then says, "I *am* the godfather of several of their children, though . . . " He pulls out his phone. "These are my grandchildren," he says, displaying a photo of four kids in Halloween costumes. They're the children of another one of his crew, Ricardo De La Torre. Originally from Mexico City, he has cooked with Smith for more than twenty years. Smith points to each child, saying each name with pride, just like a grandfather.

"He's a good friend," De La Torre says quietly, and then, after a moment of silence, looks directly at me, as if he wants to make sure I understand. "Everything I know, he's teaching me."

Smith is usually keen to point out just the opposite, relishing all that he learns from De La Torre and the rest of his staff. He defers credit for developing new dishes himself, calling his process in the kitchen a collaboration. He recounts a recent discussion he had with one cook who suggested a better way to make a piecrust. "And of course," Smith says, "he was right." He tells long stories about the time he's spent with his coworkers in Mexico, including one involving a seven-hour ride in a makeshift cab through a lawless region on the way to a wedding in Oaxaca. "I go down there all the time," Smith says. But as for what he does when he's down there, it's less culinary exploration than it is plain family time. "I sit on the hood of a car and drink beer and hold babies."

Crook's Corner is in fact on a corner, housed in a humble building that was, at various times in the past, a fish market, a taxi stand, and a tackle shop. The building itself is probably the last thing you notice when you arrive, though. What catches your eye first is the improbable Wonderland garden that surrounds the place, the sculpture of a pig atop a pole rising from the roof, the hubcaps that decorate the fence out front, and the selection of "critters"—animals sculpted from logs—that stand guard. The former owner of the property, Rachel Crook—for whom the corner is named—was last seen alive here in 1951 before being found murdered. The crime has never been solved.

"I don't know if this place is haunted," Smith says, "but it ought to be."

If Crook's Corner is haunted by anything, it's the benevolent ghost of Bill Neal, the original head chef. Along with Gene Hamer—who still owns the restaurant—Neal bought the place in 1982 and began its transformation from barbecue shack to culinary temple. Neal died in 1991 at forty-one, a young victim of AIDS, but not before making a profound impact on the national consciousness about Southern food. He was one of the first chefs to renew the South's pride in its culinary history and give it a modern, national platform. Crook's Corner's most iconic menu item, its shrimp and grits, is a classic Neal dish and still the restaurant's biggest seller.

Smith knew Neal well, and it's hard not to notice the parallels. Smith got his start with him, and worked with him for years at La Résidence, where he took over head chef duties for Neal before eventually doing so again at Crook's Corner. And much like Neal, a pioneer in the evolution of Southern food, Smith is now forging a new form of Southern cooking, combining his own personal history and the region's contemporary Latino influence. But as is fitting with Smith's laid-back personality, he seems to wear the mantle of his forebearer lightly. "I just trundle along," Smith says, describing his career path. "I don't think ahead very much."

When I arrive for dinner one Friday night, I pull into the small gravel lot behind the restaurant. The first person I see is Smith, ducking into an outdoor storage shed at the edge of the lot.

"I'm getting linen!" he shouts.

It's no surprise to see Smith always working, no matter the task. He's busier than an overbooked politician, constantly adding items to an already hectic schedule. His mornings start at 8:30 a.m., when he rides his bike to work. He doesn't even own a car. "I can't say why," he says. "I'm just weird. I'm sort of a Luddite. I don't have a car or a television, but I have like five computers." At work, as if he didn't have enough to do already, he spends at least some time almost every day preparing food for donation. He doesn't get home until 11:00 p.m., at the earliest, and somehow still finds time to write books and articles and make public appearances. None of it seems to faze him. "I've always been a night person," he says in his usual easygoing style. "And a morning person."

Inside, Smith joins me at the bar for a moment and orders a PBR. A seemingly endless stream of friends stop to say hello, as if the whole restaurant were on some cosmic lazy Susan that revolves around Smith at its center. On any given night, he'll know half the people in the room, if not more. A plate of his classic fried oysters arrives, then the tamales, with a smoky salsa ranchera that Smith makes by "throwing vegetables on the grill and just scorching them."

There's almost always a sense of fun in Smith's cooking, like his sublime homemade Orange Red-Hot sorbet, a dish he invented using leftover Valentine's candy. "It reminds me of the popsicles I buy in Mexico that have gum inside them," he says. His so-called Cheese Pork! is a schnitzel-type cut that employs shredded Swiss cheese instead of bread crumbs to coat the meat. For dessert, we have his Atlantic Beach Lemon-Lime pie. The pie, "like a lemon meringue without the meringue," was inspired by the fact that when Smith was growing up, he was always told you could never have dessert after seafood unless it included lemon. Made with a saltine crust and infused with Smith's past, his version of the North Carolina coastal classic is both simple and timeless. And very, very good.

Early the next morning, the Mexican radio station is back on, loud, and Smith is making a "quick false jambalaya" for a local charity, thrown together from assorted leftovers. Lopez-Leon cracks jokes about his broken phone, carrying on with Smith about who knows what. They speak such a personal Spanglish it's like one of those languages you hear of that twins develop and no one else can understand.

"I probably would have already retired if I didn't have these clowns around me all the time," Smith says, stepping outside to catch some air. "Otherwise . . . it'd be like a coal mine."

Huge, outlandish plants rise from oversize planters around him. The pig sculpture flies overhead. Mexican music pours through the screen door, carrying with it the scent of jambalaya and tamales. Smith leans on a fence. This world of his—a tasty muddle of family, Southern history, love, and food—is absolutely nothing like a coal mine.

At the Stove

The Truth About Cast Iron Pans:
7 Myths That Need to Go Away

By J. Kenji López-Alt

From Serious Eats

The title of Kenji López-Alt's new book, *The Food Lab: Better Home Cooking Through Science*, perfectly describes his empirical approach to cooking. As managing culinary director of Serious Eats, he's become the food world's de facto Myth Buster. Here he takes on the "accepted wisdom" about cast-iron pans.

I f you haven't noticed, I'm a big fan of the cast iron. When I packed up my apartment last spring and had to live for a full month with only two pans in my kitchen, you can bet your butt that the first one I grabbed was my trusty cast iron skillet. I use it for the crispest potato hash and for giving my steaks a crazy-good sear. I use it for baking garlic knots or cornbread or the easiest, best pan pizza you'll ever bake (just kidding, this might be the easiest pizza). I use it for a complete chicken dinner with insanely crisp skin and for crispy, creamy pasta bakes.

Point is, it's a versatile workhorse and no other pan even comes close to its league.

But there's also a mysterious, myth-packed lore when it comes to cast iron pans. On the one hand there's the folks who claim you've got to treat your cast iron cookware like a delicate little flower. On the other, there's the macho types who chime in with their *my cast iron is hella non-stick* or *goddam, does my pan heat evenly!*

In the world of cast iron, there are unfounded, untested claims left right and center. It's time to put a few of those myths to rest.

Myth #1: "Cast iron is difficult to maintain."

The Theory: Cast iron is a material that can rust, chip, or crack easily. Buying a cast iron skillet is like adopting a newborn baby and a puppy at the same time. You're going to have to pamper it through the early stages of its life, and be gentle when you store it—that seasoning can chip off!

The Reality: Cast iron is tough as nails! There's a reason why there are 75-year-old cast iron pans kicking around at yard sales and antique shops. The stuff is built to last and it's very difficult to completely ruin it. Most new pans even come pre-seasoned, which means that the hard part is already done for you and you're ready to start cooking right away.

And as for storing it? If your seasoning is built up in a nice thin, even layer like it should be, then don't worry. It ain't gonna chip off. I store my cast iron pans nested directly in each other. Guess how many times I've chipped their seasoning? Try doing that to your non stick skillet without damaging the surface.

Myth #2: "Cast iron heats really evenly."

The Theory: Searing steaks and frying potatoes requires high, even heat. Cast iron is great at searing steaks, so it must be great at heating evenly, right?

The Reality: Actually, cast iron is *terrible* at heating evenly. The thermal conductivity—the measure of a material's ability to transfer heat from one part to another—is around a third to a quarter that of a material like aluminum. What does this mean? Throw a cast iron skillet on a burner and you end up forming very clear hot spots right on top of where the flames are, while the rest of the pan remains relatively cool.

The main advantage of cast iron is that it has very high volumetric heat capacity, which means that once it's hot, it *stays* hot. This is vitally important when searing meat. To really heat cast iron evenly, place it over a burner and let it preheat for at least 10 minutes or so, rotating it every once in a while. Alternatively, heat it up in a hot oven for 20 to 30 minutes (but remember to use a potholder or dish towel!)

The other advantage is its high emissivity—that is, its tendency to expel a lot of heat energy from its surface in the form of radiation. Stainless steel has an emissivity of around .07. Even when it's extremely hot, you can put your hand close to it and not feel a thing. Only the food directly in contact with it is heating up in any way. Cast iron, on the other hand, has a whopping .64 emissivity rating, which means that when you're cooking in it, you're not just cooking the surface in contact with the metal, but you're cooking a good deal of food above it as well. This makes it ideal for things like making hash or pan roasting chicken and vegetables.

Myth #3: "My well-seasoned cast iron pan is as non-stick as any non-stick pan out there."

The Theory: The better you season your cast iron, the more non-stick it becomes. Perfectly well-seasoned cast iron should be perfectly non-stick.

The Reality: Your cast iron pan (and mine) may be really really really non-stick—non-stick enough that you can make an omelet in it or fry an egg with no problem—but let's get serious here. It's not anywhere near as non-stick as, say, Teflon, a material so non-stick that we had to develop new technologies just to get it to bond to the bottom of a pan. Can you dump a load of cold eggs into your cast iron pan, slowly heat it up with no oil, then slide those cooked eggs right back out without a spot left behind? Because you can do that in Teflon.

Yeah, didn't think so.

That said, macho posturing aside, so long as your cast iron pan is well seasoned and you make sure to pre-heat it well before adding any food, you should have no problems whatsoever with sticking.

Myth #4: "You should NEVER wash your cast iron pan with soap."

The Theory: Seasoning is a thin layer of oil that coats the inside of your skillet. Soap is designed to remove oil, therefore soap will damage your seasoning.

The Reality: Seasoning is actually *not* a thin layer of oil, it's a thin layer of *polymerized* oil, a key distinction. In a properly seasoned cast iron pan, one that has been rubbed with oil and heated repeatedly, the oil has already broken down into a plastic-like substance that has bonded to the surface of the metal. This is what gives well-seasoned cast iron its non-stick properties, and as the material is no longer actually an oil, the surfactants in dish soap should not affect it. Go ahead and soap it up and scrub it out.

The one thing you *shouldn't* do? Let it soak in the sink. Try to minimize the time it takes from when you start cleaning to when you dry and re-season your pan. If that means letting it sit on the stovetop until dinner is done, so be it.

Myth #5: "Don't use metal utensils on your cast iron pan!"

The Theory: The seasoning in cast iron pans is delicate and can easily flake out or chip if you use metal. Stick to wood or nylon utensils.

The Reality: The seasoning in cast iron is actually remarkably resilient. It's not just stuck to the surface like tape, it's actually chemically bonded to the metal. Scrape away with a metal spatula and unless you're actually gouging out the surface of the metal, you should be able to continue cooking in it with no issue.

So you occasionally see flakes of black stuff chip out of the pan as you cook in it? It's *possible* that's seasoning, but unlikely. In order to get my cast iron pan's seasoning to flake off, I had to store it in the oven for a month's-worth of heating and drying cycles without re-seasoning it before I started to see some scaling.

More likely, those flakes of black stuff are probably carbonized bits of food that were stuck to the surface of the pan because you refused to scrub them out with soap last time you cooked.

Myth #6: "Modern cast iron is just as good as old cast iron. It's all the same material, after all."

The Theory: Metal is metal, cast iron is cast iron, the new stuff is no different than the old Wagner and Griswold pans from early 20th century that people fetishize.

The Reality: The material may be the same, but the production methods have changed. Some time in the latter half of the 20th century, cast iron manufacturers in this country shifted from using solid casts for their pans to sand-based casts. The result? Modern cast iron has a pebbly surface that looks like it was cast in, well, sand. Vintage cast iron, on the other hand, boasts a completely smooth surface to cook on.

The difference is more minor than you may think. So long as you've seasoned your pan properly, both vintage and modern cast iron should take on a nice non-stick surface, but your modern cast iron will *never* be quite as non-stick as the vintage stuff.

Myth #7: "Never cook acidic foods in cast iron."

The Theory: Acidic food can react with the metal, causing it to leech into your food, giving you an off-flavor and potentially killing you slowly.

The Reality: In a well-seasoned cast iron pan, the food in the pan should only be coming in contact with the layer of polymerized oil in the pan, not the metal itself. So in a perfect world, this should not be a problem. But none of us are perfect and neither are our pans. No matter how well you season, there's still a good chance that there are spots of bare metal and these can indeed interact with acidic ingredients in your food.

For this reason, it's a good idea to avoid long-simmered acidic things, particularly tomato sauce. On the other hand, a little acid is not going to hurt it. I deglaze my pan with wine after pan-roasting chicken all the time. A short simmer won't harm your food, your pan, or your health in any way.

What you SHOULD do

These are the only rules you need to know to have a successful life-long relationship with your cast iron.

- **Season it when you get it.** Even pre-seasoned cast iron can do with some extra protection. To season your pan, heat it up on the stovetop until it's smoking hot, then rub a little oil into it and let it cool. Repeat this process a few times and you're good to go.

- **Clean it after each use.** Clean your pan thoroughly after each use by washing it with soap and water and scrubbing out any gunk or debris from the bottom. I use the scrubby side of a sponge for this.

- **Re-season it.** Rinse out any excess soap with water, then place the skillet over a burner set to high heat. When most of the water inside the skillet has dried out, add a half teaspoon of a neutral oil like vegetable, canola, flaxseed, or shortening. Rub it around with a paper towel. Continue heating the pan until it just starts to smoke then give it one more good rub. Let it cool and you're done.

- **Fry and Sear in it.** The best way to keep your seasoning maintained? Just use your pan a lot! The more you fry, sear, or bake in it, the better that seasoning will become.

- **Don't let it stay wet.** Water is the natural enemy of iron and letting even a drop of water sit in your pan when you put it away can lead to a rust spot. Not the end of the world, but rust will require a little scrubbing and reseasoning. I always dry out my pan with a paper towel and coat it with a tiny amount of oil before storage.

There now, was that so hard? Now get out there and start cooking!

Roasting a Chicken, One Sense at a Time

By Russ Parsons

From *Finesse*

A celebrated food writer and columnist at the *LA Times* for over
25 years, Russ Parsons is also the author of *How to Read a French
Fry* and *How to Pick a Peach*. For this issue of chef Thomas Keller's
glossy food magazine, Parsons thoughtfully deconstructs the
kitchen process of a supremely mindful cook.

Here are the basic instructions for roasting a chicken: season the
chicken; roast at 450 degrees for one hour. It's that simple. You
could probably program a robot to do it. But any good cook will recognize that there's a lot missing. During preparation of almost any dish,
there are hundreds of variables that come into play. Noticing them is
the difference between being a good cook and being a machine that
performs certain tasks.

And noticing them means being aware of what is going on in your
kitchen on many levels. It means being engaged with what you are doing with all of your senses. It means paying attention to what you're
smelling, what you're seeing, even what you're hearing. So put away
your cellphone. Turn off the TV. Facebook will wait. Focus on what
you're doing. Be aware. What does the food look like? What does it
smell like? How does it sound? These are all important hints the dish is
giving you. File the information away and remember it next time.

Not only will doing this make you a better cook, it'll make your time
in the kitchen more enjoyable. By paying attention to your senses, and
calling on your collected experiences of cooking, you'll be working

intuitively rather than just following orders from some dumb recipe. You'll more fully appreciate cooking as a process, not a chore.

If all of this sounds a little far out, let's go back to that chicken.

I like to salt my chicken a day before it's going to be cooked. I allow a tablespoon of salt for every five pounds of weight. But to tell you the truth, I don't remember the last time I actually measured. I can recognize the right amount of salt by the way it looks—like the chicken has been coated with a very light frost, maybe a little bit more over the thigh and breast, where the meat is thickest.

One of the things that's important to getting a crisp, well-browned chicken is having it well-dried before cooking. The refrigerator is great for this if you leave it uncovered for an hour or so. You'll know when you run your finger over the skin and it feels slightly stiff and papery rather than supple.

When you're checking on the bird while it's roasting, the first thing you'll probably notice is the smell. There's a perfume to a roasting chicken that is sweet and mellow. If the oven is too hot and the skin starts to scorch, you'll notice that smell turning acrid and harsh.

After 10 to 15 minutes of cooking, the skin will start blistering; that's the predecessor to browning. It'll start on the breasts and legs and gradually move into skin around the joints. That's how you know when you need to turn it to get the most even color.

Listen to the bird. That's a sense that isn't usually associated with cooking, but it can give you important clues as well. During the early roasting, you'll hear the rendered fat sputtering happily in the roasting pan. But at a certain point, usually around the 45-minute mark, the tone will change when the chicken starts to release its juices. The bubbles will come closer together and they'll be snappier, angrier almost.

That's the first tip-off that the chicken is almost done.

Now, grab a drumstick and wiggle it. Before the chicken is done, it will feel stiff and resist a twist. When it's done, the ligaments will have loosened enough that it will move more easily. You'll probably also notice that the skin has started to pull away from the bone and the "heel" of the drumstick. That's another good clue.

Now, just to be safe, you'll probably also want to be taking the temperature from time to time with an instant-read thermometer. But when you plunge it into the thigh near the hip joint, notice the resistance and how the probe slides more easily into the muscle as it gets closer to done.

And that's just a roast chicken!

Think about it, and I'm sure you'll come up with hundreds of ways your senses are tipping you off if you'll only pay attention.

Smell, of course, is a key sense in the kitchen. It tells you when the nuts and grains you're toasting have hit the perfect golden note. It lets you know when pastry has browned. When the raw alcohol has burned off of a sauce.

And touch, too. You can feel the spatula scraping the fond from the bottom of the pan when you're deglazing a sauce. You can tell when a steak is done by pressing it with your finger or when a piece of meat is not done browning by the way it sticks to the pan and resists turning. When you are making jam, you can feel the change in viscosity as the fruit starts to jell. How would we ever make bread, pasta or pastry dough if we couldn't feel that perfect moment when it just comes together, baby smooth?

Still, smell and touch are obvious. For the most part, we're aware of them and take them into consideration already. But what about sound? How often have you paid attention to what you're hearing (or should be hearing) in the kitchen?

One of the surest signs rice is ready for broth to be added when you're making risotto is that it will make a light "singing" sound when it is stirred. Along the same lines, you can tell when pilaf rice is almost done because you don't hear the water bubbling the same way.

When you're whipping egg whites or heavy cream, pay attention to the sound the whisk makes when it scrapes against the bowl; it will be muffled and softer as the eggs or cream thickens.

There's that crackling sound meat makes when it has browned and is ready to turn. Or the soft susurration when butter starts foaming and it's time to add the eggs for an omelet.

The list goes on. The "crackle" bread makes when it comes out of the oven. The change in volume and timing of the bubbles in jam as it jells. The "ping" of a properly sealed jar of preserves. The change in sizzle when you're deep-frying as the moisture reduces in the crust. The slightly muffled sound of a mortar and pestle when pesto or aioli starts to come together.

All of these things together, if you pay attention to them, add up to what we call intuition—that ability to sense what is about to happen in the kitchen before it actually happens. The way you know without looking that that tart crust has reached the right stage of brown, how you know from another room that that chicken is about to be roasted.

It's funny when you think about it. Your food is always talking to you when you're cooking. All you have to do is listen.

The Secret Ingredient in the Perfect Burger Is . . .

By Daniel Duane

From *Food & Wine*

In his 2013 book *How to Cook Like a Man,* journalist Daniel Duane stakes his claim as an exemplar of Guy Food: a competitive, obsessive approach to nailing every recipe. (Luckily, he adds a healthy dose of irony to all that testosterone.) What food deserves to be perfected more than the mighty hamburger?

I have a problem. I have a daughter, too, but she's not the problem. The problem is, I am happiest in the kitchen when I'm going deep on some quest: studying the finer points of offal cookery, trying to make everything from pork kidneys to ox heart palatable, or testing my theory that a great cassoulet depends upon first butchering a pig and a lamb and a duck. This is a problem because my 11-year-old daughter, Hannah, passionately prefers familiar foods: spaghetti and meatballs, tomato soup with grilled cheese sandwiches. Most of all, that girl loves hamburgers—old-school, fast food burgers like the ones she gets in classic American burger joints courtesy of certain well-meaning people we might as well call grandparents.

In all fairness to myself, I had dreamed up family burger night as a loving concession, a way to offer the kid at least one meal a month she could feel good about. It should have been a growth opportunity, too—a chance for me to learn that not every meal has to be a step forward on my personal journey. All I had to do was buy the buns, the pre-ground chuck, some lettuce, pickles and ketchup, and then put aside my ego and make my child happy. But I couldn't stop myself from upping the ante, so I flipped through my Alice Waters cookbooks until I found a hamburger recipe, in the *Chez Panisse Café Cookbook*. California-meets-Provence, bistro-style, it called for toasted *levain* bread, grilled red onions, an obscure green herb called lovage that took weeks to find and cost a fortune, and nothing but Dijon mustard as a condiment. ("Sorry, kids," I found myself declaring, "no ketchup allowed.")

Hannah liked that burger fine, but I could tell it wasn't what she really wanted. So I pushed further toward what I mistook for excellence by adding garlicky aioli and then substituting the burger-patty instructions from Thomas Keller's best-selling *Ad Hoc at Home*. The secret, he explained, was to begin with whole cuts of sirloin, brisket and chuck, cut the meat into big chunks, toss it with salt, and then grind twice before gently shaping the patties by hand. To that end, I bought a grinder attachment for my KitchenAid mixer and discovered that my daughter did not belong to the minuscule percentage of 11-year-old girls for whom the sight and sound of a working meat grinder whets the appetite.

I loved those Alice-meets-Keller burgers. I'd eat one right now. But I couldn't miss the worry in my daughter's eyes, the fear that her father might never make a burger as good as the classic ones she ate at restaurants.

The next turning point came in a San Francisco stoner-Asian joint, Namu Gaji, where I had a sensational "Namu burger" on a soft white bun with spicy kimchi relish, aioli, and red onions glazed in balsamic vinegar and soy sauce. At home, I took the Asian-fusion impulse further, boosting my own aioli with Sriracha and fish sauce and mixing the beef with dried fermented fish flakes—a.k.a. *katsuobushi*, the ultimate umami-turbocharger. Then, in what I now consider the embarrassing nadir of my burger quest, I piled all of it right on top of the existing family sandwich—keeping the *levain* bread and the Dijon mustard—to create what turned out to be pretty much Hannah's worst nightmare.

This time, however, it wasn't just the kid who felt empty inside. Taking a bite of my own gargantuan Alice/Keller/Korean burger, I suddenly realized that it bore almost no relationship to the classic American burgers that even I had loved throughout my own American life.

"Time for research," I told the wife. "Let's hit a few burger joints, find out what the pros are doing."

She sent out queries on Facebook and Twitter, looking for recommendations. A pop-up called KronnerBurger rose to the top of the pile, so she made a reservation—just the two of us middle-aged married people squinting in the darkness of a seedy bar.

Chef Chris Kronner's girlfriend, Ashley Hildreth, set down our trays, delivering burgers that I can only describe as pop-art masterpieces—the burgers Andy Warhol would've created if he'd been working with Dairy Queen takeout instead of Campbell's Soup cans. Not too big and not too small, Kronner's burgers had simple white-bread buns with creamy white mayo, iceberg lettuce and red tomato and pickles, patties cooked rare. The visual aesthetic was old-school fast food—random burger joints in random little towns—but Kronner was a master chef, too, a veteran of San Francisco standbys like Slow Club and Bar Tartine. He wasn't playing around. (Kronner is opening a permanent KronnerBurger in Oakland, California, sometime this summer.) Each ingredient was a miracle of care and quality, combined in harmonious balance. My whole jaw slackened at the first bite. Every muscle in my mouth loosened as I chewed through a veritable clinic in advanced burgerology.

By the time I was done, I knew what my daughter had known all along: that the classic fast food hamburger is one of the world's perfect things. Glory lies not in reinventing that form, but in embracing its humble constraint, making it as good as possible without altering its fundamental identity.

We took the kids to KronnerBurger. They found the bar scary. Hannah—firstborn, rule-follower—demanded to know if it was even legal for us to have brought children there. Then we ordered, and Hannah picked up her burger. This, her face seemed to say, this is what I'm talking about.

I called up Kronner and begged for his secrets, hoping to replicate his burgers at home. Then I drove across town to purchase the exact *pain de mie* buns Kronner claimed to use. I removed a quarter-inch slice from the middle of each to improve the bun-to-patty ratio, and I spread butter onto each cut side so that, when I set the halves on the griddle, the butter's moisture would steam and soften the bun's interior while the cut surface browned. I tracked down Cabot Clothbound Cheddar and, per Kronner's instructions, beat it into the mayo to create a covert cheeseburger effect. Red onions got sliced a quarter inch thick and then seared on only one side—never two—to create a sweet grilled flavor on one surface while leaving raw crunch on the other. I even pickled cucumbers from scratch, replicating Kronner's brine with lots of vinegar and salt—but no water or sugar—for a powerful acid-saline kick. As for the meat, it turned out that Kronner was blending dry-aged grass-fed chuck with short-rib fat, grinding exactly once and never pre-salting—convinced as he was that salt would break down cell walls during the grinding process, creating a dense meat loaf quality.

Moments of beauty, in the weeks that followed:

Hannah saying, "You know, Dad, I would actually be happy with these burgers being our family burger forever."

Hannah, again: "And Dad, I'm totally over that well-done thing. If the meat's really good, I actually like it pink now."

And even: "I'm done with ketchup and yellow mustard, Dad. I only put that stuff on a burger now if it's a bad burger. It's kind of my secret way of insulting a hamburger."

But, like I said, I have a problem and I have a daughter, and my daughter is not the problem. The problem is that I'm the kind of guy who, once he's gotten a handle on the basic burger, can't help noticing the brioche smoked-potato bun recipe in bread genius Chad Robertson's new book, *Tartine Book No. 3*. And sure, making Robertson's sourdough starter is a weeklong process followed by days of mixing, kneading and rising to produce what could be the finest hamburger buns ever baked—but that's exactly the kind of trouble I can't stop looking for.

Ode to the Kronnerburger

Active: 45 minutes

Total Time: 2 hours

Servings: 4

2 cups distilled white vinegar
½ small yellow onion, thinly sliced
3 garlic cloves, crushed and peeled
2 whole cloves
1 star anise pod

½ teaspoon coriander seeds
½ teaspoon caraway seeds
Kosher salt
1 English cucumber, sliced ¼ inch thick
4 dill sprigs
2 large egg yolks
1½ tablespoons apple cider vinegar
1 cup vegetable oil
½ cup finely grated aged white cheddar, such as Cabot Clothbound
1 teaspoon hot mustard powder
Pepper
4 medium white or brioche burger buns
Softened unsalted butter, for brushing
1 red onion, sliced ¼ inch thick
1½ pounds ground beef chuck (25 percent fat)
Sliced beefsteak tomato and iceberg lettuce, for serving

1. In a medium saucepan, combine the white vinegar, yellow onion, garlic, whole cloves, star anise, coriander and caraway seeds and 2½ tablespoons of salt and bring just to a boil, stirring to dissolve the salt. Add the cucumber slices and dill, remove from the heat and let cool completely. Transfer the cucumbers and brine to a jar and refrigerate for at least 1 hour or up to 3 days.

2. Meanwhile, in a blender or mini food processor, combine the egg yolks with the cider vinegar and 2 tablespoons of water and puree until smooth. With the machine on, add the oil a few drops at a time until the mayonnaise starts to thicken, then add the remaining oil in a very thin stream until the sauce is emulsified. Add the cheese and mustard powder and puree until smooth. Season the mayonnaise with salt and pepper and scrape into a bowl. Refrigerate until chilled, about 30 minutes.

3. Heat a cast-iron grill pan until very hot. Brush the cut sides of the buns with butter and grill over moderately high heat until lightly browned, about 1 minute; transfer to a platter. Add the red onion slices to the pan and grill until lightly charred on the bottom, about 2 minutes; transfer to a plate.

4. Gently form the ground beef into four ¾-inch-thick patties, packing them as loosely as possible. Season generously with salt and pepper

and grill over moderately high heat, turning once, until lightly charred on the outside and medium-rare within, about 4 minutes total. On each bun, set 3 pickle rounds, 1 slice of tomato and 1 slice of grilled onion and top with the burger and an iceberg leaf. Generously brush the bun tops with the cheddar mayonnaise, close the burgers and serve right away.

Ragù Finto

By Cal Peternell

From *Twelve Recipes*

You'd expect a Chez Panisse chef like Cal Peternell to write a cookbook full of precise, highly wrought recipes. But way better, *Twelve Recipes* is an empowering cookbook for any beginner. As the twelve recipes each diverge into a bazillion variations—like this ragu sauce—amateur cooks can be inspired to find their own voice in the kitchen.

Most pasta sauces can be made in the time it takes for a big pot of cold water to come to a boil. Some take much longer, and in learning to know the difference, there may be some moments of disappointment and of hunger (or at least satisfaction delayed). It became clear that my son Henderson hadn't completed this part of his cooking education one night as I was tasting the evening's dishes at Chez Panisse. Saturday night at five o'clock is a crunchy moment at the restaurant. Late lunchers are trying not to look toward the door, knowing they must leave soon to make room for the dinner crowd but still lingering in Zinfandel afterglow. Early diners are waiting at the bar, and everywhere bussers and waiters are working hard to clean up after the 200 people who just had lunch while getting ready for the 250 coming in for dinner. The cooks are setting up their stations and, though tensed for the headlong rush about to begin, seem calm: the open kitchen can't hide chaos on either side, so we try mightily to keep a sane appearance. This is also "tasters" time (we taste one of everything on the menu every day—the number one secret to good cooking in a restaurant and at home: taste always), and I am at the salad station in the midst of trying one of the first courses when the sauté cook leans over to say that Henderson is on the phone from New York. We are a close crew and they know my sons well. They also can't help but overhear, so the culinary comedy of the conversation that follows is lost on no one.

"Hey, Dad. Sorry, I know you're busy, but I'm making Bolognese and can I just ask you a quick question? Don't hang up."

"Sure." I wasn't going to.

"Okay. What's the best meat to use?"

"Well, what kind have you got?"

"I'm going to the store now."

"But Bolognese takes hours to cook, and in New York it's, what, eight o'clock now? Is the store even open? Oh, sorry, it's New York, right." I roll my eyes at the cooks and squeeze a little lemon on the rocket salad we are trying. The faces of cooks and waiters around me show a mix of amusement at the content of our conversation and amazement that it's even taking place just as the curtain is going up on the evening.

"I can get the meat, just what kind?"

"Even if you get it now, you won't start cooking till nine, won't be done till like midnight." Oh, sorry, it's New York. Right.

"Yeah, but I'm on my way, walking to the store now."

"I think you should get some eggs and whatever salad looks okay, bread, cheese maybe. Bolognese is going to have to be for another night. Can I call you back later?"

I called him later and he did have eggs and good toast for dinner that night, but it made me think about getting a Bolognese-like sauce recipe to him. Something you could make up pretty quickly but that would satisfy like that classic long-cooked meat sauce from Bologna. Pork should be the meat in it because, as my friend's mother says, "Pork just tastes better." Or, as my other friend says, "Chicken has become the default cheap meant, but it really ought to be pork. Pork already is what we think chicken should be. Pork is more chicken than chicken." She's probably right, but what I love about ground pork for a pasta sauce is its sweet, rich flavor and its ability to quickly cook to tenderness. The sauce I came up with can, in fact, cook in the 30 or so minutes it takes to boil the water and cook the pasta, but it's a bit better if there's time to simmer longer.

Ragu Finto

Salt

1 pound ground pork or pork sausages, taken out of the skins

2 tablespoons olive oil

Freshly ground black pepper

Crushed red pepper flakes

¾ teaspoon each toasted and ground fennel and coriander seeds
(optional)

1 yellow onion, sliced

2 tablespoons chopped parsley

2 garlic cloves, chopped finely

1 15-ounce can peeled whole tomatoes, chopped, juice reserved
separately

1 pound rigatoni or penne

Parmesan cheese

1. Put a big pot of cold water on to boil. Add salt.

2. Spread out the ground pork like a hilly landscape on the paper it was wrapped in, or on a plate, sprinkle with ½ teaspoon salt, and grind on some black pepper. If desired, for a more sausage-y effect, sprinkle with red pepper flakes and toasted and ground fennel and coriander seeds.

3. Spreading the meat out like this shows more surface area to the seasonings and requires less handling to mix it in. Overhandling ground meat can make it turn tough, so don't. Fold up the patty of pork and mix it just until the spices are well distributed. Of course, if you're using sausage, then skip these seasoning steps.

4. Heat a large skillet over medium-high heat. Add 1 tablespoon of the oil and then quickly add the pork, breaking it into chunks and placing it into the hot pan bit by bit. Tilt the pan to spread the oil around and nudge the pork around to fill in the gaps and get even browning, but don't move it around too much. The skillet should be at full-throated sizzle—if it's too quiet, turn up the heat. Resist the temptation to poke and stir at this point; just let the meat fry: it will go from pink to gray and, if you stay out of its way, to a nice caramel brown, which looks and tastes much better, sweeter. When the first side is ready, turn the pieces over and brown the other side. Set the pork aside on a plate and tip out

some of the grease if it makes you feel better, though I generally find myself adding it back in later.

5. Add the remaining tablespoon of oil, if needed, and the onion. Sprinkle with salt and stir with a wooden spoon to scrape up the bits of browned meat as the onion begins to get juicy. Lower the heat to medium and cook the onion, stirring occasionally, until very tender, about 15 minutes. Add the parsley, garlic, and red pepper flakes and stir for a minute as the garlic sizzles, but don't let it get even a little bit browned. When the garlic smells really good, add the tomatoes and the pork. Use the back of the spoon on any chunks that are too big, and adjust the heat so that the sauce is simmering but not bubbling fast. At this point, you can cook the pasta in the salted, boiling water, stirring frequently, and the sauce will be done in the 10 or so minutes it takes to cook, though it will get better if given another 10 for the pork and tomatoes to enjoin.

6. If the pan starts to dry out and sizzle, add some of the juice from the tomatoes or, if you've used all the juice, a little water. Chicken or pork stock works very well also, but water is fine.

7. Taste the pasta, and when it is done, drain and add it to the sauce, and toss, stir, and toss. Taste it; you may want to add some salt, oil, or the pork fat you set aside—or a splash of the pasta water if it needs more flow. Serve hot and pass the cheese to grate.

When I was fourteen, I had a girlfriend who was way ahead of me. She had older brothers who loved extreme skiing and the Rolling Stones, and I remember how they laughed at me when I declared the Stones' cover of "Jumpin' Jack Flash" inferior to Peter Frampton's original. I still blush like an adolescent boy when I think of my folly (she broke up with me a month later), but sometimes it's like that: you get to liking the imitation so well that you start seeing it as the real thing. I didn't know that pistachios weren't red, that "butter" was margarine, that tomato soup wasn't born in a can, and Warhol didn't design the label. Enlightened, if humiliated, I am delighted with the originals—Mick inarguably does "Jumpin' Jack Flash" better than Peter, but wouldn't it be cool if it turned out that Andy started as some guy in the Campbell's design department?

When I have time to make the original ragù, Bolognese, I dice the onion along with carrots and celery and replace half of the pork with beef. I use chicken stock to give it richness and an especially luxurious texture. The sauce can be started and finished on the stovetop or finished in the oven. If you choose to keep the pan on the burner, turn it very low so that the sauce bubbles contentedly. Add stock or water in doses, every 15 minutes or so, as the liquid in the pan reduces. When the pork is quite tender and begins to get very comfortable in its velvety-textured surroundings, it's done, usually a couple of hours. For a richer, but somehow not heavier, effect, use whole milk for your last addition of liquid. To cook the ragù in a 325°F oven, add enough liquid to the pan so that the meat is covered by a quarter inch or so, bring to a simmer, and slide into the oven. Check every half hour, adding more liquid if needed. Chef Boyardee wishes he made it like this.

Serial Killer

By Kim Foster

From KimFoster.com

Food, family, and theater intertwine in blogger/fiction writer
Kim Foster's roller-coaster life. Since moving to Las Vegas with
her circus/theater producer husband and their two daughters,
her life has become marginally even more crazy. Roasting a whole
pig in the backyard? Bring it on.

W e get the pig from a farm.
   I watch Luis kill it. He slams it over the head three times with
a crow bar, and the pig slumps into the mud. Luis sticks the pig in the
neck. Blood spurts out. The pig is dead by the time it hits the little truck
that we ride out to the hog pens.

It's an awful, hard death, but a fast one. I feel a greater urgency that
this pig comes out perfectly. It's our third pig roast, this one for 100
people from the casts of Absinthe/Vegas and Absinthe/Australia. Each
of our pig roasts is a testing ground for the next, where we try to make
the skin crispier, the meat softer, the cooking time just right—not too
long to dry out the meat, not too short to get limp skin.

Perhaps it is all the bludgeoning and whacking with a crow bar, and
the bleeding out right before my eyes, but I want this pig to be the one
to come out perfectly.

I decide to cook hard. Out of respect and obligation.

I touch the pig on the truck. It is warm and still. I watch Luis pull it
by its teeth with a crow bar into a trough with boiling water, where all

its hair is scalded off. And then it's hung, split, entrails pulled out and heaped onto the floor. Luis has done this a lot. He is all sweaty hard arms and rote memory and efficiency. He barely even needs to look at the pig to do this work. I see purple liver, something that might be a spleen, long eel-like ropes of intestine, the colors of which were veiny blue-purple, like one end of a kid's rainbow.

There is a lot of blood and a lot of washing the blood away with a hose. In fact, Luis is obsessive about washing away the blood—health code, I'm sure—but also as if he doesn't want me to see what this killing really entails. He tries to keep it pretty for me, because I am, he thinks, a farm tourist or a delicate female.

Whenever we get a pig to roast, I always feel like I am a serial killer, and David and I are secretly trying to get rid of the evidence. We heave the pig, this one a 60-pounder, over one of our shoulders, usually David's, and shove it inelegantly into the fridge. We slam the door, hoping it won't pop the door open and fall out, revealing our crime. When I am ready, we take the pig out, lay it on a table in the backyard, and mojo the shit out of it. I stick it with needles, inject it with a concoction of pineapple juice, lemongrass, coriander, thai chilies, star anise, garlic, scallions. I rub it down hard with brown sugar and copious amounts of salt.

I have my hands all over this pig. And even though I wash my hands thoroughly, often, when I pick the kids up from school I still smell the porkiness on my fingers, because I have been all over that pig's body, in and out of the crevasses and ribs, in its head, all my fingers feeling the sinews and the rubbery bands of fat, and the blood that still trickles out, reminding me I killed this thing. Really, I made that decision. I am in this pig's body. In it. I am the violator. I am both serial killer of pigs and a rapist. It is both soothing and lovely and violent and raw.

After I am done, we shove the carcass back in the fridge, again the criminals hiding the body.

The next morning, we open the fridge and the smell is like some exotic open market, just dreamy and pungent all at the same time. I want to bury my face in the pig. Another fucked-up violation of its body. Then, it's in the roasting box, split wide open and vulnerable, fully splayed out, dotted with slices of red chilies and the burnt browns of a few cinnamon sticks in its belly.

The coals go on, fat leaks out the bottom of the box in thick drips, the yard is hot with the pig smell. The neighbor dogs all congregate and sniff around. There is smoke, heat, there is excitement. Everyone loves a pig when it is a carcass. Everyone asks about the pig—how we got it, what its death was like, how I seasoned it, how long it cooks—and then the pig brings up some kind of memory or experience, where someone talks about another time they ate from a whole pig and they smile. They always smile.

It's 6:30 now. People are eating appetizers. I, and some kitchen helpers, put out fried shoshito peppers, heavily salted and oily, turmeric grilled chicken, chicken satay with a spicy peanut sauce, fried wontons with a mushroom and pea shoot filling, spicy-ass Thai-style chicken wings, agadashi dofu, on-fire corn fritters, and grilled beef salad cradled in romaine leaves. Simple food, lots of it, that is the strategy. Just platters and platters of food going out to satiate the performers and acrobats and crew arriving in crowds.

The pig has been cooking for eleven hours.

The side dishes are re-heating in the oven. I'm scratching off dishes made and served from the master lists taped to my cupboards. This is real MasterChef reality TV shit. The pig goes out on the table. It's the first time we've cooked a near-perfect pig. We are getting good at this. The skin is blackened and crisp as all hell. Maybe too black, but it doesn't really seem to matter because I pop a piece in my mouth and it tastes like crunchy, salty, fatty, balls-on, wild animal. The meat is soft and wet. David and I start chopping up pig with big knives in front of a crowd of onlookers, like we are putting on some strange theatre of butchery, but I realize after you get through the skin, you don't need anything that blunt anymore. I start pulling apart the meat with my fingers, and using the knife as a kind of spoon.

The muscle has completely given itself over to the heat. The pig just breaks down into heaps. Total submission. That it did what I wanted it to do is breath-taking. I never get tired of the surprises of cooking.

I look up and there is a long line waiting to be served, plates out. Someone wants the soft fatty cheek. Someone else wants the crispy ear. This makes me happy, all this longing. I set out the sides, Andy Ricker's Stir-Fried Brussel Sprouts with Garlic and Chile, and Stir-Fried Noodles with Shrimp, Tofu and Cashews from "Pok Pok." There are also two kinds of fried rice, Chinese sausage and no Chinese sausage, a huge wooden board piled high with spicy chopped salad, and a platter of brisket that I soaked in Bird's Eye chilies, coriander, cumin, garlic, onions, coconut milk, salt, and lime and cooked super-low for 12 hours.

People eat. People eat more. I hear that I remind someone of a Ukrainian mom in the kitchen, and I know this is meant as a serious compliment from young people far away from home. I make myself a "secret tequila," from a bottle I have hidden in the kitchen, just for the cook and kitchen helpers. The tequila is good and hard-earned. When I go back to the yard, the carcass is a butchered mess, all bones, sucked down clean, scraps of fat that the dogs (yes, people bring dogs to our parties) begged for under the table.

Lucy, my ten-year-old daughter, is the first to remind me of dessert and we set out buckets of ice cream and cones, and people make their own. I am done. The pig is done. All I see in front of me is a little house crammed with people laughing and talking, a fire dancing in our fireplace, the doors swung open so the outside of the house and the inside are indiscernible, my floors slicked with mud and dirt from when it started raining, nice people coming to me and introducing themselves, kids weaving in and out of the legs of friends and strangers alike, laughing and chasing each other, and conversations with the acrobats and performers from the shows, and them telling me how excited they are to get their first or second big break, and how they just appreciate being here, how young and excited they are, how not jaded and cynical.

Young people are lovely. I remind myself to hang around with more people under 25 years old.

For all my obsessing about the food and the pig these last few days, what I realize most, standing there, is that the food is the most important thing, and the least. You can have a great party without great food—I mean, really you can have a great party feeding people nothing but Doritos and Coors Light—but really, good simple food, served to people you care about, says we give a shit about you enough that we want you in our house and we will go to this kind of trouble for you. It's the meta-message that means everything.

And this makes killing a living thing have some kind of value that maybe it didn't before.

Or this is what I tell myself when I feel the ghosts of our guests lingering, long after they've left. Them on us, us on them. I pour myself another glass of "secret tequila" now, although it isn't much of a secret. And I'm already thinking about the next party, the next people we get to see, the next pig to kill.

It's Not About the Bread

By Megan Kimble

From *Edible Baja Arizona*

Author of *Unprocessed: My City-Dwelling Year of Reclaiming Real Food,* Megan Kimble is also managing editor of *Edible Baja Arizona,* and a champion of local artisans and producers in the Tucson area. When it comes to locavore food culture, her subject Don Guerra ticks off every box on the checklist.

D on Guerra works alone. He spends 70 hours a week baking bread in a two-car garage–turned-bakery. His process is slow—the life cycle of a loaf is 24 hours—but his work is quick. He mixes flour into dough, shapes dough into loaf, bakes loaf into bread—time after time, 750 loaves a week. He has the build of an endurance athlete and baking 750 loaves a week—alone—is an endurance sport.

Don Guerra works with people—with farmers and millers, teachers and students, with Arizonans and with bakers from across the world. Twelve hundred people regularly buy loaves from Guerra's Barrio Bread and he knows all but a handful of their names.

Guerra has one employee supporting his work. He founded Barrio Bread in 2009 and ran it as a one-man show until 2011, when he hired his first employee, Ginger Snider, who now works eight hours a week helping with packaging and distribution.

Guerra has a community supporting his work. When the 44-year-old baker shows up at markets, customers rush over to his van to help him unload baskets full of bread. Two of his neighbors volunteer as delivery drivers. Others help him distribute at markets. "A huge part of my success and how I can get so much bread out there is that people want to be a part of the process and lend a hand," he says.

Don Guerra is a community-supported baker—almost every loaf of bread he makes has been pre-ordered online; he is a baker literally powered by consumer demand. Without a brick-and-mortar storefront, he sells his bread at four schools, one farmers' market, at the Tucson CSA's Tuesday and Wednesday pickups, and at River Road Gardens.

Guerra is supported by a community that buys his bread—and Guerra supports his community by envisioning a future for local food that extends far beyond bread. "The bread is a vehicle to connect community," says Guerra. "To get people to be proud of where they live and invested in their communities." He pauses. "I guess I say 'community' a lot."

Originally from Tempe, Guerra moved to Tucson to study anthropology at the University of Arizona. He dropped out after his junior year—"I ran out of money"—and moved to Flagstaff where, by chance, he got a job working the night shift at a bakery. "My first day there, I fell in love with it," he says. "And that was it."

He bounced around bakeries, learning from the best and honing his craft. He ended up at Arizona Bread Company, where he baked at night and took business classes at the community college during the day. The business plan for his first bakery was a school project. "I took it to a bank and they said, 'Yeah, let's do this,'" he says.

Guerra was 26 years old when he opened the Village Baker in Flagstaff. Business boomed—"We were doing a thousand loaves a day," he says. One of those loaves was usually claimed by a graduate student named Jen. "We'd chit-chat," says Don. Eventually, Don and Jen started dating; eventually, she'd move with him to Ashland, Oregon, as he opened a second Village Baker and she finished her master's degree in special education. By then, Don had all but stopped making bread, consumed instead by running two bakeries in two states. "We realized that if we wanted to have kids, we needed to figure out a business model that was more conducive to family," he says. "We missed Arizona. We missed our families. So we said, 'Let's go home.'"

In Tucson, Guerra took a break from bread, enrolling instead in the University of Arizona's College of Education. "I realized that with the bakeries, all I did was teach. I'd trained over a hundred people," says Guerra. "It was so fascinating to learn about pedagogy, about meta-cognition—learning how people learn."

He got a job at Miles Elementary teaching math, health, and physical education—in 2009, he was named Arizona's Elementary Physical Education Teacher of the Year. But he couldn't stay away from bread. "I loved teaching but the whole time I was dying to be a baker again," he says. "That was how my wife and I met, and I wanted to be that person again. I thought, If I could just get back to that place, it would all come together."

So he started making bread on the side; he started selling loaves in the parking lot after school. That model—selling bread at school—would eventually become a central part of Barrio Bread's business plan. "I chose accounts that fit my lifestyle," he says. "I designed a business after my life instead of my life after my business."

Today, Guerra bakes bread in the garage of his midtown home—the sweet smell of yeast and grain wafts out the front windows, permeating the air to the street. (The bakery is licensed under Arizona's Home Baked and Confectionary Goods program.)

Guerra's day begins at 4 a.m. He bakes until 7 a.m., when he takes a break to wake up his son and daughter, 10 and 12, and get them ready for school—and then it's back to the bakery, back to the flour, dough, and solitude. "It gets wonky in here sometimes," he says, smiling and covered in flour.

On Fridays, the day before he sells 200 loaves at the Plaza Palomino farmers' market, he works from 7 a.m. to 7 p.m., takes a break to eat dinner with his family, sleeps for a couple of hours, and is back in the bakery by midnight. The obvious question—"Do you sleep much?"—gets an obvious answer. "No," he says, simply. "I've never been a big sleeper.

"The thing I like about baking is the physicality of it. It requires physical and mental endurance, plus art and science."

The bakery is warm, not hot—76 degrees, year-round. Guerra slides eight Barrio baguettes into the Italian oven that anchors his operation. It's a deck oven, he says, peering across the 500-degree stone tiles to check on the bread. An exhale of steam lingers around the loaves.

The bakery smells like memory—like the first kitchen you remember;

the first restaurant where you earned your first paycheck. It smells like bread, of course, but what does bread really smell like? Yeast and Sunday; honey and home.

"What goes into bread is a lot of intangible things," says Guerra.

Tangibly, what goes into bread is flour, water, yeast, and salt. Bread begins with fermented dough and Guerra's dough begins fermenting by way of a sourdough starter. Made of flour and water, a sourdough starter is how bakers capture and propagate wild yeast; most artisan bakers have what's called a mother culture, which they take from every time they bake, feeding and growing the culture to source the yeast needed for a batch of bread.

After he cultivates his starter, Guerra combines several flour varieties—say, Red Fife, White Sonora wheat, and Hard Red Spring—into a batch, along with water and salt. The dough "rests" for four hours, which is when it comes to life, as the yeast are activated and start munching through sugars and exhaling carbon dioxide into air pockets—the very process that gives bread its lift.

At this point, the dough is a bundle of creamy smoothness—it is a discrete thing, one you can pick up and shape. Guerra shapes the dough into loaf-sized portions and, after another hour of room-temperature rest, the dough goes into cold storage to proof for another 15 hours before it's baked. "Slow fermentation—that's where you get all the benefits," he says.

Indeed, unlike with commercially produced bread, which goes from flour to loaf in as little as two hours, slow fermentation is the hallmark of artisan bread. During extended fermentation, an enzyme is produced that breaks down phytic acid, a nutrient blocker present in the outer layer of bran that can prevent a grain's nutrients from being absorbed into the body. Long fermentation develops flavor and texture; it creates a stable pH and increases shelf life. Hours of fermentation allow yeast and other bacteria to break down gluten—the protein that gives dough its elasticity—into smaller components that are more easily digested.

"The process is everything," says Guerra. "People have been eating poorly processed grain. I could take a semi-decent grain and turn it into a great loaf because of my process."

The fermentation is slow; the transformation, sudden. Flour, water, salt, yeast. Flour water salt yeast. Flourwatersaltyeast. Bread. Disparate ingredients cohere into one sustaining unit. It is poetic. (Pablo Neruda: "Then life itself will have the shape of bread, deep and simple, immeasurable and pure.") But there is also something so *not* poetic, not abstract nor artistic, about a loaf of bread—it is one of the most tangible things there is. Don Guerra is an artisan baker, but he is also just one producer in a web of producers that make up our local food system.

"I see Don's entrepreneurial capacity as extending beyond Barrio Bread," says Matt Mars, an assistant professor in the UA's College of Agricultural and Life Sciences. "He has a vision for the whole local food system, one based on collaboration and community." Struck by this vision, Mars spent two months interviewing Guerra, summarizing his findings in a case study called "From Bread We Build Community," soon to be published in the Journal of Agriculture, Food Systems, and Community Development.

"From a purely entrepreneurial perspective, what's brilliant about Don's model is that he never has inventory. He always knows how much to make, and how much is going to be sold and who is going to buy it," says Mars.

Another brilliance is folding fickle customers directly into the business—which, in turn, embeds the business in customers' lives. Rather than buy an artisan loaf once in a while, when they're in their "artisan bread phase," says Mars, customers return to Barrio Bread regularly—"it's part of their routine. They've met Don, they get how he works, so they value the bread more." It's precisely this sense of value that Guerra is trying to export to other facets of the local food system—the value he's working to collect and cohere into a local food identity.

"Local food systems tend to struggle with this, bringing cohesion to a system and a supply chain that is otherwise fragmented and not very well articulated," says Mars. "Don is a connector, a hub. That's a special ingredient in a local food system—someone who can transcend their own business to understand that the local system is stronger when competition is put aside. Someone who can pull everyone along the supply chain together under a common vision that is relevant to the community."

A supply chain is a narrative—it has a beginning, middle, and end. Seed to farm, grain to mill, baker to buyer.

"When you open the garage door to his bakery, it's palpable—you see the beginning, middle, and end," says Pizzeria Bianco's Chris Bianco. "The bread comes from wheat that comes from a good place and good people."

Since Guerra met Chris Bianco in 2012—since Gary Nabhan first introduced him to White Sonora wheat; since he met Jeff and Emma Zimmerman of Hayden Flour Mills, Steve Sossaman of Sossaman Farms, and Brian and Ralph Wong of BKW Farms—he's become an integral part of a collaboration between farmers, millers, bakers, and seed savers working to bring native and heritage grains back to southern Arizona farms and tables. As farmers have learned how to grow heritage grains and millers learned how to process it, Guerra has had to figure out how to make bread from that which is harvested locally.

"The challenge in working with local wheat is variability," says Guerra. "We all learned about it together. What can you do with this variety? Well, let's try it and see what it does.

"Every bag of flour is different," he says. "Baking with local grains offers some good life skills. If you push too hard on something, it's going to push back. If you push too hard, it's going to shut down."

Guerra estimates that 100 of his 750 weekly loaves are made with local grains. Part of the challenge is the price point—Guerra is committed to providing his community with affordable food, which means he has to take the loss when he prices a loaf of heritage grain bread at $5.50. (He hasn't raised his prices from $4 to $5 a loaf in four years, even when the price of a bag of high-quality organic flour has more than tripled since he started baking.) "I'm growing a strong root system, so that when I need to change, the community will be there for me," he says.

Chris Bianco made every pizza he served at his famous Pizzeria Bianco in Phoenix for 17 years. "There's a vulnerability there," says Bianco. "Say you're a professional athlete. There will be a day that comes when you won't be able to run as fast and jump as high. How can you still serve your craft? What will you leave behind?"

For Guerra, the answer is education. He teaches community baking classes and weekend workshops for adults; he worked with Avalon

Organic Gardens to help them develop their bread program; he teaches seed-to-loaf classes at Tucson Village Farm for kids. ("There are always two kids out of 60 who are going to be bakers," Guerra says. "They come up to me at the end of class and say, 'I've figured it out.'")

"I want more people to make a good loaf themselves," he says. "And I want the business to grow organically. If I can get more people making good bread, maybe they'll come back and work for me someday."

Guerra has traveled across the world to teach other bakers about his business model—the idea of a community-supported baker is exportable to other communities, he says. The idea of entrepreneurial leadership driving food system change is replicable in other locales.

But for now, when he's at home, Guerra focuses on the craft. For now, he loves the solitude. As his kids become independent teenagers—as they move out of the house and into the world—he'll think about doing the same. For now, "I love that my hands are in every loaf," he says. "When I'm in here alone, I can really just laser focus on the craft."

It's all about the bread. And it's not really about the bread. It's about the craft—but really, it's about the community. "I want to be a village baker in all senses of that term," Guerra says. "People want to belong. I want to do more than just live here—I want to belong. The local food movement makes me belong to a local tribe. Maybe that's why we're so fanatical about it. Taste, sure, but belongingness."

"I might make a loaf with Hayden's Red Fife," says Guerra, "and it smells like dirt, like soil, like dust. It smells like Arizona."

Traditions

The Lunch Counter

By John T. Edge

From *Garden & Gun*

Director of the University of Mississippi's Southern Foodways
Alliance, John T. Edge is also a columnist for *Garden & Gun* and
the *Oxford American*, and teaches at the University of Georgia. In
his upcoming book *The Potlikker Papers*, he tells the history of the
modern South through food. What could be more iconic than
the dime store lunch counter?

L unch counters, with starburst stainless backslashes, vinyl spinner
stools, and long tables of elbow-polished linoleum, are architec-
tural and cultural icons. Everyman spaces, where lawyers and laborers
sit side by side to savor burgers and fries and sweaty tumblers of tea,
they were conceived as sites of workaday communion.

At their best, lunch counters reflect our egalitarian ideals. The problem is, for much of the South's history, they were not at their best. Until
the Civil Rights Act of 1964, many restaurants were reserved for whites,
while black citizens ate their burgers and fries standing up, or at a cordoned section of the counter, or after walking around to the back door.

I spent grammar school mornings in the post-segregation 1970s on
a Waffle House spinner stool, eating breakfasts of over-easy eggs and
butter-troweled toast as blacks and whites alike slurped coffee from
stoneware mugs, dropped quarters in the juke, and exchanged the af-
firming pleasantries that make restaurants incubators of community.
Watching the grill cook at our local in Macon, Georgia, as he spatula-
flipped patty sausages with his left hand and cracked eggs with his right,

my father, who worked on federal civil rights cases in the sixties and seventies, would tell me stories of the struggle to desegregate the region and sketch the promise of gathering all at a common table.

I think of those morning discussions each time I take a seat at a restaurant with a counter. Even as I order a bowl of the cheddar-bound macaroni and cheese that Ashley Christensen serves at Poole's Downtown Diner—a swish modern restaurant in Raleigh, North Carolina, that attracts an inclusive crowd—I can't help but fix on that design form and on the role those counters played in our region's tragic past. When I slide onto one of the stools at Poole's serpentine counter and order an old-fashioned, I conjure how such places of pleasure were once sites of contention.

I'm not falling on my sword. I believe that an acknowledgement of our past better prepares me to enjoy the pleasures of this present. In that spirit, I recently took a stool at Brent's Drugs, in Jackson, Mississippi, a model of the lunch counter form, with a boomerang-imprinted aquamarine counter and Tab placards mounted on the back bar. Two bites into a breakfast of fried eggs and stone-ground grits, I flashed to the ugly moment back in May 1963, when an integrated group, led by college students, attempted to gain service at a Woolworth's lunch counter in downtown Jackson, while a mob of protesters threw salt in their eyes, dumped mustard on their heads, and stubbed lit cigarettes on their forearms.

Three miles and fifty-one years separate Woolworth's then and Brent's today. Neither distance seems great. Two generations after the Civil Rights Act legally desegregated America's restaurants, hard appraisals are as necessary to our current understanding of good food as facing down the evils of factory-farmed pigs before ordering that next slaw-capped barbecue sandwich.

The role of lunch counters in the social life of our region began to change in February 1960, when four black freshmen at what is now North Carolina Agricultural and Technical University walked into an F. W. Woolworth Company store in Greensboro, North Carolina, and requested service. Protesters in Southern border cities like Baltimore and Oklahoma City had staged previous sit-ins, demanding equal treatment. But this one struck in the heart of the Deep South, where Jim Crow reigned. The students were quickly refused. A larger group of students returned the next day. All took their place at the counter and ordered food that never came.

Within two weeks, students in eleven cities had staged sit-ins, mostly at lunch counters in downtown department stores. They were organized and insistent. Students in Nashville, wary of violent reprisal, developed protocols: "Do show yourself friendly on the counter at all times. Do sit straight and always face the counter. Don't strike back, or curse back if attacked. Don't laugh out. Don't hold conversations. Don't block entrances."

By the end of February, sit-ins spread to thirty cities in eight states. Some white merchants responded with harebrained strategies. Instead of serving an integrated crowd, department store and drugstore managers in Charlotte and Knoxville unscrewed the seats from their lunch counter stools. In the *Carolina Israelite*, North Carolina journalist Harry Golden unpacked the absurdity of the moment. "It is only when the Negro 'sets' that the fur begins to fly," he wrote, proposing a tongue-in-cheek solution, the Golden Vertical Negro Plan, in which segregated sit-down lunch counters would be refashioned for integrated stand-up meals.

When President Johnson signed the Civil Rights Act, on July 2, 1964, he outlawed discrimination and segregation in places of public accommodation. Many restaurants integrated within the first week. On July 3, Cafe du Monde, the coffee and beignet stand in the French Quarter of New Orleans, served its first black customers without incident. On July 5, the Sun and Sand motel in Jackson, Mississippi, served its first black dining room client, but closed the swimming pool.

Others adopted the principles of massive resistance. The most well-known included Maurice Bessinger of Maurice's Piggie Park in Columbia, South Carolina, who integrated his barbecue restaurant after losing a Supreme Court battle but continued to fight through the 1970s, when he served as president of the National Association for the Preservation of White People and ran a losing campaign for governor while wearing a white suit and riding a white horse.

Some responses were more sophisticated. The owners of the Emporia Diner in Virginia developed a two-menu system. Blacks got menus with higher-priced fried chicken. Down in North Carolina, proprietors of Ayers Log Cabin Pit Cooked Bar-B-Que in the city of Washington took a cruder tack when they agreed to serve blacks but posted a sign by the register: ANY MONEY FROM NIGGERS GIVEN TO THE KKK.

When my friend Brownie Futrell was a boy, he asked his father, publisher of the local newspaper, what the sign meant. "It means we can't eat here anymore," came the answer. Futrell, a white son of the South, had to wait a long time before pondering a return. The sign remained in place until 1970, when the U.S. Attorney General filed suit to force its removal. True redemption came later, after Ayers closed, when the Solid Rock Holiness Church, a black congregation, began worshipping in that same space.

Old habits die hard. When I moved from Georgia to Mississippi in 1995, the Crystal Grill in Greenwood still displayed one sign that identified it as the Crystal Club, a name adopted in 1964 that defined the restaurant as a so-called key club, off-limits to blacks. As recently as 2001, I was turned away from a New Orleans restaurant when I arrived with a Korean American friend. "We can't accommodate you," the owner said as we peered past him into a half-empty dining room, draped in linen and set with gleaming flatware.

Today, the symbolism of the long unbroken table remains important, especially among Southerners schooled from infancy in Last Supper imagery. Sharing a meal signals social equality. Like sex, eating is a deeply intimate act. And no eating space is more intimate than the lunch counter, where diners stoop to sit and eat with people of other sexes and other races.

Many of us now live in gated communities and relax at private clubs. One of the drivers for that privatization was the struggle that began over lunch counters and escalated to include all restaurants. Remnants of the South's post–Civil Rights Act flirt with key clubs can be glimpsed at schools like the University of Mississippi in Oxford, where I work.

Here, many of the white elite opt out of the university cafeteria system to eat at sorority and fraternity houses. Passage to those dining rooms is no longer determined by skin color, as it was in the 1960s. Today, class is as likely to drive campus segregation as race. And, yes, some black students now eat in fraternity and sorority dining rooms. But each time I watch a lunchtime stream of white students file into the sorority houses that line the street alongside my office, I can't help but think that a new generation is losing out on the same opportunity I squandered back in the 1980s when I took my lunches of country-fried steak and green beans at the all-white Sigma Nu house at the University of Georgia.

All that said, there are frequent and sustaining flashes of contemporary hope. After a long absence, Southerners are returning to communal dining. Large unbroken tables, considered class equalizers during the French Revolution, copied by American hotels in the nineteenth century, and interpreted as lunch counters in the twentieth century, are regaining popularity. At restaurants like Snackbar here in Oxford, the communal tables are where the real gossiping and elbow rubbing and oyster slurping and community building go on.

On that recent trip to Jackson, I noted the same thing at the Beatty Street Grocery, a backstreet café that abuts a scrap metal yard. All of the action was at the counters, where white construction workers in dusty brogans and black government bureaucrats in gleaming cap-toes gathered at the same high-tops to eat three-buck fried bologna sandwiches on toasted white bread. Fifty years after the South fitfully desegregated its restaurants, the welcome table ideal has yet to be realized here. But that ideal may finally be in reach.

Hot Country

By Jane and Michael Stern

From *Saveur*

Since the 1970s—way before "eating local" became a catch phrase—Jane and Michael have crisscrossed America, hunting for beloved regional spots to feature in their Road Food books and columns. But are they brave enough to go for the extra-hot version of Nashville's famous hot chicken?

"Make me hurt," murmurs a slender young woman in business pinstripes and high heels before placing her order at the window inside Bolton's Spicy Chicken & Fish, a tumbledown eatery on Nashville's east side. Twenty minutes later, we watch as she carries a wax paper package to a table. She peels back the wrapper, revealing a massive hunk of fried chicken enveloped in a glistening veil of pepper-red crust beside a slew of dill pickle chips. There is a slice of white bread on top of the chicken, as well as below, to soak up the spicy grease. It looks like a sandwich, but the bones are still in there, and its heft makes picking it up seem absurd. While plastic knives and forks are available, like everyone else here, she doesn't use them. This is chicken to tear apart with your fingers, to pick at, to gnaw every bit of meat off of every single bone. This is Nashville hot chicken.

With each bite, beads of perspiration build on the woman's brow. She undoes the top buttons of her blouse, removes her earrings from her earlobes and drops them on the table; she begins to sniffle and breathe heavily, to fan herself and whisper, "Mercy!" several times, as if in a euphoric trance. Finally, when she wobbles to her feet to throw away the bones, she sighs, "I'll be okay," to no one in particular and steps out into the sunny Music City streets.

Bolton's is one of a handful of Nashville restaurants specializing in hot chicken, as well as hot fish. While the fish—usually fried whiting splashed with hot sauce and served as a sandwich—has comparables in other cities with thriving soul food scenes, hot chicken is in a class by itself.

Each hot chicken joint has its own carefully guarded recipe, but the basic idea is to marinate chicken in a brine of buttermilk infused with cayenne, paprika, garlic powder, and other spices. Then it is dredged in more spice and double-fried. Finally, when the chicken is fresh from the hot oil, it is slathered in a fiery buttery paste that melds with the crust, creating a crunchy, pepper-charged coat, resulting in an infernal delight. Yet, stunning as hot chicken is, heat alone is not what hooks devotees. Aqui Simpson, who opened a hot chicken restaurant in 2007 called 400 Degrees, is convinced it's as much about flavor as ferocity. Good hot chicken should be spicy, yes, but that heat should be tempered by sweetness, juiciness, and an umami richness.

It is said that hot chicken was created as a form of revenge in the 1930s to purposely hurt the first person ever to eat it. Thornton Prince, the proprietor of a fried chicken restaurant, had a lady friend so irritated by his carousing that early one morning, upon his return from who-knows-where, she served him a plate of chicken with enough pepper punch to drop his sorry ass. But the booby-trapped bird backfired: Mr. Prince liked it. He liked it so much that he put it on his menu. Today, Prince's Hot Chicken Shack, now operated by Thornton's great-niece André Prince Jeffries, is the Olympus of Nashville's hot chicken universe. Proprietors of all the other hot chicken places in town learned to love it here first. It was Prince's that first tucked the ferocious bird between slices of bread, and Prince's that scattered pickle chips around it. The seemingly unassuming strip mall joint is also responsible for establishing the near-ubiquitous heat scale of mild, medium, hot, and extra-hot. Prince's medium is as incendiary as a four-alarm Texas chili. And the hot version tests our pain-pleasure tolerance so emphatically that we have yet to find the will to try extra-hot.

Its intensity explains why hot chicken is one preparation in which an otherwise bland breast is like a blank canvas to paint with spice. That's not to say that versions made with dark meat aren't a thing of extraordinary pleasure. At Hot Stuff Spicy Chicken & Fish, a spiffy-clean storefront southeast of the city, we poke the tines of a fork through the brittle red crust on a thigh and watch as juices come pouring out. This piece is crazy moist, sopping the bland supermarket bread with a slurry of spices and chicken fat, transforming it into a starchy, savory pudding that almost no one leaves behind.

Hot Stuff's chicken comes in degrees of heat that go from Lil Spice and Lemon Pepper to X-, XX-, and XXX-hot. Ordinary hot (no X) clears our sinuses and takes our breath away. While a manager suggests sweet fruit tea as a salve, it has little effect on a ravaged tongue. What does work, we find, is cake. Hot Stuff's counter is arrayed with slices of layer cake made by local baker Spencer Middlebrooks. And the cooling effect of his tall, silky yellow cake with caramel-tinged mocha frosting is just what our blazing taste buds need.

Though the city's hot chicken joints are informal, this is by no means fast food. For good hot chicken, you wait. Each order is fried to order because a heat lamp would risk a softened crust on a dish in which frangibility is fundamental. Regulars know to phone in their order 20 minutes before they arrive. On the small tarmac around Pepperfire Hot Chicken, which has no indoor dining, cars crowd willy-nilly as their drivers read newspapers, talk on cellphones, or doze while listening for their names to be called on the loudspeaker.

Isaac Beard opened Pepperfire in the fall of 2010 and is one of the few white men among Nashville's hot chicken purveyors. Beard, a Nashville native, is convinced that this specialty of the city's African-American communities can captivate the country just as its profile in his hometown has grown into a source of citywide pride and the inspiration for an annual hot chicken festival every Independence Day. He may be right. Recently, hot chicken joints have started popping up as far away from Nashville as Brooklyn's Peaches Hot House and Cackalack's Hot Chicken Shack in Portland, Oregon.

Hot chicken does have a way of inspiring devotion that verges on addiction. A woman we met in line at Prince's gleefully told us she eats extra-hot five days a week (the restaurant is closed Sunday and Monday). I can't help it, she said. "I just need it."

Nashville Hot Chicken

The secret to Nashville's famous hot chicken is in the layering: The bird is marinated in a spicy buttermilk brine, then dredged with more flour and spice, double-fried, and finally slathered with a fiery butter paste to create a crunchy, peppery coating. One bite into its burnished orange crust reveals first a tangy crunch, and then a deeper, complex spice that leaves a lingering fire behind. Adjust the heat by adding as much—or as little—cayenne as you like.

Serves 2–4

3 cups buttermilk
¾ cup cayenne
9 tablespoons granulated garlic
9 tablespoons paprika
6 tablespoons onion powder
3 tablespoons sugar
1 (2½–3 pounds) chicken, cut into 8 pieces, or 3 pounds chicken wings
Kosher salt and freshly ground black pepper, to taste
Canola oil, for frying
2 cups self-rising flour
6 tablespoons unsalted butter, melted
Sliced white sandwich bread and dill pickle chips, for serving

1. Combine buttermilk, ¼ cup cayenne, 3 tablespoons each granulated garlic and paprika, 2 tablespoons onion powder, and 1 tablespoon sugar in a bowl; whisk until smooth. Add chicken and toss to coat; cover and chill at least 4 hours or up to overnight.

2. The next day, drain chicken, rinse, and pat dry; season with salt and pepper. Heat 2 inches oil in a 6-quart saucepan until a deep-fry thermometer reads 300°F. Stir remaining cayenne, granulated garlic, paprika, onion powder, and sugar in a bowl; transfer half to another bowl and whisk in flour. Working in batches, dredge chicken in flour mixture; fry, flipping once, until golden and almost cooked through, 6–7 minutes, or until an instant-read thermometer inserted into the thickest part of a thigh reads 150°. Transfer chicken to paper towels.

3. Increase oil temperature to 350°. Stir remaining cayenne mixture and melted butter in a bowl; set paste aside. Dredge chicken once more in flour mixture and fry until cooked through, 2–3 minutes more; drain briefly on paper towels and brush with reserved paste. Serve with bread and pickles.

Oyster Heaven

By Bethany Jean Clement

From the *Seattle Times*

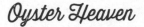

In her post as the *Seattle Times'* head food writer (and, before that, at the alternative weekly *The Stranger*), Bethany Jean Clement is a lively, entertaining guide to the Northwest coast's foodways. Which includes oysters, of course, as freshly caught as you can get 'em.

The sky is the ceiling of the Oyster Saloon. It has no walls. It is surrounded by enormous Douglas firs with strands of gray-green moss trailing from their shaggy branches; the craggy peaks of The Brothers, framed in a firred notch above the two-lane highway winding past; a pile of oyster shells bleached pure white by sun and rain, big enough you can drive a car up onto it; the sparkling or cloud-coated waters of Hood Canal, sometimes with tideflats. The oysters you eat at the Oyster Saloon come from right there. The distance from where they grow to your mouth is a matter of yards.

This is the almost unbearably scenic Hama Hama oyster farm, family-run for five generations. It's located where the Hamma Hamma River meets Hood Canal. The spelling hadn't been settled yet when the land was, and the joke (or maybe the truth) is that great-great-grandpa left out the extra M's to save on ink. If you go just a little ways farther along the curve of Highway 101, you'll see the elegant, antique arc of the bridge that crosses the south fork of the Hamma Hamma—a drawing of the bridge is the logo for the family's work.

The saloon itself has been in existence for just one year. Last spring,

Lissa James Monberg, who's in charge of retail and marketing, got the idea that it'd be fun to feed oysters to visitors on site, in addition to what they can get at the company store to take away. (The company store itself opened after passers-by would stop, knock and ask if there were oysters for sale.) So alongside the Hama Hama Co.'s notably modest world headquarters, a bit of the world's prettiest parking lot was cordoned off, with wire contained columns of oyster shells around the perimeter.

More oyster shells hem in a fire pit, around which you may sit on a plank-and-stump bench or a cinder block. There are a few picnic tables, laid with hot sauce, salt and pepper, and paper napkins. Two cedar-and-fir pavilions offer shelter in inclement weather; the windows came from an old bathhouse. Lissa likes the way their raised plank floors sound like a boat's deck, she says, tapping them with her rubber boot.

The saloon name came from the big, old-time places in New York City where oysters were cheap bar snacks and the floors were covered in sawdust. The bar here, beneath an overhang, has eight metal stools, beer and cider, and an unbeatable smell to go with the unbeatable view: salty air mixed with pines and the smoke of oysters cooking on the grill.

G rilled oysters are the standby of Lilliwaup, the unincorporated community along this particular stretch of shore, though people around here would more prosaically call them barbecued. Locals pretty much eschew oysters on the half-shell, while lots of visitors—barring traffic, Seattle is 2½ hours away by the pretty route, two by the fast one—have never had them cooked.

The goodness of a grilled oyster is difficult to explain to the uninitiated; they're custardy in the middle, crisped around the edges, somehow both more and less oceanic than raw ones. You tend to eat them so fast that the memory is only a ghost that, when summoned, demands more.

Of course, the saloon serves raw oysters, too, and Hama Hama's are prized for their sea-sweet, clarion flavor on the half-shell. It's a taste that rings like a bell. Their fried oysters, with the oysterness concentrated and encased in a crisp, delicate, cornmeal crust, are a deeper brown than most; they're pan-fried instead of deep-fried, which would be easier. The saloon sells them to pop in your mouth serially or on a po'boy.

Lissa's brother, Adam James, runs the day-to-day that gets the oysters from Hood Canal to the platter. Their mom, Helena James, makes Dungeness crab cakes for the saloon, for the store and for the Ballard and University farmers markets. Asked if it's a secret recipe, she laughs. She got it from Gourmet magazine years ago, though she didn't have Old Bay seasoning, so she used Spike. "I think you could probably find something very similar on epicurious.com," she says, smiling.

She and Lissa both make it clear that service at the Oyster Saloon can be a little rough-and-tumble. Last summer was much busier than they thought it would be, just from signs by the roadside and a couple Facebook posts, "And it was full of mishaps," according to Helena. Getting your order or your bill sometimes took awhile, Lissa says. Her grandpa—Helena's dad, Bart Robbins, who recently moved from Lilliwaup to a retirement home in nearby Shelton—came with friends, and he got his lunch, but the friends' order got lost.

"We've had a steep learning curve on being a restaurant," Helena says, laughing.

Luckily, Lissa says, people visiting Hama Hama are generally in a good mood. They've often been on a hike nearby—the company store has a book of them, or the affable guy manning the grill will tell you where the waterfalls are. There's the canal to look at and, on a sunny day, the beer you have here is the best one you've ever had.

The oysters, originally, were incidental. Bart Robbins remembers the logging camp up the Hamma Hamma River Valley, where 300 men harvested timber, and life was rough-and-tumble indeed. Bart's a tall man, somewhat taciturn. His nose is carved away on one side, the aftermath of a lifetime on the water in the days before sunscreen.

His grandfather, Daniel Miller Robbins, came west from Minneapolis and started accumulating timberland in the late 1800s. "He worked for J.J. Hill, building railroads," Bart says. "It was all logging back then." His grandfather didn't even know he was getting the family into the oyster business.

Back in the day, the oysters were sold off the beach in bulk. Then, during the Great Depression, it helped a lot to not have to feed the stock at Hama Hama; oysters eat algae and waterborne particulate plant matter. The virtues of pulling a nail out of a board and saving it, of building something yourself instead of paying someone to do it, were still handed down. In the 1950s, Bart moved out to the farm and made money any way he could, selling shake bolts, Christmas trees and more. He started shrimping, driving his catch into Seattle to sell, and then began including oysters in the deliveries. Invoices were payable to the Hama Hama Logging Company. Around 1975, the family leased the shellfish operation out; in the mid-1980s, they took it back under their wing.

There's logging at Hama Hama still, done sustainably on a 60- to 80-year rotation. It's true second growth up on the hills, and the way it's managed, Adam James says, "allows the woods to get a little older, a little more decadent."

He can show you where the railroad tracks used to lead right up to the beach for the shipping of the timber, and if the timing's right, that might be exactly where you see a plump, sinuous river otter, closer than you can believe. The Hama Hama land's also home to massive Roosevelt elk (sometimes visible from the bridge), blue herons, bald eagles (sometimes known to eat the baby blue herons) and several kinds of scoters (who like to eat Hama Hama clams—hence the nets out on the tideflats).

The gravelly soils brought down the valley with the river help make this such a sweet spot for oysters, building up the tideflats into the beds on which they rest and flourish. For a long time, the oysters that are now gourmands' half-shell pleasure were all shucked and sold in jars, ready for frying or oyster stew. This is how the shell pile got so monumental. The half-shell part of the Hama Hama operation, with oysters shipped whole and alive, didn't begin until around 1960, at Bart Robbins' suggestion.

"We were selling through the Oyster Growers Cooperative," he says. "All you heard about in the East was half-shell oysters, and it wasn't out here at all. So we got started doing that. It's certainly grown since then."

The use of the land and the waters are now the charge of a board made up of members of the extended family. Historically, the presidency of the board went father-son, but the newest president is Kendra James. She's Adam and Lissa's boss when it comes to the oyster company, and she's also their sister-in-law. It's the first time the board president has been a woman or an in-law. Lissa says Kendra's doing a great job.

While the Hama Hama Co. oyster farm has certainly grown, it's not what you'd call large. About 30 people make it happen, including Juan Aguilar, who's been shucking oysters and driving them to Seattle for Hama Hama for 18 years, and Teresa Rabbie, who has packed oysters into jars for 22 years. (Taylor Shellfish Farms, by way of comparison, has around 500 employees.) The oysters are gathered by hand from the beach, in what would be backbreaking work if it weren't time-limited by the return of the tide. But the tide also means that sometimes oysters must be harvested in the dead of night, in freezing winter wind and rain.

You can get a tide-table app for your phone now, but Adam James says it can't fully account for the waters' mysteries. Barometric pressure can make a tide change more slowly and go significantly lower or higher. At a conference recently, Adam heard a talk about all the factors that guide the tide; it only confused matters. He's waiting for the day when he can feel it in his knees, he says with a laugh.

A day for him, tides depending, might start in the early morning with sorting through orders from renowned restaurants like the Walrus and the Carpenter in Seattle, L & E Oyster Bar in Los Angeles, Bavette's in Chicago, and Aquagrill and the Grand Central Oyster Bar in New York.

Then he or one of the crew will go out on the barge, which is a platform with a wheelhouse, motor and a crane; on a pretty morning, its noise and angles contrast the canal's ethereal pearly gray. The horizon can be barely distinguishable, no clear border between water and woods and sky. Mist can suddenly envelop everything.

"It's kind of like by Braille—we've got these buoys out here, and these marker stakes," Adam says. They could, of course, use GPS, but "that would take the fun out of it."

As with all farming, there's a lot of moving stuff from place to place. Some buoys mark big, rusty cages of oysters that will come in to be sorted, then restored to the water, grouped by size, to make dealing with them more efficient down the line. Adam says you'd be surprised to know how much, in its raising, your oyster is touched by human hands: possibly a dozen or more times.

"A lot of the things we do are what Grandpa did," he says, but they've also added modern techniques to old-school wild capture. That pile of shells, for instance, isn't mounding up as fast as it used to; the leftovers from Juan's shucking sometimes go back out on the barge to be dumped unceremoniously back in Puget Sound, because, in season, they're dotted with almost microscopic live baby-oyster seeds. Some seedlings come from hatcheries, too, now. And in 2011, Hama Hama started farming Blue Pools: Like the sought-after Kusshi oysters, they're tumbled, grown in mesh bags suspended on frames so that the tide agitates them, chipping their edges and making them grow deeper cups.

Customers want different kinds of oysters nowadays, Adam says. The Blue Pools accommodate that, and the tumbling could be called a value-add, though he wouldn't put it like that. He looks pained talking about other companies' marketing and brands; there's one named Naked Cowboy, another featuring imagery of a sexy lady. Hama Hama, in a further accommodation of the contemporary oyster customer, has started distributing another variety of tumbled oyster, from south Puget Sound, but its name is anti-sexy: Sea Cow. The company also partners with independent oyster farmers in Pickering and Hammersley, and has leases for more oyster-growing in Pickering and up north on the Olympic Peninsula, near Port Townsend. The growth is measured, Adam says, not undertaken lightly.

Back on land, he figures out what the crew needs to harvest for tomorrow's orders and deals with loose ends in the office. Today he runs home and returns with his eldest, Emmett, who's 3½ years old. The barge is beached in its slip, with more offloading and loading going on.

"Da-Da, why is the water so shallow down there?" asks Emmett.

"Because the tide's out," Adam says.

Down on the beach, Emmett runs free, finds a multi-legged sand worm, digs in the sand and goes in the water over the tops of his boots, with glee. Adam reminisces about daring a friend to eat a sand worm sandwiched between two Doritos, a dare the friend took. "He lived," Adam says.

Bags of Blue Pools, still half-submerged, are slowly loaded onto a boat. Meanwhile, three crew members dig clams, then two of them head out to pick oysters. The Blue Pools get moved from the boat to a truck, and someone runs the oyster-laden vehicle into the only piling anywhere near on the beach, which everyone finds hilarious.

Lissa walks out to the oyster beds as dusk falls. "The gloaming," she says.

"It's atavistic," she says. "You know, we have bags, we have buoys, but people have been picking up oysters forever."

The wind ruffles the surface of the water, which is the same color as the sky: a darkening, piercing blue. The crew finishes up, and the tide takes the beds back for the night.

The Story of Chicken

By Karen J. Coates

From *The Cook's Cook*

Author of *Eternal Harvest* and *Cambodia Now*, investigative journalist Karen Coates specializes in Asian food and environmental issues. Formerly *Gourmet* magazine's Asia correspondent, she blogs at ramblingspoon.com. For thecookscook.com she gives geopolitical context to a food we often take for granted.

I'm sitting on the bank of the Chao Phraya, digging into a slimy plastic bag of fall-off-the-chopped-bone grilled chicken with sticky rice, which I bought at a little street stall just upriver from Bangkok. It's a one-person feast. I devour the meat, one bite at a time, as I roll the rice into little balls between my fingers, dipping it into super-spicy *nam prik*. I sop up the sauce and revel in the sweet-tangy heat of the whole affair (undoubtedly enhanced by MSG). My mouth tingles, my fingers glisten with grease. I sweat in my seat on this riverside pier, the air 90 degrees on the Fahrenheit scale, the chile many multitudes higher on the Scoville scale. All around me, people dig into little plastic bags of their own. I briefly wonder how many others are having unique little chicken epiphanies this same afternoon.

As a species, we humans love chicken. As a meat, it surpasses all others in the number of animals raised for consumption. It's the most plentiful bird in the world, and we've made it so: more than 19 billion worldwide, which equates to an average of nearly three chickens per person on Earth (or nearly 40 for every person in Bahrain and Brunei, the biggest chicken lovers on the planet). Those numbers are rising, with poultry as the world's leading livestock industry.

Why such ardor for a bird? Well, it tastes like chicken. But it's also cheap—chickens are quicker and easier to raise than cattle, pigs or goats. And unlike other creatures of the human dining repertoire, few cultures maintain chicken taboos.

But our chicken addiction has led human beings into a thicket of trouble. The more we eat, the more we produce, the more we wrestle with our conscience about what we do to animals in order to consume them—practices that may threaten our very survival as human beings. The human-chicken story is one of love, evolution and risk.

The typical chicken we eat is a descendent of the "aggressive, pugnacious" red jungle fowl of Asia, writes Harold McGee, the godfather of food science. It was *Gallus gallus*, a member of the pheasant family, which eventually morphed into the breast on our plates today. "Chickens seem to have been domesticated in the vicinity of Thailand before 7500 BCE, and arrived in the Mediterranean around 500 BCE," he writes. Fitting, then, that Thailand today serves such finger-licking luscious little bits of bird. In the West, it wasn't until the 19th century when imported Chinese fowl sparked a frenzy of bird breeding, turning the "unpampered farmyard scavengers" of the day into the meat we Americans now love. We humans have tamed the wild and pugnacious into a feathered food machine.

I have seen *Gallus gallus* in the wilds of Asia. It's a mighty impressive bird, especially the cock, with radiant orange plumage like a coat of lava—unlike anything I ever saw growing up in the '70s and '80s in the American Midwest. We didn't live on a farm. We lived in the suburbs. Our already-plucked chickens came on yellow Styrofoam trays, wrapped in plastic and arranged in parts. Usually breasts. Usually more breasts on a tray than on an individual chicken. I never thought about that as a child, and I never fully thought much about the math until years later, living in Asia, where the chicken in our local market was a bird, the whole bird and nothing but the bird. With two breasts. And then one day, one vendor started selling separated breasts, legs and wings. It was the absence of the rest of the bird that really got me thinking.

In Europe, "Breast fillets are so profitable that they finance all the other parts of the bird," according to a Heinrich Boll report called *Meat*

Atlas. "For the producer, if it is not breast, it is waste." In years past, all those wings and legs were ground into feed. But that ended with the emergence of mad cow disease, and the subsequent EU ban on feeding animals bits and pieces of their cousins. So, instead, European producers sent their poultry bits and pieces to Africa at such low prices that the imports undermined the local chicken industry—and Africans developed a palate for wings and legs.

Frozen bird bits have made forays into other parts of the developing world, too—such as deep in the heart of Borneo. I'm squashed in the back of a beat up old Toyota double-cab with ripped interior and, on the outside, a rusty hunk of metal where the bumper should be. The tires are slathered in mud as Francis, the driver, shimmies down a slick logging road in an oppressive rain. We're in the Kelabit Highlands where undulating mountains form the border between Malaysia and Indonesia. For thousands of years, small local tribes have occupied the old-growth jungles that straddle these two nations. But the forests are falling, and the village is changing as traditional diets make way for the modern. "People here love chicken wings!" Francis says with a grin. So he buys them frozen from a warehouse in town on the coast, he trucks them 15 hours into the jungle. Afterward he returns to the coast with a cooler full of bush meat, for his family, completing the circle.

But still, many Asians harbor a deep admiration for the bird that sustained their youth. "Local chicken." "Village chicken." These terms are used with the same reverence we Westerners accord "free-range" and "organic" (whatever that actually means anymore).

I'm in mountainous farm country in the far north of Laos when, one day, I start describing the typical American chicken operation to local farmers. "It's not possible to do that," a man named Davong tells me. He sees no future in Laos for an American-style broiler operation, which can easily house 100,000 birds at a time. Why wouldn't it work? "If you have a chicken coop," he says, "you have to look for food for the chickens." And, he points out, that's just not economical. By his estimation, it's far easier and cheaper to let chickens eat what they peck on the ground.

Farther down the dirt road I ask a woman named Lee similar questions about chicken, and she agrees with Davong. "That's for economy only," she says after I describe typical conditions for industrial chickens of the West.

Plus, her neighbor Mon says, the meat won't taste good if chickens can't run around and find their own food. Cooped-up birds also need medicine and chemicals, she says, and that's not good either. "If you raise chickens for eating, fed by nature is best."

Another neighbor, Noi, confirms this: free-roaming chickens develop strong legs, thick muscles and, consequently, tasty meat. Chickens kept in a coop have soft legs and little muscle.

"Their legs are not too strong," she says, and their meat is not delicious (though she's never actually tasted factory chicken).

Yet flavor is so often influenced by the world around it. It's not just what we eat, but how we eat it and with whom. That's true for chicken, for lobster, for a humble bowl of rice with a dollop of fish paste: how we, as humans, think of a meal depends on context. I learned that as a child.

I remember the stench of charred chicken skin. Not burnt, but utterly black; entire wings and breasts crusted over, obscured by a shroud of carbon. It smells of fire and dirt and damp air. It smells, too, of potatoes wrapped in foil over open flames, and of summer in the mosquito-ey Midwest. I see my Mom standing in the screen door of the Minnie Winnie camper, shaking her head as my Dad mutters insults at the fire.

Most every weekend during the summer of my 5th year, we camped. And most every weekend that summer, we ate my Dad's charred grilled chicken. When I think of those scorched hockey pucks of flesh today, it's not the chicken that forms the meaning of my memories. It's everything else: the air, the light, the towering oaks, the ambient sounds of camper doors and the *pssshhhht* of Deep Woods Off! as mothers spray their kids. Food isn't always about food; sometimes it's about the life around it. Consequently, I look back on my Dad's black chicken with a smile. And I miss those summer nights by the fire.

Just as I almost—*almost*—look back fondly on the night my husband and I spent in Sukhothai, Thailand, in the height of the hot season a dozen years ago. We're young, we're cheap, we're having an adventure. And the adventure goes like this:

We toss and turn in pools of sweat, a budget room with a fan, a bed and a great ruckus outside, all night long. Our luck: we have chosen a guesthouse beside a chicken slaughterhouse. We didn't know this when we checked in because the slaughterhouse operates only at night so the chickens are ready for the morning markets. The butcher begins lopping the heads off birds, one by one, starting at 10 pm—just as we attempt to sleep.

I see it through our window and through a small slit in the ramshackle wooden building where this death occurs. I see a small light. And in that light, I see a man sitting beside a bin. I see him grasp a feathered beast from the bin, and I hear it wail. It sounds so real and human: "No. No, no, no, no, NO." A crescendo of pitiful tones, ending abruptly on a high quick plea shouted in anger. "NO." I cannot actually see the man perform the act of killing (a wooden slat blocks my view), but I know. The cries cease immediately and the headless carcass flies into an adjacent bin. And then it begins again as the man's hand reaches again toward the other bin for another bird.

This continues without fail every 24 seconds (I count) until sunrise. Soon thereafter, we depart Sukhothai by train, heading south 8 hours to Bangkok. We ride third class, no aircon (we're young, we're cheap, we're having an adventure). Sweat pearls on my face, neck, arms and hands. It drips down my legs and fingers. The sweltering air never ceases, and the passing scenery seems all the same: green fields and workers in straw hats. And then another town with another market and another row of rainbow-colored umbrellas shielding storefronts and stalls selling smoking-hot grilled chicken.

I have never killed a chicken, and I admit the disconnect between what I eat and what I know—the reality that a once-living bird must die for it to become paprikash on my plate. Production and slaughter are neither pretty nor nice, especially not on a massive scale. They offend the sensibilities of those who care about the treatment of animals, and all of us non-vegans make our own moral justifications for consuming flesh.

What I witnessed in Sukhothai is hardly the worst in terms of animal welfare. "The muscles and fat tissues of the newly engineered broiler birds grow significantly faster than their bones, leading to deformities and disease. Somewhere between 1 and 4 percent of the birds will die writhing in convulsions from sudden death syndrome, a condition virtually unknown outside of factory farms." Just read a little Jonathan Safran Foer and learn how bad it gets (and, no, you *really* don't want to know about farmed pigs). In the factory farm scenario—the predominant operation supplying our Safeways, Albertsons and Piggly Wigglys—chickens that survive a full 47-day factory life are loaded into crates and onto trucks and shipped to a plant where their ankles are shackled and the birds are hung upside down on a conveyor system, which drags them through an electrified water bath. "This most likely paralyzes them but doesn't render them insensible," Foer writes. Then, they're taken through an automated throat slitter. They're decapitated, their feet and innards are removed—and that's when further trouble occurs. In this step of the process, intestines are frequently sliced and fecal matter sprays the cavity, contaminating the meat.

It's not just gross, it's dangerous. A 2014 *Consumer Reports* study found that 97 percent of tested chicken breasts "harbored bacteria that could make you sick,"—everything from Enterococcus to E. coli, Campylobacter to Salmonella and more. Not all contaminants would cause food poisoning, but their presence indicates widespread contamination with fecal matter (which is why food safety experts always recommend cooking chicken to at least 165 degrees).

The study, fittingly titled "The High Cost of Cheap Chicken," also found multi drug resistant bacteria on one in three samples of chicken tested. And that's where things get really ominous. We are, many experts predict, heading into a post-antibiotic world in which seemingly simple infections will turn killer on us—because antibiotics will no longer work. Because we're eating conventional meat, circa 2014. Because we're feeding huge amounts of antibiotics (30 million pounds each year, in America alone) to livestock, including chicken. Because diseases are growing resistant to antibiotics. Because these are the same antibiotics we use on ourselves. (If you want an entire archive of documentation on this matter, just Google the journalist Maryn McKenna.) This is serious stuff: we're talking a return to the age when bug bites, skinned knees and sore throats could kill.

This is what goes through my head when I eat chicken. It's hard to make the voices stop.

Chicken—in its evolution from a belligerent bird of the Asian forests, to a creature of abundant sustenance, to a possible harbinger of doom—is, in many ways, symbolic of humanity. We took an ancient bird and built a modern food machine. That modern food machine is harboring ancient bacteria and building modern killers out of them. We created the modern chicken. We did this to ourselves. And now we must figure it out.

And yet, sometimes, I still order restaurant chicken, no questions asked, here in America when I'm out to lunch on business (as I was today) and it's the most appealing thing on a limited menu. I eat chicken (organic, free-range) breasts in Boulder, chicken (of unknown provenance) saj in Baku, and chicken (freshly slaughtered, in my presence) soup in mountaintop Hmong villages of northern Laos. I do my best to do the best I can. But we are only human.

I'm back on the river Chao Phraya. I take one last bite of Thai barbecued chicken, slathered in sticky chile. And for a few moments I just eat, thinking no deep thoughts at all.

Thai Grilled Chicken

(Inspired by David Thompson's recipe in *Thai Food*, Ten Speed Press 2002)

Serves 4

Cloves from 2 small heads local garlic, peeled
3 small cilantro roots
13 strong black peppercorns
Pinch of sea salt
Pinch of ground turmeric
1 lemongrass stalk, chopped
5 hot Thai bird's eye chilies
1 chicken, cut into serving pieces

1. In a mortar and pestle (or food processor), combine the garlic, cilantro roots, peppercorns, salt, turmeric, lemongrass, and chilies. Pulverize (or process) to make a coarse paste.

2. Rub marinade under and over chicken skin. Cover and refrigerate for about 2 hours.

3. Prepare a hot grill and grill to desired taste.

Chicken in Pandanus

Adapted from Smart Cook Thai Cookery School

Makes 6 packets (2 to 3 appetizer servings)

3 teaspoons minced garlic

1 teaspoon minced cilantro root

½ teaspoon white peppercorns

3 teaspoons roasted sesame seeds

1 tablespoon soy sauce (or fish sauce for a gluten-free version)

1 teaspoon sesame oil

½ teaspoon sugar

100 grams (4 ounces) boneless chicken, diced small

6 fresh trimmed pandanus (also known as pandan leaves), available in
    Asian markets and at importfood.com

470 ml (2 cups) oil, or as needed for frying

Sweet-sour sauce or chili sauce, for serving

1. In a mortar and pestle (or food processor), combine garlic, cilantro root and peppercorns. Pulverize (or process) to make a paste.

2. Place the paste in a mixing bowl and add the sesame seeds, soy sauce or fish sauce, sesame oil, sugar, and chicken. Mix well, cover, and refrigerate for at least 1 hour.

3. Wrap the chicken with pandanus leaves to form a triangular packet. This is most easily done by making a loose triangular knot out of a single long leaf, stuffing in the filling, and enclosing the filling by tightening the knot and weaving loose ends as necessary to cover any exposed chicken. If necessary, toothpicks may be used to secure each wrapper.

4. Heat the oil in a wok over medium heat. Deep fry the packets until the leaves are crispy on the outside and the chicken is opaque inside; you may need to cook one alone to test the cooking time. Remove from heat and drain oil on paper towel. Serve with sweet-sour or chili sauce of your choice.

Gumbo Paradise

By Keith Pandolfi

From *Saveur*

Nothing in Keith Pandolfi's resume—born in Cincinnati, now living in Brooklyn, former staffer at *Saveur* and *This Old House* magazine—would really explain his fixation on gumbo, practically the state food of Louisiana. But that's the thing about obsessions—they tend to follow a logic all their own.

As the sun sets on the small Cajun town of Scott, Louisiana, Sheriff Tommy Hebert labors with his young son, Noah, in the backyard garden of a brick farmhouse. The 50-year-old lawman is shirtless, exhibiting the kind of jagged musculature only a person who works the land can attain. He and Noah are gathering okra from a modest row Hebert plants each May and harvests throughout the summer. Using a Smith & Wesson pocketknife, Hebert slices off the end of a woolly pod that seems about a foot long and hands it to me. I've never tried raw okra before; it never occurred to me to do so. But when I bite into it, I decide it's something I'd like to do damn near every day. It's got a snap that leads to a taste reminiscent of fresh-cut grass. Hebert will stew some with tomatoes for dinner; the rest he'll slice up, freeze, and, when the weather cools this autumn, thaw to make a gumbo. According to him, you can't make a good one without it.

Most people down here will tell you that okra is the origin of the word gumbo. In her book *New Orleans: A Food Biography* (AltaMira Press, 2012), historian Elizabeth M. Williams attributes the term "gumbo" to Bantu-speaking West Africans, who brought okra seeds on slave ships. Their word for okra was *ki ngombo*. Other scholars believe gumbo is a deviation of the Choctaw Indian word *kombo*, for sassafras leaves, which tribal members ground up to make an aromatic powder called filé. While either okra or filé can be used to thicken gumbo, there are strong opinions as to which is best.

Hebert's wife, Jessica, joins us as we walk beyond the garden to take a look at the marshes farther back. Hebert flooded this land with well water years ago so he could grow rice and raise crawfish. A chicken comes strutting by, and Hebert gazes at it for a second. "I can make a good gumbo out of just about anything in my yard," he tells me. "It's all right here."

During the five years I spent living in New Orleans, and the decade that has passed since, this is what I've come to love about gumbo: It is a dish in and of the state of Louisiana: its waters, its smokehouses, its rice mills, and its backyard gardens. It is everything to everybody: It is a transcendent soul food served buffet-style at Li'l Dizzy's Café in New Orleans' Treme neighborhood, or an august Creole delicacy presented by tuxedoed wait staff during Friday lunch at Galatoire's in the French Quarter. It is something enjoyed at family celebrations where Cajun music plays from an old clock radio in the kitchen; or something you mindlessly slurp down while seated drunk on a bar stool listening to an old Irma Thomas song work its magic from the jukebox.

I may have grown up in the suburbs of Cincinnati, but for me, gumbo is a favorite comfort food and a saving grace. The year I made my first was among the most dismal of my life. After more than a dozen years of arguing with my girlfriend over whether we wanted to get married (I did; she didn't) or have kids (same), she moved out of our Brooklyn apartment. A month later, on a cold November morning, my sweet old border collie mix, Gracie, died at the end of my bed.

The kitchen fridge, once filled with farmers' market produce and butcher shop meats, was now blindingly white inside, save for the six-packs and takeout containers. The sink in which my girlfriend and I had rinsed fresh greens and bell peppers was nothing more than a receptacle to ash cigarettes into as my cat, Walker, looked on, wondering if he should move out, too.

One good thing did happen that year. My favorite football team—the once notoriously awful New Orleans Saints—was winning. A lot.

And as 2009 mercifully yielded to 2010, they were well on their way to their very first Super Bowl. It was a modest miracle, yes, but one that lifted the spirits of a city and a state still yearning for signs of hope five years after the ravages of Katrina. To join them in celebration, I decided to put my troubles aside and host a Super Bowl party for which I would make my first gumbo. For guidance, I turned to a new cookbook, Donald Link's *Real Cajun* (Clarkson Potter, 2009) and his recipe for a fried chicken and andouille version.

Early that Sunday morning, I fried some chicken in vegetable oil, crisping the skin before removing it. Then I slowly added some flour to begin my roux. Following Link's instructions, I whisked it for 40 minutes, downing a couple of beers in the process. Fifteen minutes in, the roux smelled exactly like it was supposed to: nutty with overtones of burnt popcorn. I added the Louisiana trinity of chopped onion, bell pepper, and celery, as well as a spice mix that included pepper, paprika, and filé powder. Then I transferred the roux to a soup pot and added my chicken broth. A half hour later, I plopped in the fried chicken to continue cooking, and an hour after that, the sliced andouille. Then I anxiously awaited the results.

In the end, I created something extraordinary: a dark, thick, rustic stew with just the right amount of heat, redolent of spicy sausage, fried chicken, and stewed vegetables. As friends started to arrive, I proudly ladled out my day's labor. The Saints won that night. Life, it seemed, was getting better. And Link's gumbo became part of my repertoire.

During this recent trip back to Louisiana, however, I am reminded that everyone makes gumbo differently, that Link's is just one of a million variations. It's like Janice Macomber tells me in her daughter's New Orleans kitchen as she stirs what will turn out to be one of the best seafood gumbos I've ever had: "There are as many gumbos in Louisiana as there are mamas." (Everyone has her own gumbo saying, too.)

Today, Janice, who lives in the Cajun town of Abbeville and teaches at The New Orleans Cooking Experience, is making hers using the bounty of Louisiana's waters: blue crabs, shrimp, and some fried oysters she took home as leftovers last night from a restaurant called Shucks. Gumbo, after all, is a mishmash of whatever happens to be available, whether it's freshly caught redfish or leftover oysters, butcher shop sausage or hunted-down fowl.

With a Beau Jocque CD playing in the background, the Cajun grand-mother, her thick gray hair tamed beneath a bandana, tears the claws off the crabs before peeling her shrimp and tossing the shells of both into a stockpot filled with water. She pours some oil into a beat-up old skillet, lines up two cold Miller Lites stove-side, and starts her fragrant roux. "I just love that smell," she tells me. "I had a Cajun friend in Colorado who was dying. She asked me to come and cook a roux in her kitchen—just so she could smell Louisiana."

Written mentions of gumbo go back centuries, but no one knows when exactly it was born. Many theorize its origins might be the bouil-labaisse made by early French settlers in Louisiana. And with Africans laboring in New Orleans' Creole kitchens, it's easy to see how okra made it into the mix, too. As far as roux goes, blond versions are often used as a base for French sauces and vegetable dishes. Some scholars surmise that, one fateful day, a cook might have burned his roux, then added it to the pot anyway, satisfying Louisianians' desire for more intense flavors. Cajuns—largely French Acadians who were exiled to the bayou in the early 1700s for refusing to swear loyalty to the British crown—were forced to make their gumbos with whatever ingredients they could muster, while Creole versions, prepared in the cosmopolitan kitchens of New Orleans, with their mixture of European and African influences, were more refined.

At La Provence restaurant, in the town of Lacombe, an affable young chef named Erick Loos serves a gumbo that embodies that refinement. The recipe was the brainchild of the restaurant's late founder, Chris Kerageorgiou, who, like many of New Orleans' finest chefs, employed French Creole cooking techniques to take his Cajun mother-in-law's rustic gumbo to an entirely new level. Sitting in the provençal-style din-ing room, I watch as my waiter sets down a large white bowl containing a quail roasted a deep brown and stuffed with dirty rice, and pours on a chocolate-colored purée of roux, andouille, duck, and vegetables from a silver pitcher. As I slice the quail with my fork, the dirty rice falls out, the meat breaks up into the sauce, and the entire dish becomes, well, a gumbo.

The day after my dinner at La Provence, I drive west over the swampy Atchafalaya Basin to the city of Lafayette. As my Cajun friend Mason as-sured me, if you want to find gumbo-serving restaurants worth traveling for, Lafayette is where you set your GPS. My first stop is Café Vermilionville, which is located inside an 1830s farmhouse that has served as a Confederate Army headquarters, and, during the city's 1980s oil boom, a singles bar. In the wood-beamed dining room, co-owner Andrea Malcombe Veron offers a smoked turkey and andouille gumbo. The turkey breast is cured right out back, yielding a dish that embodies two of my favorite flavors: dark roux and barbecued meat.

To some people, smoked turkey breast in a gumbo is heresy. While gumbo is all about melting-pot metaphors, there is disharmony in people's beliefs as to what does and does not belong in it. Cajuns feel disgust toward the Creole tendency to add a ghastly fruit known as the tomato. But I find myself in support when, weeks after my trip, I test out a Creole okra version from *The Picayune's Creole Cookbook* (Random House, 1989) that skips the roux altogether. The tomatoes give the gumbo a bright, sweet complexity.

"I use oxtail," Barbara Sias, a cook at the Rice Palace in Crowley, Louisiana, tells me, proving that the proteins in gumbo can vary wildly, too. Indulging my curiosity, she offers me her recipe for oxtail and turkey neck gumbo. Cooking it back home in New York, I find the dish deliciously dangerous in its intensity—the stiff drink of gumbos.

Just as there are many ways to make a gumbo, there are many ways to devour one. It's something I discover at Prejean's in Lafayette, where a young waitress named Kyrie hands me a complimentary demitasse of mustardy potato salad after watching me enjoy my duck and andouille gumbo without it for longer than she can stand. "This is how we eat it here," she tells me. Adding potato salad to gumbo is a deranged act that pays off in spades. Doing so cools the gumbo down to room temperature and adds a creaminess—a texture sort of like melting ice cream. It's just another example of how far afield this homegrown dish can take you.

On my last day in Louisiana, I find myself in Donald Link's New Orleans kitchen. Photographer Chris Granger has scored us an invite to the chef's house so I can watch him make the same fried chicken and andouille gumbo I made for that Super Bowl party five years ago. Link owns several New Orleans restaurants, including the Cajun-inspired Cochon and the white-tablecloth Herbsaint. I've met him a few times before. He's a big guy. Quiet. And since his mind is pretty much unreadable, he has always intimidated me. Does he like me? I don't know. I like him. His gumbo practically saved my life.

When we arrive that afternoon, he is already adding flour to the sizzling chicken-skin-speckled oil to make his roux. As Link cooks, Granger and I sit at the table drinking what will turn out to be far too many glasses of wine. After a few hours, Link ladles the gumbo into bowls and sprinkles on some rice (down here, rice is a garnish for gumbo, not a base). Devouring it, I am reminded of days gone by, both good times and bad. Afterward, we all go out back for a swim. We toss a football with the chef's son, Nico. We drink more wine. All the while, Granger and I keep disappearing into the kitchen, spooning up more gumbo until the pot is empty, which is a shame since gumbo's always better the next day, or the day after that. As a pink sky gives way to blue darkness, I start feeling some remorse for ever having left this place. It's like Tommy Hebert told me back in Scott: "It's all right here."

Fried Chicken and Andouille Gumbo

New Orleans chef Donald Link was born and raised in the Cajun town of Lake Charles, Louisiana, and this rustic gumbo, which is often served at his St. Charles Avenue restaurant Herbsaint, always reminds him of home. To give the gumbo added flavor, Link makes his roux with the same oil he uses to fry the chicken, which he later shreds and adds to the pot, along with his homemade andouille sausage. The result is a dark, thick, rustic stew with just the right amount of heat.

Serves 6–8

1¼ cups plus 2 tablespoons canola oil
1 (3½–4 pounds) chicken, cut into 8 pieces
2½ teaspoons freshly ground black pepper
Kosher salt, to taste
2 cups flour
1½ teaspoons dark chile powder
1½ teaspoons filé powder
1 teaspoon cayenne
1 teaspoon ground white pepper
1 teaspoon paprika

3 cloves garlic, minced
3 stalks celery, minced
1 green bell pepper, minced
1 jalapeño, minced
1 poblano pepper, minced
1 yellow onion, minced
12 cups chicken stock
1 lb. andouille, halved and sliced
12 ounces okra, trimmed and sliced ½ inch thick
Sliced scallions, for garnish
Cooked white rice, for serving

1. Heat 1¼ cups oil in an 8-qt. Dutch oven until a deep-fry thermometer reads 350°. Season chicken with 1 teaspoon black pepper and salt; toss with ½ cup flour. Working in batches, fry chicken until golden; transfer to paper towels to drain.

2. Add remaining flour to Dutch oven; whisk until smooth. Reduce heat to medium-low; cook, whisking, until color of roux is dark chocolate, 1–1½ hours. Add remaining black pepper, the chile and filé powders, cayenne, white pepper, paprika, garlic, celery, bell pepper, jalapeño, poblano, and onion; cook until soft, 10–12 minutes. Add stock; boil. Reduce heat to medium-low; cook, stirring occasionally and skimming fat as needed, until slightly thickened, about 30 minutes. Add reserved chicken; cook until chicken is cooked through, about 45 minutes. Add andouille; cook until chicken is falling off the bone, about 1 hour.

3. Using tongs, transfer chicken to a cutting board and let cool slightly; shred, discarding skin and bones, and return to pot. Heat remaining oil in a 12-inch skillet over medium-high. Cook okra until golden brown and slightly crisp, 8–10 minutes, then stir into gumbo; cook 15 minutes. Garnish with scallions; serve with rice.

In Search of Ragu

By Matt Goulding

From Roads & Kingdoms

Though he's based in North Carolina and Barcelona, journalist Matt Goulding—chief editor and publisher of this digital travel magazine (roadsandkingdoms.com)—seems happiest on the road, especially if food's involved. He's a sucker for rooted food traditions, like the classic ragu sauces of Emilia Romagna.

L *a Grassa.* The fat one. Bologna has earned its nickname like no other city on earth. The old city is awash in excess calories, a medieval fortress town fortified with golden mountains of starch and red cannons of animal fat, where pastas gleam a brilliant yellow from the lavish amount of egg yolks they contain and menus moan under the weight of their meat-and-cheese-burdened offerings.

I long dreamt of nuzzling up to Bologna's ample waistline. As a high school kid with a burgeoning romance with the kitchen, I was hungry to consummate my love with what I regarded as the world's finest cuisine. The intermediary was a young, heavyset Italian-American named Mario Batali. Every morning at 10:30 during summer break, I sunk into our Chianti-red couch and watched the chef with orange clogs and a matching cheddar ponytail motormouth his way across Italy, breaking down the regional cooking of the country in exquisite three-plate daily tasting menus. I wanted to taste the bulging breads of Puglia, the neon green pestos of Liguria, the simmering fish stews of Le Marche. The pepper-bombed pastas of Lazio. But above all, I wanted to feast on the Italy of Molto Mario's most spirited episodes, the Italy of *Parmigiano* ("the undisputed king of cheeses!"), of mortadella and *culatello*, and, of course, the Italy of *ragù alla bolognese*, the most lavish and revered of all pasta creations.

It took a broken heart to bring me to Bologna's bulging belly. I fell in love with a girl in Barcelona who didn't share my lofty feelings, so I escaped to Bologna to drown my rejection in a bottomless bowl of meat sauce. For three weeks I sought out ragu in any form possible: caught in the tangles of fresh *tagliatelle*, plugging the tiny holes of cheesy tortellini, draped over forest green handkerchiefs of spinach lasagna.

Since the dawn of Christianity, Emilia Romagna—birthplace of ragu, home of the city of Bologna—has been one of Europe's wealthiest regions, a center of trade with a heavy agricultural presence. Few things say wealth as loudly as a sauce comprised of three or four cuts of meat, two kinds of fat, wine, milk, and a flurry of one of the world's most treasured cheeses—all served on a pasta so dense with egg yolk it looks a sunset run through a paper shredder.

Slow-simmered meat stews were common throughout Italy in the 15th and 16th centuries, but pasta, a luxury enjoyed by the upper class until the industrial revolution made wheat more accessible, didn't enter the equation until the early 19th century, when the aristocrats of Emilia Romagna found it in their hearts and wallets to combine the two. Pellegrino Artusi, a successful businessman and noted gastronome, is often credited with the first published recipe for *ragù alla bolognese*, dating back to 1891 in the self-published *The Science of Cooking and the Art of Fine Dining*. Not satisfied with the panoply of meats and cooking fats, Artusi recommends goosing the dish with porcini, chicken livers, sliced truffles, and a glass of heavy cream.

Just as Artusi's version reflected his privileged times as a wealthy merchant carousing about Emilia Romagna in the mid 19th century, ragu has always been a barometer of sorts, a dish that closely mirrors the conditions of its makers. Substantial meat-heavy ragus took hold in the relatively fat times of the early 20th century, but in the hardscrabble years after World War II, pasta found itself nearly naked, slicked with lard and vegetable scraps and little else. Only as Italy climbed out of the post-war depression in the 1950s and '60s did meat rejoin the script as the recipe's central constituent.

Over the years, other parts of Italy developed their own take on the bubbling meat sauce. (And let it be said now that sauce is a misnomer—sauce implies a level of liquidity that you'll never find in a true ragu. Instead, the Italians would call it a *condimento*, a condiment meant to accompany the pasta, not smother it relentlessly) *Ragù alla Barese*, from the heart of Puglia, is made from thin slices of meat—pork, beef, lamb, even horse—with the sauce served over *orecchiette*, ear-shaped pasta, and the protein eaten separately. Italy's second most famous ragu after Bologna's belong to Naples, where a giant vat of tomato sauce is used to render huge chunks of meat fork-tender (the inspiration for Italian-America's Sunday gravy). But the scope of ragu goes well beyond these famous offshoots: Travel Italy today and you'll find ragus made from fish, duck, and wild boar, laced with everything from cumin to dried chili to chocolate.

Through all these years and all these iterations, Emilia Romagna has remained ground zero for Italy's ragu culture, but even here, the differences between one village's ragu and the next can be a catalyst for controversy and recrimination.

Of course, uniformity was never part of the equation: from the start, *ragù alla bolognese* has been a reflection of subtle differences in terrain, weather, and wealth that defined one town from the next throughout the region.

Today, the list of variables runs longer than the list of ingredients. Is ragu pure pork? Pure beef? A mixture? Is the meat ground, chopped by hand or braised and shredded? Does pancetta or another type of cured pork product belong in the mix? How about liquid: stock or water, red wine or white? In some parts of the region, where dairy cows are aplenty, milk makes it into the sauce; in other parts, it's considered sacrilege. Spices: salt, maybe pepper, usually bay leaf, sometimes, in rare cases, nutmeg.

The biggest source of dispute, undoubtedly, is the tomato: How much, if any? Fresh, canned, or tomato paste?

So is there one true ragu? One best way to make it? One expression of this meaty amalgam that best represents the DNA of this region? That's what I've come back to Emilia Romagna to find out.

Twenty miles outside of Bologna, at a roadside restaurant, I meet Alessandro Martini, short and thick and boiling over with life. He runs Italian Days Food Experience, a full-day binge on Emilia Romagna's most famous ingredients: cured meats, *Parmigiano Reggiano, aceto balsamico di Modena* ("12 years aging minimum!" as Alessandro likes to say). His Facebook page is dominated by pictures of tourists feeding each other pasta, hoisting massive hunks of cheese, slurping 100-year-old balsamic from plastic spoons. On any given day, depending on the whims of TripAdvisor's algorithms, Alessandro's tour is the most popular activity in all of Europe.

For a short period in 2010, Alessandro was my truffle dealer, sending freshly-dug specimens across the Mediterranean one kilo at a time, which I would keep under my pillow for a few days until my dreams smelled of tubers, before selling them off to Michelin-starred chefs around Barcelona. I remember waking up to messages from Alessandro during those heady days after an early morning truffle hunt: "I have the white gold!"

Alessandro hails from the heart of ragu country and lives for these types of belt-loosening food adventures. This is a man who celebrated the birth of both his son and his daughter by gifting them batteries of *aceto di balsamico*—a series of wooden barrels that hold balsamic vinegar as it ages over the course of a lifetime. When I emailed him two weeks before the trip and asked him to be my guide, his answer was short and definitive: "Si! Si! We go to see the best Italian grandmas and the ragu kings. Don't worry!"

We start in the hilltop town of Zocca at Ristorante Bonfiglioli. An hour before lunch service, the kitchen looks like what I see when I close my eyes and see Italy at night. All women, mostly grandmas, all performing backbreaking acts of an intensely nurturing and homemade nature. One rolls out long sheets of emerald green spinach pasta for *lasagne verde*. Another fries little rectangles of dough for *gnocchi fritti*. A pair of older women in bonnets stuff hundreds of pasta squares with a mix of ground pork, mortadella, and parmesan before pinching them into tortellini. In the corner, over a lone burner, a younger woman stirs a pot that, judging by the savory perfume, can only contain one thing.

When Alessandro announces that we've come to talk ragu, the flurry of activity comes to a sudden halt and the women gather around the mountain of tortellini.

"Well, what do you want to know?" the young sauce-stirrer asks.

"Everything," I say.

And that's pretty much all it takes. The women launch into their personal recipes, exchanging barbs about protein choices and seasoning philosophies. Finally, Zia Maria Lanzarini, the oldest cook in the kitchen, quiets the crowd and offers some well-earned wisdom.

"The meat can change based on the circumstances. The liquid can, too. But the one thing a ragu never has in it is garlic."

The only other point of agreement among the group: ragu should be made with pignoletto, an acidic, lightly fruity wine that you can see growing from the restaurant's windows. "It's a Bolognese sauce, it should be made with a Bolognese wine."

The official version at Bonfiglioli, what Alessandro calls "the noble ragu," would be a source of controversy for most in the area—including, apparently, a few of the cooks in this kitchen. It is made from 100 percent beef, a rarity in the region but an act of recycling in a restaurant with mountains of beef scraps leftover from the strip steaks they are famous for. Those scraps are combined with onion, carrot, and celery, a few glugs of pignoletto, plus peeled and seeded fresh tomatoes, and simmered for four hours, the cook adding water at her discretion if the ragu starts to dry out.

"The cooking is the most important part in that it must be slow," says Signore Elena, Maria's tortelloni accomplice. "It's the slow cooking that gives the sauce its flavor."

She passes me a spoon and the ragu, a gentle orange color from the emulsion of tomato and fat, sits up like a well-trained dog. It tastes of the mineral intensity of good Italian beef corrupted by nothing more than light tomato acidity and the sweetness from the vegetables. The women try to ply us with other delights of the Emilian kitchen, and I start to give in, but Alessandro intercedes and ushers me to the door. The day is young.

Three hilltops over, at Trattoria Garofani Lina, we sit down to a light lunch of spinach *gramigna*, hollow fish hooks of pasta, with sausage ragu; *polpette*, massive, dense meatballs made from pork, beef, chicken, mortadella and an absurd amount of parmesan; thick shanks of osso buco; tomato-braised rabbit al cacciatore; and *tortellini en brodo*.

We are surrounded by cyclists; runners; large, spirited families—people in need of sustenance. Alessandro loves this restaurant, and for good reason: the food is intensely satisfying, especially the chewy pile of *gramigna,* hiding nubs of sausage in its knots, and the tortellini, another Emilia Romganan specialty, which are belly buttons of ground pork, mortadella, and parmesan afloat in a clear, soul-soothing chicken broth.

But after a few bites of the ragu, he flashes me a look of disappointment: "I'm sorry my friend. The ragu is good, it is fine, but there is too much *doppio concentrato.* Tomato paste has no place in ragu!" To hear Alessandro say these words about a restaurant he himself selected, one in which the owners greet him with hugs and ask about his children, underscores just how hard it is to please an Italian—especially with ragu.

As we waddle our way back towards his van, he tells me: "These are great examples for a beginner, but later, I will show you the true ragu."

The rest of my week in Emilia Romagna is a blur of ground pork and durum wheat. I spend days in Bologna, plodding from one restaurant to the next, faithfully ordering *tagliatelle al ragu* even when my stomach cries out for clear liquids or a few green leaves of vegetation.

Bologna is my kind of town: ancient in its cobbled avenues but youthful in its constituency, big enough to capture a certain urban energy, but small enough to never need anything other than your two feet to take it all in. Above all, it's a civilization seemingly constructed for the sole purpose of eating.

Everywhere you turn you will see signs of its place at the top of the Italian food chain: fresh pasta shops vending every possible iteration of egg and flour; buzzing bars pairing Spritz and Lambrusco with generous spreads of free meat, cheese, and vegetable snacks; and, above all, osteria after osteria, cozy wine-soaked eating establishments, from whose ancient kitchens emit a moist fragrance of simmered pork and local grapes.

Osteria al 15 is a beloved dinner den just inside the *centro storico* known for its sprawling plates of charcuterie, its crispy flatbreads puffed up in hot lard, and its classic beef-heavy ragu tossed with corkscrew pasta or spooned on top of béchamel and layered between sheets of lasagna. It's far from refined, but the bargain prices and the boisterous staff makes it all go down easy.

Trattoria Da Gianni, down a hairpin alleyway a few blocks from Piazza Maggiore, was once my lunch haunt in Bologna, by virtue of its position next door to my Italian school. I dream regularly of its *bollito misto*, a heroic mix of braised brisket, capon, and tongue served with salsa verde, but the dish I'm looking for this time, a thick beef-and-pork joint with plenty of jammy tomato, is a solid middle-of-the-road ragu.

The best ragu I taste is a white ragu of rabbit folded between a dozen thin layers of lasagna, served at Pappagallo, a polished restaurant in the shadow of the two towers that climb from Bologna's center. It is a paradigm of sophistication and refinement next to the heavy-hitting classic versions, but with bunny as its base, it is not a ragu that could bear the name of this city.

Any of these dishes would qualify as the best plate of pasta in your town or my town or any town outside of Italy, but there's nothing that makes me want to change my return flight. Eventually, the Bologna ragus all begin to bleed together in a delicious but indiscernible pool of animal fat.

Alessandro has a simple explanation for my conundrum: "Bologna is not where you will find the best ragu. Too many tourists, too many students, not enough *nonne*. You must come with me to my town."

Savigno is a lovely little village of 2,000 people nestled in a valley framed by rivers and oak trees and the gentle humpbacks of humble vineyards. Beyond being the capital of the region's white truffle industry, Savigno is also a major pillar in Emilia Romagna's ragu culture.

At Amerigo dal 1934, a restaurant famous throughout the region for its slow-simmered sauces and truffle-driven cuisine, Alberto Bettini and his family before him have spent the past 80 years refining the region's most famous dish.

"There are thousands of recipes for ragu," Alberto says. "I can't tell you one is right and the other is wrong. This is Italy: if you go 5 kilometers from here, you'll find a completely different ragu."

Nevertheless, a few axioms hold true across the spectrum of possibilities. Above all, Alberto espouses what could be the bedrock ethos of Italian cuisine. "The *materia prima* is the most important part. You can't make good ragu with bad ingredients."

His ragu begins the same way all ragus begin: finely diced onion, carrot, and celery sautéed in olive oil. "It's important to really caramelize the vegetables. That's where the flavor comes from."

Later comes two pounds of coarsely ground beef ("from the neck or shoulder—something with fat and flavor") and a pound of ground pork butt, browned separately from the vegetables, and deglazed with a cup of white wine (pignoletto, of course). Peeled tomatoes, tomato paste, bay leaves and three hours of simmering over a low flame. Seasoning? "Salt. Never pepper."

In the dining room, after an array of truffle-showered starters, Amerigo serves us three ragus—a blind tasting of today's and yesterday's sauce, along with a jarred version he sells in upscale markets, so we can judge the effects of time and temperature on the final product. He doesn't serve the ragu on *tagliatelle*, though, but on little rounds of toasted bread—the better for us to appreciate the subtleties of the sauce, he says.

Alessandro and I both immediately choose the day-old ragu. It's not dramatically different, but the flavors are deeper, rounder, more harmonious. In both you taste the quality of the meat, the silken texture from the long simmer, the ghost of bay. It's a lovely creation, but there is perhaps too much tomato sweetness for a purist like Alessandro's taste. He's happy, but not euphoric—which is a state he hits a few times a day when he's eating and drinking well.

For Alessandro, we seem to be perpetually one or two steps away from the one true thing, constantly circling the simmering pot, as if the dozen ragus we eat together are all preludes to a more realized vision. "Come, my friend. I will show you how we do it at home."

As we walk through Savigno, the copper light of dusk settling over the town's narrow streets, we stop anyone we can find to ask them for their ragu recipe. A retired policeman says he likes an all-pork sauce with a heavy hit of pancetta, the better for coating the pasta. A gelato maker explains that a touch of milk defuses the acidity of the tomato and ties the whole sauce together. Overhearing our kitchen talk below, an old woman in a navy cardigan pokes her head out of a second story window to offer her take on the matter: "I only use tomatoes from my garden—fresh when they're in season, preserved when it gets cold."

Inspired by the Savigno citizenry, we buy meat from the butcher, vegetables and wine from a small stand in the town's plaza, and head to Alessandro's house to simmer up his version of ragu: two parts chopped skirt steak, one part ground pancetta, the sautéed vegetable trio, a splash of dry white wine, and a few whole canned San Marzano tomatoes.

"People talk about materia prima, materia prima, then they dump in a bunch of *doppio concentrato. Vaffanculo!*"

We leave the ragu to simmer and race off into the hills above Savigno to meet with Alessandro's truffle dealers ("the truffle season doesn't start until Tuesday, so don't tell them you're a journalist"). The sauce we return to, one that took all of 15 minutes of active preparation to create, is straightforward and beautifully balanced, an honest expression of the handful of ingredients we put into the pot.

It's clear that after years of dedicated pasta consumption across all corners of this region, Alessandro has learned a few things about ragu.

"We're getting closer," he tells me.

The *tagliatelle al ragù* at Osteria Francescana in Modena stands six inches tall and costs $55. It also takes a battery of chefs and nearly 72 hours to make. Its height and price and layers of manipulation, at the very least, are befitting of a restaurant of Francescana's stature: it has three Michelin stars and is currently ranked number three in *Restaurant* magazine's list of the World's 50 Best Restaurants.

Massimo Bottura, Francescana's wild-eyed Captain Nemo, is no stranger to controversy when it comes to his treatment of the sacred pillars of Italian cuisine. When he first opened Osteria Francescana in 1995, Modenese grandmas were lining up to bash him with their rolling pins. One of his first enduring creations, a dish that morphed five different parmesan cheeses into five different textures (a 24-month pudding, a 50-month "air"), prompted the type of rabid public reactions you'd expect for a politician selling state secrets to the enemy.

More than any cuisine in the world, Italian food is built around an almost religious reverence for tradition: dishes pass from one generation to the next without as much as a grain of salt out of place. Part of that comes from the belief that Italian cuisine is already a fully realized vision, a museum-worthy collection of perfectly conceived dishes that can only be weakened by modern intervention. It's not untrue: Few people on this planet can do as much with five ingredients as the Italians. *Cacio e pepe*, pasta carbonara, pizza margherita: in their most honest iterations, they are near-perfect foods, deeply revered as expressions of the richness of Italian culture, and most God-fearing countrymen will be damned to watch a half-mad chef fuck with their formulations in search of his own stardom.

But Massimo—a man who finds culinary inspiration in Walt Whitman and Miles Davis—never saw it like that. Like the heavyweights of the post-modern cooking world—Ferran Adria in northern Spain, England's Heston Blumenthal—he sees food as a medium for man's greatest ambitions: experimentation, transformation, accelerated evolution. "We don't want to lose our history, but we don't want to lose ourselves in it either. That's why we are always asking ourselves questions about the best way to do things."

The best way, according to Massimo, isn't always the traditional way, and that didn't sit well with certain people in this country, especially in conservative Modena. It wasn't until Massimo won over international critics and achieved global fame that he managed to convince locals. "Suddenly, they started to defend me." (And for anybody that continued to doubt him, he won the gold medal for best balsamic vinegar in Modena, the most revered craft in one of the most tradition-driven cities in Italy—a barrel-aged middle finger to those who think he only knows how to manipulate.)

He's in the middle of recounting his vinegar triumph when an old man with a bike at his side peeks his head into the door to ask Massimo a question. *"Mi scusi, maestro! Maestro!"* The chef stands up from his desk and greets the man like a great don of the neighborhood. When he returns, he flashes a grin and raised eyebrows: "See that? Now they call me maestro!"

The master has strong opinions about everything, especially ragu. While the differences from restaurant to restaurant and grandma to grandma tend to be granular, especially to the outside eater, Massimo's two main pillars of ragu are nothing short of controversial in this highly charged world. First, he insists the meat shouldn't be ground, but rather cooked in large pieces, then shredded by hand. "99 percent of ragu starts with machine-ground meat. But why?" Instead, he insists that big pieces of braised meat give deeper flavor and better texture to the final dish.

The Second Law of Ragu according to Massimo is even more explosive: no tomato. "We never had tomatoes in Emilia Romagna, so how did they end up in the sauce? Tomato is used to cover up bad ingredients."

In some dusty corner of the Emilian culinary history Massimo's version may have its antecedent, but the ragu he fabricates is a severe departure from everything I've tasted so far. While the individual components of the dish constitute a showcase of the avant-garde technique and fuck-the-rules philosophy that characterizes so many of the world's most-lauded restaurants today, the final result tastes deeply, gloriously of ragu.

"Vision is the crossroad between the rational and the emotional," says Massimo, in one of his frequent moments of existential reflection in the dining room. The rational mind says that hand-torn meat rich in gelatin will make a lusty, powerful sauce with no need for excess ingredients. Emotion tells him that it must still look and taste like home.

Later in the meal, the full extent of Massimo's whimsy-driven modernist vision will be on display—in a handheld head of baby lettuce whose tender leaves hide the concentrated tastes of a Caesar salad, a glazed rectangle of eel made to look as if it were swimming up the Po River, a handful of classics with ridiculous names like "Oops I Dropped My Lemon Pie"—but it's the ragu that moves me most. The noodles have a brilliant, enduring chew, and the sauce, rich with gelatin from the tougher cuts of meat, clings to them as if its life were at stake.

Most Italians would laugh at the price tag and blush at the modernist art-strewn room in which it is consumed—a poor replacement for their nonna's kitchen, they'd say—but with a twirl of a fork, the sculptures and the canvases and the credit card payments would disappear and all that would remain is a taste of childhood.

Time and nostalgia add intensity to the flavors of our earliest memories, and in many ways, the mission of modernist kitchens playing with sacred staples of home cooking is to find ways to make the reality live up to the impossibility of the memory. In the case of Massimo's ragu, that means making the noodles with a thousand egg yolks then cooking them in a concentrated parmesan broth. That means braising nothing but the richest cuts of meat at very low temperatures for very long times, then pulling them apart by hand to make a sauce of extraordinary depth and intensity. That means twisting the noodles into a tight spiral so that the pasta towers above the plate, the same way it does in the memories of those that eat it.

While I work my way down the tower to the bottom of the bowl, all

I can think about is that this is why so many of us fantasize about being Italian, because to be Italian means to have memories that taste of this plate of pasta.

At 5:30 pm in the village rec room of Savigno, a cabal of ragu-making grandmas has assembled at a long wooden table. Alessandro has convened an emergency council, calling on the time-tested *nonne* of this scenic town to hopefully bring a final bit of clarity to the murky issue of Emilia Romagna's slow-cooked sauce. He seems concerned that I still haven't fully understood ragu—that perhaps my mind has been clouded by the tourist-friendly osteria of Bologna and the Michelin-friendly pageantry of Modena. "Don't you worry, *amico*. If anyone knows something about making ragu, it is this group of *nonne*."

It is a comic book cast of grandmother shapes and sizes: There's Lisetta, tall with a thick wave of black hair. Maria Pia, midsized and modest and crowned with a dark half-fro. Anna #1, short, plump, square-faced and generously jowled. And Anna #2, smallest in size, largest in stature among the old ladies, a woman who not only directed the famous pasta program at Amerigo 1934, but twice traveled to Tokyo to bring ragu to the people of Japan. "I walked into the subway and there I was, larger than life, making pasta on a Japanese billboard. *Madonna!*"

Anna's far-flung adventures notwithstanding, these are women born and raised in this fertile valley of golden grapes and hidden tubers. They have ragu in their soul.

I have a long list of questions that have been vibrating in my head over the past week—about the deployment of dairy, the browning of proteins, the ever-controversial issue of tomato. But ultimately, I manage only one feeble query—"how does everyone here make their ragu?"—before the council takes over and I'm rendered a silent spectator.

"*Piano piano*," says Lisetta, slowly, step by step. "You cannot rush a good ragu."

"The 1950s were full of misery," says Anna #2. "Back then ragu was just a bit of tomato and onion and lard. It changed slowly over the years when people had more money to buy meat. A little pork, a little pancetta."

"A proper ragu should be made with half pork, half beef," says Anna #1.

"No, no! One quarter pork and the rest beef."

"More pork than beef—it has better flavor. I use one kilo of beef and one and a half of pork."

"Pancetta. Always."

"No! Not if you already have pork. That's too much pork."

"Can we all agree that skirt steak is the best?"

"No no no. In ragu Bolognese there's no place for skirt steak."

"Piano piano."

"Fresh tomato is better in the summer. If not, *concentrato* works."

"Canned DOP tomatoes are more consistent."

"When do you add milk?"

"I don't use milk. Only with the *ragù di prosciutto*. It helps mellow the saltiness."

"You know there are people who serve their ragu with spaghetti."

"Spaghetti! Oh please no. Tagliatelle. *Sempre tagliatelle!*"

"Good ragu comes from someone's house, not a restaurant."

"Piano piano."

As the debate rages across the table, I feel a sudden and overwhelming need to be one of their grandsons. Whatever food argument you've ever had with a friend or family member feels trivial by comparison; the differences at the heart of the discussion may sound miniscule, but it's clear that they matter to everyone in this room. I have zero doubt that the best ragu for me would be whichever one of their homes I happen to be eating in at the moment.

Despite the raised voices and the wild gesticulations, nobody here is wrong. The beauty of ragu is that it's an idea as much as it is a recipe, a slow-simmered distillation of what means and circumstances have gifted you: If Zia Peppe's ragu is made with nothing but pork scraps, that's because her neighbor raises pigs. When Maria cooks her vegetables in a mix of oil and butter, it's because her family comes from a long line of dairy farmers. When Nonna Anna's slips a few laurel leaves into the pot, she plucks them from the tree outside her back door. There is no need for a decree from the Chamber of Commerce to tell these women what qualifies as the authentic ragu; what's authentic is whatever is simmering under the lid.

Eventually the women agree to disagree and the rolling boil of the debate calms to a gentle simmer. Alessandro opens a few bottles of pignoletto he's brought to make the peace. We drink and take photos and make small talk about tangential ragu issues like the proper age of parmesan and the troubled state of the prosciutto industry in the region.

On my way out, Anna #1 grabs me by the arm. She pulls me close and looks up into my eyes with an earnestness that drowns out the rest of the chatter in the room. "Forget about these arguments. Forget about the small details. Just remember that the most important ingredient for making ragu, the one thing you can never forget, is love."

Lisetta overhears from across the room and quickly adds. "And pancetta!"

Ragù alla Bolognese

This is not a definitive recipe, but rather a synthesis of the parts I loved most about the dozens of ragus I tasted in Emilia Romagna: the rich, gelatinous flavor of Massimo's hand-torn super ragu, the whisper of tomato from Alessandro's version (despite Massimo's convincing protestations, the light sweetness and extra umami hit of tomato has a certain place in the sauce), and, of course, the pancetta from the grandmas of Savigno. Whatever you do, don't serve this with spaghetti. Try penne, rigatoni or pappardelle— something substantial enough to grab hold of the chunky ragu.

1½ lb beef (oxtail, short rib, shank—something with fat, flavor, and
    preferably some marrow and gelatin), in one or two large pieces
Salt to taste
1 tablespoon olive oil
2 medium carrots, peeled and minced
2 ribs celery, minced
1 medium onion, minced
1 pound ground pork (preferably from the shoulder)
½ cup minced pancetta
1 small can whole peeled tomatoes (preferably San Marzano),
    drained and crushed
1 cup dry red wine
1½ cups chicken stock
1 bay leaf

1. Heat the oil in a large, heavy-bottomed pot or Dutch oven set over medium-high heat. Season the beef on all sides with salt and cook until deeply browned all over. Remove from the pan.

2. If the pan is dry, add another splash of oil. Sauté the carrot, celery, and onion until soft, about 5 minutes. Add the pork and pancetta and cook until lightly browned, then stir in the tomato and continue cooking for another 3 minutes. Return the beef to the pan, add the wine, stock, bay leaf and cover. Turn the heat to low and simmer for two hours, until the beef is falling apart.

3. Shred the beef by hand or with two forks and fold back into the sauce, discarding any bones, excess fat, or cartilage. If the sauce looks too dry, add a splash of broth or water to get the right consistency. Serve over pasta with freshly grated Parmigiano Reggiano. Makes about 8 servings.

How to Make Carnitas
That Will Fix Everything That's
Wrong in Your Sad, Horrible Life

By Nicolás Medina Mora

From BuzzFeed.com

Born in Mexico City, BuzzFeed reporter Nicolás Medina Mora is based now in New York, but he describes himself as "a perpetual foreigner." Which perhaps explains why the cultural anchor of food—and, very specifically *carnitas*—looms so large in his complicated personal history.

They called him Güero, which means "blondie," but he looked nothing like a Californian surfer. He owned a nameless taco stand in El Olivo, one of those ugly Mexico City neighborhoods that stand at the tense border between rich and poor. The place consisted of a small kitchen where four aproned men sweated in close proximity, cooking tortillas over an open fire and butchering whole pigs. Close by, on the sidewalk, sat a giant copper vat where vaguely discernible pieces of pork boiled away in a broth of lard and Coca-Cola. Everything was filthy—flies gathered over the wet-fresh cilantro and the finely chopped onions and the yellowing lime wedges. People ate on their feet, holding bright plastic plates close to their chins. For a city where pale and dark-skinned people generally do not mix, it was a diverse crowd—there were bureaucrats in ill-fitting suits, construction workers covered in paint splatters, and private-school boys in Lacoste polo shirts. On any given day, the line went around the block.

I ate his food every week for years, and yet I know nothing about Güero. People told apocryphal stories about him. Some said he had been born into a rich family in Michoacán and gone to culinary school in France but had dropped out, preferring the simple life of a taquero to the chef's pursuit of cultural capital. Others insisted he was a former narco, and that he'd learned to wield his butcher's knife in the darkest corners of Culiacán. Still others said he was just a kid from the neighborhood with a gift for braising pork and blending chiles. Güero cultivated an air of mystery: I never once heard him speak. People would yell orders at him; he would nod, chop the appropriate amount of meat, and hand it to the customer over two tortillas—all without a word. He also refused to handle money, insisting that people give their crumpled pesos to a teenage assistant.

My friends and I went to see Güero every Friday after school, before we went drinking. We were young at the time—15, 16, 17—but we drank like sailors with a death wish. I still don't know what compelled us to do such damage to ourselves. Part of it was the culture of excess of wealthy Mexico, but in our case there was a deeper existential crisis at play. The course of our allotted years seemed to stretch in front of us with hopeless inevitability. We would go into the family business. We would marry women who had been taught never to raise their voices. We would raise children who would develop a drinking problem before graduating high school. We would never lack for anything; we would somehow manage to be miserable. My grandmother would have said we were in desperate need of a priest, but we were faithless, and so Güero became our minister.

And yet those afternoons were also full of that Mexican joy that comes from basking in your own heartbreak. It is an exuberant, redemptive sadness best captured by a group of punch-drunk teenagers stumbling on a deserted street in the gray light of the morning, singing sorrowful *rancheras* at the top of their lungs, having the time of their lives. That's what carnitas are really about: the paradox of celebrating and mourning at the same time. They are sacrificial food—you butcher and braise a pig when you have a reason to feast, and those occasions tend to be bittersweet moments of parting. You eat carnitas when your daughter turns 15 or your father dies; when you graduate from college or you retire from the civil service. You eat carnitas the night before you set out for the north. You eat carnitas once a week, because even though you are too young to understand the passing of time, you can already feel your life slipping away.

I left Mexico when I was 18, because I was unhappy and believed that my unhappiness had roots in history and geography. I chose to come to the United States because I was privileged enough to be able to secure a student visa, and because from a young age I had been fascinated with America. It was a place, I imagined, where things were mutable, where each person was allotted more than one life, in case they chose to start again. My America was the opposite of Mexico, which I thought of as a place where everything was fixed, where memory was inescapable and history ran in repeat. I applied to 10 colleges in New England and packed all my books. I did not intend to return.

Of course, once I actually arrived in the United States, I discovered that my America was nothing but fantasy. Still, I tried my hardest not to look back. This meant, among other things, that for a long time I did not eat much Mexican food. I began to approach the meals of my childhood like a gringo would: as a welcome variation on pizza and hamburgers. Güero's carnitas and their metaphysical significance became a distant memory, much like the faces of my high school friends.

And then, last winter, I found myself in desperate need to feel at home. I had just turned 23 and had recently moved to New York. The woman I loved had settled on another continent and found another man. I had a month-to-month contract writing for a news agency, but the company would not sponsor me for a visa, and the prospect of having to return made me nauseous. It had been snowing for weeks, and the windows in my apartment near the Gowanus Canal wouldn't shut properly, such that I woke up each morning covered by a thin blanket of snow. Everything felt ungrounded and fleeting, but not in the light-hearted, liberating way they advertise at the immigration desk at John F. Kennedy Airport. I got off the subway one afternoon after work and felt a deep craving for a heaping plate of carnitas and half a bottle of mezcal.

I set out to look for a taqueria. I wandered aimlessly around streets lined with abandoned factories, auto-shops, and crumbling row houses, feeling the snow leak into my sneakers and soak my feet. And then, by one of the large avenues that run north-south in that part of Brooklyn, I stumbled upon the Country Boys Restaurant. The place has since shut down, but on that afternoon it had just opened for the day, and the windows were covered in handwritten signs that advertised, in Spanish, a taco-for-a-dollar special.

I walked in and felt like I had stepped into a mummified soda fountain from the '50s. There was a long bar, and in front of it, 10 or 12 spinning chairs upholstered in pink patent leather. Behind the bar there was a dusty mirror. There was nobody to be seen, so I sat down in one of the chairs and waited. A middle-aged man appeared five minutes later, wearing a black T-shirt and a Yankees baseball cap. In English, he asked me what I wanted. In Spanish, I replied I wanted carnitas. He went into the kitchen and came back, sooner than I expected, carrying my tacos in a bright green plastic plate exactly like the ones at Güero's. I bit into the tortilla and was mildly disappointed. The tacos were good, but they just weren't the real thing. That was my first intimation that "the real thing" may well not exist, except in memory.

The Brooklyn taquero and I talked about soccer for a while. And then, as I was finishing my last taco, he asked me a question out of the blue.

"So, do you have papers?"

I stared at him for a second. I finally answered that I did.

"That's great," he said.

I then tried to explain that I had only a yearlong work permit and that it was about to run out.

He interrupted me. "That's still great."

I tried to pay him the five dollars I owed him, but he refused to take my money. I walked out of the restaurant and went home. I still felt lost and alone, but the world seemed a shade more tolerable. Soon afterward everything improved. I found a job that sponsored me for a visa. I met someone else. Winter ended.

It was around that time that I began making carnitas, using a recipe I cobbled together from dozens of YouTube videos narrated in Spanish by men who sound like they don't like to talk. Once a month, I invite my American friends to my apartment and feed them the food of my adolescence. The tacos I make are but a pale ghost of Güero's— the store-bought tortillas you find in the Northeast are always a little rubbery, the chiles are never quite as varied, and a Dutch oven over a Brooklyn stove is no match for a copper vat over a roaring fire. Still, they do the trick. They induce that same kind of melancholic joy I felt when I was in high school.

How to Make an Insanely Delicious Feast of Mexican Carnitas; or, How to Make a Mexican Feast at Home in Gringolandia

In Mexico, you eat carnitas when your daughter turns 15 or your father dies; when you graduate from college or you retire from the civil service. You eat carnitas, like I did, every Friday after school, at the same filthy-delicious taco stand owned by a silent taquero named Güero. And you eat carnitas the night before you set out for the north.

Below you will find directions on how to make carnitas without access to Güero's giant copper vat or a whole pig or a tortilla-making machine or a well-stocked chile stand or decent avocados or juicy limes or any of the things that make life in Mexico wonderful. This recipe will tell you how to make something that approaches carnitas but will never really be the real thing, because the real thing only really exists in the memory of people who have left the old country.

To be clear, this takes a full 24 hours: You have to soak the beans the night before you plan to eat, and the pork needs to simmer for 6–8 hours. During that time, you can get drunk, make two salsas, beans, and spicy green rice. And then you will feast. Also, most of it is appropriately (i.e., extremely) spicy, especially the green salsa, the pickled onions, the green rice, and the beans.

For the pork

8 pound pork shoulder, de-boned
2 pounds pork belly
1 cinnamon stick
1 piece star anise
1 tablespoon ground cumin
2 tablespoons mustard seeds
2 cups lard*

1 white onion, coarsely chopped in rough ½-inch pieces
10 garlic cloves
1 bottle of Mexican Coke (or any cola made with real sugar)
2 sprigs dried epazote leaves (or a big pinch, if they're crumbled) (epazote is a Mexican herb, like an anise-y tarragon)*
2 dried bay leaves
2 tablespoons dried Mexican oregano*
1 orange

For the smoky red salsa

5 dried guajillo chiles
5 dried chipotle chiles
5 medium, ripe tomatoes
½ white onion, peeled
10 garlic cloves
2 tablespoons apple cider vinegar

For the tart green salsa

8 tomatillos
4 fresh serrano peppers
4 jalapeño peppers
½ white onion, peeled
6 garlic cloves
4 limes
¼ bunch cilantro, coarsely chopped (leaves and stems)
2 tablespoons apple cider vinegar
1 ripe avocado

For the spicy pickled onion

1 red onion
2 habanero chiles
2 cups apple cider vinegar OR distilled white vinegar
1 teaspoon dried Mexican oregano
Kosher salt

For the beans

1 pound dry pinto beans
3 cups chicken stock

1 white onion, divided
2 dried bay leaves
1 tablespoon lard
1 pound raw chorizo sausage
5 tomatoes
6 garlic cloves
4 jalapeños
1 red onion

For the rice

2 cups uncooked white rice
12 fresh poblano chiles
½ white onion, peeled and cut in large chunks
4 garlic cloves, peeled
4 cups chicken stock
1 tablespoon lard
1 bay leaf
1 sprig dried epazote leaf

For the garnishes

½ pound of chicharron (that's fried pork skin, gringo)
1 white onion
2 ripe avocados
5–6 limes
3 pounds small corn tortillas

For the ingredients with an asterisk (*) like chiles and herbs, you may need to go to a Mexican grocery store. For the lard, call a butcher.

At least 12 hours before you start cooking:

Soak the beans: Put 1 pound of pinto beans in a large bowl or Tupperware container, and cover them with water by at least 2 inches. Let them sit out at room temperature to soak overnight, 12–24 hours.

Pork

1. Before you start cooking, you need to cut your meat. Start by cutting the pork shoulder into rough 2-inch cubes. The size doesn't matter

so much, as long as all the pieces are pretty consistent. Leave all the fat on. Yes, all of it. Cut the pork belly into cubes the same size, but keep the cubed pork shoulder separate from the cubed pork belly.

2. Heat a large (at least 3-gallon) stock pot or Dutch oven over medium heat, then add the ground cumin, mustard powder, star anise, and cinnamon.

3. The moment the cumin becomes fragrant, add the lard. Two cups may seem like a lot, but push your lard tolerance as far as it will go.

4. When the lard is completely melted and quite hot, add the chopped white onion. Fry the onion in the lard until it becomes soft and translucent, but not brown, about 3 minutes.

5. Add the cubed pork shoulder all at once, and season generously with about a tablespoon of salt and some freshly ground pepper. You want some browning, but no need to work in batches or be elegant about it. Cook, stirring occasionally, until all the cubes of pork are mostly cooked on the outside, about 5 minutes.

6. Add the pork belly and whole garlic cloves, then stir everything together.

7. Slowly add the bottle of Mexican Coke, then add just enough water to cover everything. Add epazote leaves, bay leaves, and dried oregano. Give the whole thing a good stir.

8. Chop the orange into thick slices and place the slices on top of the meat.

9. Cover the pot and bring the braise to a boil over high heat. As soon as the liquid starts to boil, reduce the heat to a low simmer and half-cover the oven.

10. Cook the braise for two hours, stirring it *maybe* once just to make sure nothing is sticking to the bottom. The less you touch the braise, the better. After 2 hours, remove and throw away the orange slices, otherwise they'll make everything bitter.

11. Continue to simmer the braise for as long as it takes for the broth to evaporate almost completely, the meat to become impossibly tender, and the pork belly to become a glorious pig goo, about 6–8 hours more. There will still be some liquid in the pot, but it will be mostly fat. Which is delicious.

12. In the meantime, start drinking and make the salsas, toppings, and side dishes.

13. When you are ready to serve, use a slotted spoon or strainer to take your carnitas out of the pot while draining some of the excess fat. Fish out the leaves and the whole spices and throw them away.

14. Preheat your broiler to high, and line a large, rimmed baking sheet with parchment paper or foil.

15. Use a pair of tongs to toss and shred your pork, until you have little pieces of meat—*carnitas*. What did you think that meant, gringo?

16. Take about half of the carnitas, spread them over a baking sheet, and broil them until they get crispy—8–10 minutes.

17. Serve warm tortillas and all the garnishes below. DO NOT ADD CHEESE, SOUR CREAM, CHOPPED TOMATO, OR, GOD FORBID, LETTUCE. Why? Because if you were foolish enough to eat lettuce at el Güero's, you'd be setting yourself up for a weekend in the toilet. And we're going for the real thing here, right?

Smoky red salsa

1. Preheat your oven to 500°F.

2. Cut the top off the dried chiles, cut them in half lengthwise, and use a knife or your finger to scrape out the seeds. Throw the seeds away.

3. In a cast-iron skillet without any oil or lard, toast the dried chiles until they are lightly blackened on all sides, about 3 minutes.

4. Fill a small sauce pot about ⅔ of the way with water, and bring the water to a simmer. When the water is simmering, turn off the heat and submerge the blackened chiles in the water. Let the chiles sit for 15 minutes, until they're soft and mostly rehydrated. Drain and discard all but half a cup of the water.

5. While chiles are soaking, place tomatoes, white onion, and garlic cloves in the cast-iron skillet. Roast in the hot oven until the vegetables start to blacken, 15–20 minutes. Be careful not to burn the garlic.

6. While they are still hot, transfer the tomatoes, onion, and garlic to a blender. Add the chiles and about 2 tablespoons of the chile soaking liquid, then add the apple cider vinegar. Season with a teaspoon of salt and some freshly ground pepper.

7. Blend until there are no large chunks, adding a little bit more of the chile-soaking liquid if the mixture is too thick. Pour the finished salsa into a bowl or Tupperware container, and refrigerate until you're ready to serve.

Tart green salsa

1. Take the husks off the tomatillos and cut the stems from the serrano chiles and the jalapeños.

2. Fill a medium (at least 3-quart) sauce pot about ⅔ of the way with water, and bring to a boil. When the water is boiling, add the serrano chiles, jalapeños, tomatillos, white onion, and garlic. Reduce to a simmer and cook until the tomatillos and the chiles turn a bright green and start to soften, 10–15 minutes.

3. With a slotted spoon, take the veggies out of the water and place them in a blender.

4. Cut the limes in half and squeeze the juice out of them, directly into the blender.

5. Add apple cider vinegar and chopped cilantro, then season with a teaspoon of salt. Blend until everything is evenly combined and the salsa has no large chunks. Taste for salt, and add more if you need to.

6. Pour the salsa into a bowl or Tupperware container. Peel the avocado and cut it into rough ¼-inch cubes, then mix the cubes into the salsa. Refrigerate until you're ready to serve.

Spicy pickled onion

1. Chop the onion into rough ¼-inch pieces. Cut the stems off of the habeneros, then finely mince the flesh, leaving the seeds in.

2. Transfer the mixture to a bowl or plastic container, and cover with distilled white vinegar or apple cider vinegar. Add dried oregano and a pinch of salt, then stir together just to combine.

3. Leave the mixture out at room temperature for at least an hour before serving, so that the onions pickle slightly.

Beans

1. Drain the beans from the water in which they soaked overnight, and put the beans in a medium (at least 3-quart) pot or Dutch oven.

2. Add chicken stock and 3 cups cold water. Add bay leaves and half the white onion (peeled but not chopped), cover and bring to a boil. Reduce to a simmer and cook with the lid ajar for as long as it takes for the beans to become tender, about 2 hours.

3. Meanwhile, remove the chorizo from the sausage casings and crumble it into bite-sized pieces. Chop the remaining half of the white onion, tomatoes, and jalapeños into rough, ¼-inch cubes. Mince the garlic cloves.

4. Heat lard in a large skillet over medium-high heat, then add the chorizo, and fry until it's almost cooked through and starting to brown, about 2 minutes. Add the chopped onion, and fry until it starts to get translucent and soft, about 3 minutes. Add the chopped tomato, jalapeño, and garlic, stir everything together, and reduce the heat to medium low. Cook until the tomatoes are broken down and the onions are very soft, about 30 minutes. (This is called a sofrito, gringo.)

5. When the beans are nearly done, taste for salt and add more if needed. Remove the onion half and the bay leaves, then turn the heat up to high just to boil away the excess liquid, no more than 3 minutes.

6. When you are ready to serve, heat the sofrito until it starts to sputter, then pour it over the beans. Give it a good mix, then serve.

Green rice

1. In a large bowl or container, cover the rice with cold water by about an inch. Soak the rice for 20 minutes, then drain it into a strainer or colander and rinse until the water runs clear. Shake the rice in the colander to get rid of excess water.

2. Meanwhile, heat a large skillet over high heat, then add the poblano chiles. Let them sit in the skillet until the underside has started to blacken, about 3 minutes. You should hear popping noises. Turn the chiles and repeat until they are blackened on all sides, about 12 minutes total. Place the hot, blackened chiles in a ziplock bag, seal the bag and let them "sweat" for about 15 minutes, until they are deflated and cool enough to handle.

3. When the chiles are cool, slice off the stem and about half an inch from the top of each chile, then throw away the tops. Slice the chiles lengthwise so that they lie flat on a cutting board, then scrape out the seeds. Try to peel off as much of the gooey skin as you can. It's no big deal if you can't get all the skin off.

4. Put the chiles in a blender along with the white onion, garlic, chicken stock, and a teaspoon of kosher salt. Blend until the mixture

is a thin liquid with no large chunks. This is the cooking liquid for your rice. Set the liquid aside while you fry your rice.

5. Heat lard in a medium (at least 3-quart) pot or Dutch oven, over medium heat. Dump in the rice and toast it, stirring constantly so that it doesn't burn. You want it to become the color of hay, like the hair of gringos from the Midwest.

6. Once the rice is golden, add the blended liquid. Stir, add bay leaves and epazote leaves. Cover and cook over high heat until the mixture boils. Reduce the heat to medium low and cook, still covered, for 20 minutes.

7. After 20 minutes, turn off the heat and let the rice steam for 15 more minutes. Do not take the cover off. If you like a slightly crispy crust at the bottom (which I do), leave the pot on the burner, even if it's off. If you don't, move it off the stove and let it cool.

8. To serve, fish out the epazote and the bay leaf, then fluff the rice with a fork or spoon.

Garnishes

1. To heat your tortillas: Heat a large griddle or a couple of large skillets over high heat. Add a single layer of tortillas and cook until the tortillas are starting to blister on the underside, 1–2 minutes. Flip the tortillas and repeat on the other side. When the tortillas are heated, transfer them to a large basket or bowl lined with a towel or cloth napkin, to keep them warm. Repeat until all the tortillas are warmed.

2. To prepare the chicharron dust: Put the chicharron in a large ziplock bag and roll over the bag with a bottle or rolling pin until the chicharron are crushed to a coarse dust. You will dust your carnitas with this glorious star powder. It has all the healing properties of unicorn horn.

3. Coarsely chop the rest of the cilantro, leaves, and stems, and place in a bowl for people to sprinkle upon their tacos.

4. Slice the avocado in impossibly thin slices.

5. Cut the limes into quarters.

A note on building tacos

Proper tortillas have two sides to them—one that is more resilient, and one that will peel away easily if you rub the tips of your fingers against it. The latter is the inside of the tortilla—it will absorb the pork juices much better, granting your taco more structural integrity.

Lastly, you don't want to overstuff your taco. It's like trading in mortgage-backed securities: It sounds like a great idea at first, but your greed will result in catastrophic consequences.

The Family Table

The Imperfect Family Kitchen

By Debbie Koenig

From ParentsNeedToEatToo.com

Author of the cookbook/new parent lifeline *Parents Need To Eat Too,* Brooklyn-based blogger-writer Debbie Koenig is all about down-to-earth fixes for modern families. Which is why she couldn't resist calling out food writers who blithely prescribe high standards for the family dinner.

Food writers are lying to you.

In our quest to inspire people to cook, we offer images of glorious plates of food, dramatically lit, propped with carefully-chosen cloth napkins and color-coordinated dishes, with the most adorable little trail of crumbs to suggest that someone's actually eating this slice of perfection.

My dinner plate never looks like that anywhere but the computer screen, on a really good day. In real life it's chipped, with maybe some sauce spilling over an edge onto the crumpled paper napkin.

Most people edit their lives, to show only the corners they like to the world—think about how you decide what to share on Facebook. Food writers leave out the grimy spot near the toaster, the overstuffed, disorganized fridge that's barely chugging along. I don't think we're ashamed of these parts of our lives, necessarily, just that in order to capture attention, we chase a notion of unrealistic beauty. That leads to cookbooks and food blogs as staged and Photoshopped as the models in Vogue.

The picture above is my kitchen, this morning. Those battered cabinets, in that weird mauvey shade, were painstakingly painted by my husband and me before Harry was born. I couldn't stand the dingy, 1970s almond laminate, and somehow imagined that coating it in pink would fix things. It didn't, but the process of removing all the cabinet doors, priming, painting, and reattaching them, was so exhausting I just couldn't see doing it all again. Especially with a kid around. We've lived with them for almost a decade now, and I still don't like them.

My food processor dates to 1993, a wedding present from my first marriage. The non-functioning hood over the stove (an appliance my landlady replaced last year, after the 40-year-old predecessor finally kicked the bucket) has been scrubbed so many times the paint's worn off. A sheet of plastic tarp funneled into a bucket hangs in front of the window, since there's a mystery leak the handyman has never been able to locate, which floods the area during major rainstorms.

So yeah, my kitchen is imperfect. Just like my cooking.

That's where food writers really let down our readers. Too often, we gloss over mistakes or talk about how easy a recipe is, when in fact it failed miserably the first three times we tried it, and sometimes even now, when it's "perfect," it just doesn't come out as good as we remember. We give time estimates based on how long it takes us to prepare something, neglecting the fact that many, if not most, people don't work as fast as we can, don't share our confidence in the kitchen. We urge people to cook for their families, and preach about how crucial it is to the well-being of our children and heck, the entire world. Whether we intend to or not, we suggest that if someone doesn't cook—or doesn't like to cook—that person isn't doing it right.

That person is usually a woman. And given the whole mantra of "family dinners are THE answer" to obesity, drug use, juvenile delinquency, and general shiftlessness, that woman is usually a mom. Case in point: Virginia Heffernan's essay in this week's *New York Times Magazine*, in which she confesses that she doesn't like cooking, and that family-oriented cookbooks only make her feel bad about herself.

Here's my confession: Lately, I hate cooking. The frustrations and challenges of coming up with creative, appealing, and easily reproduced meals that my insanely picky kid might deign to eat have sucked all the joy out of my kitchen. That's why things have been so quiet around here lately. I'm tired, and I don't have much to crow about. I don't want to admit that I've failed as a mother—and I know I haven't really, but that's what many of my fellow family-food writers smugly imply if your child isn't omnivorous. (I'm looking at you, Mark Bittman.)

When I wrote my cookbook [*Parents Need to Eat Too*], my goal was simple: To reassure frazzled new parents that yes, they'd get their mojo back, and yes, they'd learn to make dinner again someday, and then to help them do it. From the feedback I've received since it came out, I think I succeeded. I think I managed to write a family cookbook that doesn't make parents feel bad about themselves. And you know what? Sales are meh. When it comes to laying down money, I suspect most people want pretty; they want promises of perfection, of problems solved. They don't want to be told that this period of your life is challenging, but you'll get through it.

So when people ask about my next cookbook, I shrug and mumble into my shoulder. The obvious subject would be feeding your picky eater, but since I struggle with that myself multiple times every day, with two giant leaps back for every baby step forward, it seems disingenuous to suggest I might have any answers. Or that my answers will work for any family other than my own. Lord knows nobody else's have worked for mine.

Maybe my next book should be about the Imperfect Family Kitchen. The one with a leaky window, chipped plates, and a kid who won't eat. The one where the UPS guy comes just when the timer's about to go off, where the whining of the eight-year-old as he sets the table makes you wish you'd just set the table yourself. The one with a mom who moans at least twice a week, "I have to make dinner again?"

But who wants to read that?

Friday Night Meatballs: How to Change Your Life with Pasta

By Sarah Grey

From SeriousEats.com

Despite a decidedly feminist-activist streak to her resume, Philadelphia-based writer-editor Sarah Grey didn't intend to start a movement when she and her husband launched their Friday Night Meatballs project. (Really, it was just a way to cook and eat with friends.) But the proof is in the pudding—or rather, the pasta....

F riday, 7 p.m. I light the candles.

For the last two hours I have been rushing: cleaning up toys and clutter, vacuuming, dusting. Now the table is set with my great-grandmother's good china. My four-year-old daughter Lucia is busily folding paper napkins and placing them next to each of ten plates. Between the candlesticks are a plate of sliced bread, a dish of olive oil, a small bowl of grated fresh Parmesan. My husband Joe bends over a pot of simmering sauce. A pot of salted water rests on the stovetop, ready to be boiled when the guests arrive. I've changed into a clean T-shirt and cotton skirt. My feet are bare. After I light the candles I stop cleaning, dim the lights, put my phone away, and pour two glasses of wine.

It isn't long before our little rowhouse on the far northern edge of Philadelphia's Fishtown section is full. My friend Stephanie, a massage therapist and space designer, brings her husband Joe and their daughter, five-year-old Olivia, who shows Lucia her new toy pony. The girls rush to the toy corner. Steph presents us with a salad loaded with goat cheese, walnuts, and fresh strawberries.

Brian and Carina arrive from down the street with two bottles of wine. Lily and Nico tease us about the unusually clean house. Peter, Catherine, and Catherine's mother Diane, visiting from Connecticut, arrive laden with diaper bags and car seats. We drink wine and take turns bouncing baby Rosie on our knees while Joe boils the big pot of pasta. The room feels changed somehow, smaller and brighter and warmer.

When the table is laden with platters of pasta and steaming bowls of meatballs, we sit and raise our glasses:

"To Friday Night Meatballs!"

Breaking Out of Busy

Joe and I have been doing this every Friday, give or take a few, for nine months. They have been extraordinary months.

We had a few simple problems to solve. Working from home (as a freelance writer and editor) can be incredibly isolating, and we'd spent most of the year so busy with work and other obligations that we had almost no time for a social life. People were always inviting us out, but by the time we factored in the cost of babysitting and the loss of what precious time we get, as working parents, with our daughter, we rarely said yes.

We had no idea how much the simple act of gathering for dinner would transform our family's life.

Joe grew up in a traditionally minded Italian-American family in Long Branch, New Jersey, where they call red sauce "gravy." On Sundays, his father Alfonso got up early to start the sauce before Mass. Sunday dinner was spaghetti and meatballs. Joe hasn't been to Mass in thirty years, but he has always expressed love through cooking—and his meatballs are to die for. He's a talented home chef with an eye for R&D: he's worked hard on his father's recipe to achieve just the right tenderness, the perfect amount of sauce saturation. Lucia often stands on a stepstool to watch him roll the meat and bread in his hands: she is squeamish about meat (except for bacon) but asks question after question as he works.

My household in the suburbs of Pittsburgh was less traditional, but it too was suffused with the sense-memory of meatballs and sauce. Once a week my father, who had joint custody, picked up me and took me out for spaghetti and meatballs at Hoffstot's in Oakmont. I was the world's pickiest eater and mealtimes were often battles, but at Hoffstot's I was always happy.

When we started hosting family dinners, then, meatballs were the obvious choice. We'd noticed that visiting friends often requested them; they seemed to us too pedestrian for guests, but our friends from other food cultures—Indian, Jewish, West African—adored them. So meatballs it was.

On my thirty-third birthday, I took to Facebook:

> So here's what Joe and I have decided to do, in my 33rd year, to make our lives happier: we are instituting a new tradition we call Friday Night Meatballs. Starting next Friday, we're cooking up a pot of spaghetti and meatballs every Friday night and sitting down at the dining room table as a family—along with anyone else who'd like to join us. Friends, neighbors, relatives, clients, Facebook friends who'd like to hang out in real life, travelers passing through: you are welcome at our table. We'll just ask folks to let us know by Thursday night so we know how many meatballs to make. You can bring something, but you don't have to. Kids, vegetarians, gluten-free types, etc. will all be taken care of. The house will be messy. There might be card and/or board games. There might be good Scotch. You might be asked to read picture books. You might make new friends. We'll just have to find out. This is our little attempt to spend more time with our village. You're invited.

The response was immediate: I was inundated with "likes" and comments from down the street and across oceans. I showed Joe and he raised an eyebrow: "We're going to need more chairs."

In the weeks that followed, we got used to hosting. It became less of an ordeal. We got more chairs. More wine glasses, too. We began making meatballs ahead of time and freezing them. We capped the guest list at ten adults and as many children as can play well together without too much supervision. And we stopped worrying about making everything perfect. Our parents and grandparents, we realized, hadn't made a big deal about hosting family dinners; it was just something they did. It was normal. After a few weeks it started to feel normal for us, too. I jettisoned any visions I might have had about cloth napkins and Pinterest crafts and began to relax.

Those problems we'd set out to solve? It wasn't long before we realized our solution was working. Little Lucia began looking forward to Friday Night Meatballs as a weekly playdate. She was learning how to interact with adults, too: she took on the job of dishing the correct number of meatballs onto guests' plates. Joe and I saw more of our friends and strengthened our social networks as word began to spread. And my isolation? Well, this was the winter we learned the term "polar vortex." Philadelphia had record-breaking snow, bitter cold, and no less than nine canceled school days. I spent the endless blizzards trying desperately to meet deadlines while entertaining my child. There were entire weeks when I barely left the house. For this hardcore extrovert, Friday Night Meatballs became a lifeline. And things started to happen.

Coming Together

Part of the fun of hosting a weekly dinner is the rotating cast of characters. We have our beloved regulars, but the mix is always different. Seinfeld's George Costanza famously flipped over his "worlds colliding"—friends from one sphere of life mixing with friends from another—but today, social media has our worlds colliding on a regular basis as coworkers, college friends, and conservative uncles argue politics on Facebook threads.

At Friday Night Meatballs, bringing together those disparate groups can yield all sorts of connections. One friend asked me to let her know any time I got an RSVP from a cute single guy. I did, and soon found myself following the dating drama via text message. Professional connections happen too: one recently laid-off guest found herself passing the bread to someone who was hiring in her field. Chef and food blogger Nancy found an agent for her cookbook over dessert. (I suspect the perfect crust on her blueberry-lemon pie was what won him over.) Filmmaker Matt Pillischer, who was promoting a screening of his documentary about the criminal justice system, found a table full of activists eager to help spread the word.

There's something about the mix of candlelight and comfort food (okay, and wine) that encourages people to relax and share their stories. I've always found hosting parties to be stressful, but Friday Night Meatballs has become a relaxing escape at the end of the week. In his book *The Sabbath*, rabbi and civil rights activist Abraham Heschel observes that "there is a realm of time where the goal is not to have but to be, not to own but to give, not to control but to share, not to subdue but to be in accord." This, he says, is the point of taking a day off for rest and reflection and the company of loved ones: it's when we manage to stop worrying about making a living that we start actually *living*.

Perhaps that's why Friday Night Meatballs has struck such a chord. When we hosted a Friday Night Meatballs at my mother's house in Pittsburgh over the holidays, we lifted the limit on guests—and thirty people came out. All of them said the same things: *We love the idea. There's something perfect about it. Why don't we get together like this more often?*

This isn't a new idea by any stretch of the imagination, of course; Shabbat dinners, Sunday suppers, Ramadan iftars, and the like are cherished all over the world. But in late-capitalist America, it can be *hard* to find community. The institutions that used to provide communal social life, like churches and unions, have long been in decline. People work long hours, often with long commutes or multiple jobs. An increasing number of us are freelancers, working from home without company. Social events aren't always hospitable for families with young children, and those who don't have kids can go years without even interacting with them. And with an economy that's really only recovered for a wealthy few, many Americans are more likely to down a burger in the drive-thru on the way to a second job than to sit down around a family table.

Friday Night Meatballs is intergenerational, kid-friendly, low-key, and cheap. You don't have to join anything: the biggest obligation it asks you to shoulder is showing up with a dessert or a bottle of wine. And it even has a hashtag.

If you'd like to give it a try, here are a few things I've learned along the way.

Hosting Without Stress

1. Use tech tools to take control of the guest list.

The first rule we made for Friday Night Meatballs was that our table would be open. We would welcome old friends, new acquaintances, Internet friends, and friends of friends, with no set guest list. This has worked well, though we often have to explain to surprised new friends that, yes, we really are inviting you to a family dinner like you used to have at Grandma's house.

But since it caught on quickly, we discovered early on that we needed to limit our head count. Our narrow Philadelphia rowhouse can fit about ten people before things get a little too cozy. We also began enforcing a 24-hour RSVP rule, which helps us avoid running out of meatballs. Facebook and Twitter are great for getting the word out; if you like to know what to expect, a shared Google Drive spreadsheet with ten numbered slots lets you track RSVPs. You can also add a column for people to tell you what they're bringing, which is a nice way to avoid winding up with three salads and no wine. Sites like Perfect Potluck and Punchbowl also let you track guests and will even send out automatic reminder emails. Just remember not to overthink things too much!

2. Don't sweat the housework.

Women are often taught from childhood that the state of one's home is a matter for pride or shame, but I've found that hours spent writing or spending time with my kid are far more valuable than hours spent scrubbing things that will be dirty again in two hours. I'm also just really not very good at organizing or decorating. Our house is more or less permanently disheveled. Cleaning seemed like it would be the most daunting part of hosting Friday Night Meatballs, but I've discovered two secrets.

The first: set aside one hour on Friday afternoon to do a speed-clean: whatever you can get done in an hour is what gets done. You'll be amazed at how much you accomplish.

The second secret is even simpler: *stop giving a shit.* Really. Your family and friends want to see you, relax, and eat meatballs. They do not care if your apartment is small or there is dust on the mantelpiece. They might not even see the dust: that's what the candlelight's for! And if they do, screw 'em. (Or draft them to wash the dishes.) I'd rather spend my life eating with friends in a messy house than refusing to have anyone over because the place isn't nice enough for guests.

3. Specialize.

When you host a traditional dinner party, there are usually multiple courses involved: hors d'oeuvres, entree, dessert, etc. You find recipes that are a little more special than usual. You pray that the souffle rises. It's stressful. You do not want to do that every week. That's why it's better to pick one relatively simple dish and stick to it. Let your guests bring the salads and side dishes. Not only will you save money and time, you'll also get *really, really good* at that one dish. Have you seen *Jiro Dreams of Sushi?* That's sort of what Joe is like with meatballs.

4. Your freezer is your friend.

There's another benefit to specializing, which is that you can make components of your dish ahead of time and freeze them. Hosting is a lot easier when you're not tied up in the kitchen all night. We make meatballs early in the week, then let them spend all day Friday in the slow cooker, soaking up sauce. Your freezer is also a handy place to store alternatives for guests with dietary restrictions. If you make vegan or gluten-free meatballs, freeze them individually on a cookie sheet covered with wax paper, so they won't stick together, then store them in portion-sized bags so they'll be ready when guests need them.

5. Unplug.

One of the most magical things about Friday Night Meatballs is that *people put their phones away.* We don't make this a rule, though you certainly could, but most of the time everyone is so busy eating and talking that phones just get in the way. I'm notorious for constantly snapping photos, but I've taken very few during Friday Night Meatballs. My theory is that the desperate need to stay connected that keeps us tethered to our phones melts away when we're all sitting around a table sharing a meal, *actually* connected. Once your candles are lit, put your phone away and just be there. You'll be amazed at how renewed you feel once the last guest has left.

In the past nine months, friends who've been inspired by Friday Night Meatballs have told me about slow cookers full of meatballs in hotel rooms at conferences. There's a Taco Tuesday in Minneapolis and a Brisket Brunch in Austin. Many others have shared their favorite low-stress ways to bring people together: game nights, "bring a weird snack" night, bad movie night, Sunday brunch club, even a backyard fried-chicken competition. It doesn't matter what dish you serve or what idea brings you together: the point is simply to break bread.

Super Simple Friday Night Meatballs

So many readers asked for my husband Joe Cleffie's meatball recipe that we had to oblige. After making a few small tweaks for foolproofing and streamlining, we're proud to present it here. This isn't the most complicated meatball recipe around—quite the opposite in fact. Our goal here is a recipe that anyone can make, no practice required, and get great results. I hope it inspires a thousand dinners in communities worldwide.

Why this recipe works:

- Simplicity is the name of the game here. The adobo seasoning in the meatball mixture adds plenty of garlic and spice flavor, while breadcrumbs and eggs help keep the balls tender.
- A long simmer in the sauce leads to good flavor exchange, making the sauce meatier and the balls saucier.

  Note: Meatballs can be frozen after frying and before adding them to the sauce. After browning, transfer to a parchment-lined plate or baking sheet. Place in freezer until balls are fully frozen, then transfer to a zipper-lock bag. Sauce can be frozen separately in a zipper-lock bag. To finish, thaw sauce and transfer to a pot. Add meatballs and simmer for at least one hour. Alternatively, transfer thawed sauce and meatballs to a slow cooker. Set to "keep warm" setting and allow to cook for 8 hours.

Yield: Serves 8 to 12

Active time: 45 minutes

Total time: 2 hours

For the Sauce

2 (28 ounce) cans whole peeled tomatoes
2 tablespoons extra-virgin olive oil
6 to 8 cloves minced garlic (about 2 tablespoons)
1 (6 ounce) can tomato paste
Kosher salt and freshly ground black pepper

For the Meatballs

4 slices bread, crusts removed
2 eggs
2 pounds 80/20 ground beef
1½ tablespoons adobo seasoning (such as Goya), see note above
½ cup minced fresh parsley leaves
Kosher salt and freshly ground black pepper
Olive oil for frying
Pasta and grated Parmesan cheese for serving

For the Sauce

1. Crush tomatoes by hand, with a food mill, or in the food processor to a very rough puree. Heat oil in a large Dutch oven over medium heat until shimmering. Add garlic and cook, stirring, until softened but not browned, about 1 minute. Add tomato paste and cook, stirring, until fragrant, about 1 minute longer. Add crushed tomatoes, bring to a simmer, cover, and reduce heat to low. Season lightly with salt and pepper. Meanwhile, make the meatballs.

For the Meatballs

1. Tear bread into rough chunks and pulse in the food processor until reduced to fine crumbs. Transfer to a large bowl. Add the eggs and mix with your hands until combined. Add beef, adobo seasoning, and half of the parsley. Combine mixture with your hands, working

the breadcrumbs into the meat until meat mixture can form a ball that holds together when tossed back into the bowl. Do not over mix.

2. Place a small amount of mixture on a microwave-safe plate and microwave on high until cooked, about 20 seconds. Taste and add salt and/or pepper to mixture to taste. Using wet hands, form the mixture into balls roughly 2 tablespoons each, about 1½– to 2-inches across. Place the balls on a large parchment or wax paperlined tray as you work.

3. Add enough oil to a large cast iron or stainless steel sauté pan to form a thin layer across the bottom. Heat over medium-high heat until shimmering. Add as many meatballs as will fit in a single layer and cook until well browned on first side. Gently turn balls with tongs or a thin metal spatula and continue cooking and turning until well browned on all sides. As the meatballs finish browning, add them to the pot of sauce and replace them with raw meatballs. Continue, adding more oil as necessary, until all meatballs are browned and in the sauce.

4. Simmer over low heat for 1 hour. Season to taste with salt and pepper and stir in remaining fresh parsley. Serve with pasta and grated Parmesan cheese.

A Mother's Cookbook Shares More Than Recipes

By Kim Severson

From the *New York Times*

New York Times* Atlanta bureau chief Kim Severson has a hefty food-writing history, with stints at both the *Times* and the *San Francisco Chronicle*, not to mention two books: *Spoon Fed* and *Cook Fight.* When a box full of worn recipe cards and beat-up cookbooks landed on her doorstep, it triggered a nostalgic quest.

T he last full sentence I heard from my mom was around Easter. "You better call Michael," she said.

The only Michael in our family is a distant cousin I can't be sure I've even met. But I went with it. Sure, Mom. I'll call him.

That's what it's like these days.

My mother has a kind of dementia that comes with advanced Parkinson's. That's lousy in a million ways, but I especially miss talking to her about cooking.

My dad recently sent me a big box filled with her old cookbooks and stacks of handwritten recipes on index cards and slips of paper. The recipes are held together with thick rubber bands or filed into a cheerful metal recipe box. They are the sum total of the cooking life of a woman who fed seven people every day for a long time.

I wish I could tell you that the collection is a brilliant, well-ordered trove of culinary instruction.

That special glazed Bundt cake I remember from childhood, the one she would always have under the green plastic dome when I returned home for a visit? The recipe came from a card attached to a bottle of Bacardi rum.

Next to the King Ranch casserole recipe in an old PTA cookbook, she made a note to add chopped green peppers, green chiles and a can of Rotel tomatoes. It was her attempt to give the sauce of canned soup a little life. The page ripples with the aftermath of some long-ago spill. Bits of dried sauce still cling to it.

In a flash, I'm back at our oak dinner table, my dad still in his shirt and tie from work serving that workhorse of a dish to five kids.

Turns out it was the mess that mattered to me the most.

The worn pages of a cookbook have a unique ability to drill into a place where food memory mixes with love and loss. As our kitchen adventures increasingly get recorded in sleek digital files or even the fleeting history of a recipe search, beat-up cookbooks become more valuable, both personally and historically.

"We love to see marked-up, dog-eared, grease-splattered cookbooks," said Paula Johnson, a curator at the Smithsonian Institution's National Museum of American History in Washington, where Julia Child's kitchen and beloved books are housed. How a cookbook is marked, by handwritten notes or physical evidence that a recipe was prepared over and over, tells much about the intent and life of the cook.

At the museum, visitors marvel at how worn Child's books are, especially her two copies of *Joy of Cooking*.

"They're thrilled to see the wear and tear, because Julia used her books just like they do," Ms. Johnson said.

From a curator's perspective, the mess also brings worry. "We know that big old grease stains and bits of buttery dough on the pages will have an impact on the long-term viability of the volume," she said. The mess could even attract bugs, which could harm the volumes around it. So conservators must sometimes clean the books, documenting every splotch they remove so the full story of the book is preserved.

Celia Sack, 45, collects old cookbooks, and she opened Omnivore Books in San Francisco, in part, to feed her habit. She sells plenty of

new cookbooks, but her shop has also become a repository for anti-
quarian volumes and other important work.

She bought the chef Jeremiah Tower's entire cookbook collection
in 2011. Mr. Tower didn't make notes as he cooked his way through
Child's *Mastering the Art of French Cooking,* but he made plenty of
splatters.

"What made it valuable was, it was his and you could travel back in
his mind and see where he was going by what he was cooking at the
time," Ms. Sack said. "It is a journey."

In Nashville, three writers joined this year to celebrate the analog
beauty of a well-used cookbook page. They asked 18 cooks, some professionals and some novices, to select a meaningful recipe of their own
and write about why it mattered. The women and their recipes were
photographed. The project, called "Dirty Pages," became an art installation that made the rounds in Nashville and will have a permanent home
at the Southern Food and Beverage Museum in New Orleans.

The idea came when Jennifer Justus, a food writer, saw a friend's
Facebook post depicting a splattered cookbook page. Kim McKinney, a
home cook in Nashville, left a comment: "I tell my daughters that when
I go, they'll know the good recipes from the dirty pages."

Erin Byers Murray, a founder of the project, said, "What's crazy is
that it's taken social media for a lot of us to recognize what treasures
they are."

The novelist Alice Randall, 56, is one of the women in the exhibit. In
February, she and her daughter, Caroline Randall Williams, published
*Soul Food Love: Healthy Recipes Inspired by One Hundred Years of Cook-
ing in a Black Family.*

At the heart of the book, which covers four generations, is a collection of more than a thousand cookbooks left to Ms. Williams by her
grandmother, a Nashville librarian who read cookbooks like novels. As
one might expect from a good librarian, she didn't mark her books. But
they hold treasures pressed between the pages, like Queen Anne's lace
and grocery lists.

"Every time I come upon one, it is a marker of a shared, similar experience," said Ms. Williams, who recently received a Master of Fine Arts
degree from the University of Mississippi. "It connects you to a moment
when they were alive and were occupying space with this same object."

Even the titles of the books her grandmother collected speak to her. "Knowing that my grandmother loved Italian fish stew and salmon mousse and Russian food, what does that tell me about a black women in Nashville during the civil rights movement?" she said.

Her mother, Ms. Randall, is a much messier cook, and her books reflect it. She describes her mother as distant. For comfort, Ms. Randall watched old Julia Child cooking shows and taught herself to cook from her books. Later, at Harvard, she did an independent study with Child.

She contributed Child's lobster bisque recipe from "Mastering the Art of French Cooking" to the exhibit. She has made vats of it, starting when she was the young bride of a State Department official, because it seemed suitable for entertaining. The book's pages are older than her daughter, who is 27.

"If I had to take one item out of my burning house to give to Caroline, it would be that book," she said.

I feel the same way about the trove my father sent me. (He has been passing on family memorabilia since he moved into a condominium a short walk from the little nursing home where my mom lives, in a Colorado ski town. He goes there to feed her every meal.)

When I finally got the strength to dig into the box, everything in it seemed important. Even the order felt too sacred to mess up.

My mom was a cook who got better as her children grew up. Eventually, she would head up the cookbook committee for the hospital auxiliary and even teach a few classes when she got a part-time job at a kitchen cookware store.

She clipped recipes from magazines or wrote them on whatever happened to be at hand. Instructions for the popovers she made with our Christmas roast beef were scratched out on the back of a contract bridge score sheet. Several were taken down on notepads from moving companies, evidence of how many times we packed up and headed for a new city. Sometimes, a recipe like chicken chili or an aunt's carrot cake would show up in my dad's neat block script on his work stationery. She had odd little notes—"3 qts water 1 qt vinegar 1 cup salt boil and put on pickles"—and mysteries I have yet to solve, like who was Shirley, why were there quotation marks around her "sugar cookies," and did they really need a cup of lard?

She even had practical advice from friends, like this on a recipe for cassoulet: "Really good if you like beans. A real pain in the ass to make, however."

The most sacred to me are the recipes from her Italian family. I picked up a sheet that listed mashed potatoes, oil, salt and egg with only two lines of instruction. The word "rats" was written at the bottom. That's what some of her sisters called cavatelli. Early on, I learned how to press the potato dough on the counter with my thumb so the little dumpling flipped over and curled like a rat's tail.

I finally got to the card that held a recipe for the coconut cream pie she would bake because I loved it so. It was the first pie I ever attempted.

My mom's handwriting is a messy version of the formal cursive they taught in northern Wisconsin public schools in the 1940s. I traced the loopy, uneven instructions with my fingers. And then I made the pie for my daughter.

Of Links and Legacy

By Steve Hoffman

From *Minneapolis Star-Tribune*

Freelance writer (and sometime tax preparer) Steve Hoffman
wasn't born a Lapadat, but he married into the family through
his wife, photographer Mary Jo Hoffman. And even in-laws are
needed to help out when the whole clan gets together to make
their traditional Romanian Christmas sausage.

According to family legend, Eva Lapadat arrived in New York by
ship from Beba Veche, Romania, in 1937, with three dollars in
the pocket of her housecoat.

She would settle on lower Rice Street in St. Paul, raise three children,
open a hair salon, command an armed robber not to come back until he
could ask for money politely, and, over the decades, more or less domi-
nate the social life of St. Mary's Romanian Orthodox church, both in
her own mind and even to a great extent in real life.

But standing on deck, in the shadow of the Statue of Liberty, she was
just Eva, thick featured, pregnant with her second son, holding the hand
of 2-year-old John Lapadat, my future father-in-law, in hers.

It is the exact volume of one of those cupped hands that we are trying to quantify—four grown men in aprons, standing around a trough-
sized enamel tub filled with 60 pounds of coarse ground pork.

"Is this a Grandma Eva handful?" asks Eva's fifty-something grand-
son, Johnny, handsome in a broad-nosed, Jack Dempsey way. He holds
out a thick paw containing a dainty-looking mound of coarse salt.

"A little more," guesses his brother Pauly.

"A little less," guesses his son Mikey.

Satisfied, Johnny sifts the salt over the pork, followed by five more Grandma Eva handfuls of salt, and four of black pepper.

Then, from a steaming bowl of water, he lifts a plastic colander half full of crushed garlic and lets fall an aromatic rain that splashes into the tub, filling this 50-degree garage in Minnesota with one of the world's great smells.

At his waist, held in place by a lowball glass of Manischewitz, lies a stained, handwritten recipe titled, "Romanian Sausage," which begins, "Two handfuls . . . "

The conversation from the adjacent kitchen has risen a score of decibels. Dogs chase each other. Kids are screaming. The Vikings are losing again. It's like any other holiday party, except for what Johnny says next.

"Pull on your gloves, boys. It's time to mix some sausage."

We plunge eight hands, which ache immediately, into the 35-degree meat, and, groaning, fold the garlic water and what we hope are the right quantity of Grandma Eva handfuls of salt and pepper into the 2014 vintage of Lapadat family sausage.

Variations on a Theme

The history of this sausage can be divided, like any great tradition, into several distinct eras.

There is antiquity, when generations of Romanian peasants teamed up at communal hog killings to process their winter meat.

There is the classical period, when, in dirt-floored Rice Street cellars during the mid-20th century, Lapadats put up sausage and made what we can only assume was awful concord grape wine.

We endured a 1980s Baroque, when such decadence as pouring cabernet into the mix, or using meat other than pork, or seasonings other than salt, pepper and garlic, gained traction.

But finally, John Lapadat, known to everyone as Papa, that 2-year-old boy in the New York harbor, the family patriarch and undisputed sausage king, stepped in, and in a semimythical moment in family history, ushered in our current Neoclassical era, declaring that we would return to Eva's original recipe, unadulterated by anything beyond the four basic ingredients.

He announced this with one of an endless supply of Now cigarettes bobbing from his lips, which, during his proclamation, let drop an untended ash tip that bounced off the front of his sweater and into the pork.

Dictator for a Day

"More salt!"

Marianne, under her blond do, holds an empty toothpick in her right hand. She is this year's appointed "meister," a title that rotates annually, and although everyone—her four children, their spouses and 11 grandchildren—will shortly weigh in with an opinion, Marianne is the day's acknowledged autocrat.

Everyone grabs a toothpick and samples a morsel of the pan-fried first batch.

Dee-Dee says more garlic. Roxy says perfect. Mary Jo says watch the pepper. Patrick says more of everything.

But none of it matters. What the meister says goes, and Marianne says more salt.

She leans affectionately toward her daughter-in-law, and smiles a little tiredly. This will be Marianne's second sausage making as John Lapadat's widow.

A former Hamm's executive, Papa Lapadat trusted me from the start because I had German in me, and Germans knew beer and sausage.

During one of my first sausage makings, he explained to me in a growling baritone how all the different cuts of meat that went into the grinder added qualities to the final mix, and just as you couldn't have good beer without good water—you know that, Stevie—you couldn't have good sausage without good ground pork.

That might have served as a tempting metaphor for a naturalized Romanian American, born on the Serbo-Hungarian border, who had processed through the grinder of Ellis Island. But he didn't want to talk to me about melting pots.

He wanted to talk to me—and did through four cigarettes and several backhanded thigh pats—about this family of his, and how everyone who joined it, by marriage, birth or friendship, came out of the experience a little bit Lapadat.

Being American was a privilege. Being a Lapadat was a gift.

Cranking Out History

The heavy black cast-iron sausage stuffer has seen its living quarters improve with the family's fortunes. From East Side root cellars, it migrated up Rice Street into John and Marianne's finished Shoreview basement, and now resides in the comfort of Johnny's two-story Lino Lakes colonial.

Now it's Johnny's responsibility—the care and maintenance of the ancient, hand-cranked machine, and by extension, of the tradition itself. It is Johnny who each year disassembles the machine, meticulously washes pork splatter the consistency of dried caulk from all of its edges and threaded parts, and oils it down again for storage.

It is Johnny, in a similar spirit, who taught himself to make *colac*, which he bakes every year, artfully braiding locks of egg dough with hands made to stack stone walls.

He always serves the first pan of steaming, golden-crusted bread straight from the oven to a family that falls on it with butter knives and devours it in minutes. The second pan waits on a trivet, because the only really acceptable bread to serve with Romanian sausage is *colac*.

In the garage, kids are blowing into the ends of 25-foot, salty white pig intestines. The final seasoning mix has met with the meister's approval and filled the cast-iron stuffer. A casing is threaded onto the aluminum spout, lubricated with a little crank of sausage meat, and sealed with an overhand knot.

We raise glasses of kosher wine to Papa Lapadat and, sacrificing taste buds in the service of tradition, choke down the grapey syrup that most closely resembles the homemade wine Papa remembered from childhood, with the exception that Manischewitz "tastes a little better."

Hands are everywhere. Young kids grab the crank handle with both hands and with all their strength barely turn it. The hands of parents or cousins or uncles fold over the straining fists and help turn the crank, so that the meat is pressed out of the spout smoothly.

A pair of hands cradles the knotted casing, and applying just a slight back pressure, lets it fill and then spill slowly into a thick pink spiral in the catch pan. When the right length is reached, the crank pauses. A hand with a shears cuts the casing, another pair of hands knots the cut end, and the cranking resumes, filling hundreds of feet of lacy white hog casings with a steady crackling sound.

We make 2-foot lengths for entertaining. Foot-long loops for family dinners. Links for breakfast. And patties for meatballs, cabbage rolls and stuffed green peppers. Johnny mans the bagging station, restoring himself with sips from his now smudged lowball glass while the vacuum sealer drones.

At his side, a cardboard box fills with vacuum packs that will chill down in a snowbank tonight, and then spend the winter in the freezers and on the tables of a tiny Romanian diaspora unfathomable economic circumstances removed from the kind of need that once made this a life-or-death activity.

The last person to know that need personally has just missed his second event in a row, which does not lend any sense of diminished importance to the squeals of reunited cousins, or the roar of shouted conversation, or the chime and clatter of dropped silverware and stacked ceramic plates.

A New Generation

It is generally agreed when dinner is served that the correct number of handfuls of salt have found their way into this year's batch.

I have hung up my apron and switched to something a little drier than Manischewitz. Standing next to my wife, Mary Jo, I have a view across the kitchen island into the dining room where everything is laid out.

Our daughter appears at the sideboard, grabs a bias-cut length of her own history, folds it unthinkingly into the still-warm pocket of a slice of *colac*, and slathers it, properly, with horseradish sour cream. She moves away across the dining room, munching, and is gathered into the compliant chaos of shouted conversation and several generations of bodies still partly shaped by the necessities of manual farm work in 19th-century Romania.

She is a strong and independent 16-year-old.

Her grandfather used to call her the Moldavian Princess.

Her name is Eva Lapadat Hoffman.

Monkey Eve

By Carolyn Phillips

From *Alimentum*

Blogger Carolyn Phillips (MadameHuangsKitchen.com) describes herself as a Chinese food wonk, partly due to her marriage to Chinese author J. H. Huang and partly to her own insatiable curiosity about Asian foodways. But in-law status is one thing—to truly earn a place in the Huang family, cooking turned out to be the key.

M y Chinese father-in-law looks over his glasses at the oblique chunks of bean curd piling up in front of me. He frowns slightly and gently clears his throat, for unlike his small squadron of perfectly hollowed-out pyramids, my disheveled army is most definitely not up to his exacting standards. It isn't that he expects much from me, the inappropriately foreign wife of his eldest son, but I am definitely irritating him more than usual today as we prepare his annual Chinese New Year's Eve extravaganza.

"You are going too fast," he at last says in his Cantonese-accented Mandarin. "Watch me." I stop and take in his glacially slow movements, trying to rationalize why it should always take forever to cook a meal in his tiny apartment kitchen. The bustle of Chinatown's traffic vibrates thirteen stories below us, the strange flat blue of the Los Angeles sky casting harsh afternoon shadows on his brushes and pots of ink, the tan smell of sandalwood soap invading every corner. Firecrackers rip and rebound through the alleys, and wisps of gunpowder filter in through his living room window.

As always, I am on my best behavior with him—not as wary as when I am around my volcanic mother-in-law, just very mindful of our generational and cultural differences. He patiently shows me again what it is that I should be doing: a fingertip slips into the yielding mass and then scoops up microscopic bits as he carefully prods away, hollowing out the doufu triangle with infinite care so that its sides are not breached. He readies them so that they can be stuffed with marbles of ground pork seasoned in the style of his Hakka home town in Guangdong hill country. He was forced to abandon this ancient ancestral fold when civil war exiled him, first to Taiwan and then to the States with his wife and grown children. As he approaches his eighth decade, these deeply savory Hakka dishes tether him to the old country and in turn form the sole connections the rest of us will ever have to his former life.

He carefully arranges a finished piece next to the others and slowly picks up a new triangle. I silently start to time him; five minutes per piece. Each one still has to be dusted with cornstarch, filled, fried, and then slowly braised. And this is just the first dish of many. We'll never make it at this pace, and our ravenous clan will soon be banging on his door.

"Dajia jidianzhong lai?" I ask, already knowing the answer. He slowly turns toward the clock on his oven, adjusts his bifocals, and says softly in Chinese, "In three hours." I look over the rest of the ingredients for the huge meal in progress—a whole rock cod, a fat plucked chicken, fresh pink pork, gray fish paste, aromatic bundles of garlic chives, a new bag of polished rice, a webbed sack of white eggs interspersed with a few pale blue duck ones, tangles of brown ginger, bunches of cilantro and scallions, a pile of coppery shallots, a pink bakery box that smells of his beloved sweets, and even more plastic bags filled with goodness knows what hanging from assorted door handles—and feel the first flickers of panic.

He patiently returns to the task in front of him while my eyes take in his spotted hands, which tremble slightly as he tries to coax the memory of his mother's cooking out of them. Ever since the last series of small strokes, he has lost his natural grace, the dancer's movements that were once the toast of Shanghai. Gone is the handsome tango partner and dashing fighter pilot who dazzled the city's fallen women in wartime dancehalls along the Bund.

I tell myself that he's an old man, that I must be patient, that I should just learn to breathe and relax as I watch him redo all of my efforts. Suppressing my desire to take over the kitchen, I try my best to transform myself into a submissive daughter-in-law, but my right eye twitches violently.

Murmuring something about the time, I let my husband's father work at his own pace while I settle into the grunt work: washing the vegetables and rice, scaling and prepping the fish, tidying the fridge and bathroom, wiping down counters, furtively recycling his massive stash of empty doufu boxes and plastic bags, and setting out a rickety assortment of borrowed folding chairs around his table on this eve of the Year of the Monkey. My hands stay busy while my eyes keep track of how he makes the family's favorite holiday dish. I surreptitiously allow my glances to wander up his arms to his shoulders and then to the back of his head, his stiff black hair much grayer than last year.

He seems so familiar and yet so strange. We never got to know each other much beyond these kitchen encounters because Chinese tradition forbade anything other than minimal interaction, and so he almost never even acknowledged my presence beyond what simple courtesy demanded. We never chatted, never shared ideas or thoughts, and never even looked each other in the eye. But we both liked to cook, and we had each discovered that hiding by a stove allowed us to maintain Swiss-like neutrality in our family's never-ending internecine warfare. Like me, he had no dog in those fights. Bowing out of whatever fracas was taking place, we found our refuge behind kitchen doors, the loudly whirring stove fan and whacking knives creating a bell jar that deflected all discord.

My beautiful mother-in-law had long ago gladly surrendered the kitchen to him and his endless stream of aromatic southern cooking, entering it only when this warlord's daughter longed for the foods of her northern birthplace in Tianjin, her plain steamed breads and hearty pork braises a stern rebuke to the sensuous dishes that customarily fed the family: simply cooked fresh fish spangled with green onions, chicken wings swimming in pools of golden fat and gently scented with vinegar, stuffed omelet purses, brilliant emerald mustard stems studded with crunchy bits of garlic, and bowl after bowl of steamed rice to sponge up all of those glorious juices.

His home readied for guests, I arrange some plum blossoms and for-sythia in an old glass jar and center it on the dining table. Chopsticks and soup spoons are placed at each setting, and the holiday tabletop looks as it ever does. I sneak a peek at my father-in-law calmly working on the bean curd, oblivious to everything but the ingredients for this one dish. My pulse slows as I remember that this kitchen of his has become my safe haven, a place where I can screen myself behind the pots and pretend I am being appropriately dutiful.

Pausing on the kitchen threshold, I see for the first time the wisdom of his measured pace. His unhurried tempo advises me that the dinner will have to be gradually presented over several leisurely hours, that the cook and his helper will need to be regretfully absent from the festiv-ities as they tend to woks and steamers, and that they will then have to spend an inordinate amount of time meticulously cleaning up the kitchen in order to guarantee good luck in the new year. With the clang of steel and the clatter of china drowning out all attempts at conversa-tion, they will emerge sweaty and unscathed only when the last guests have left. With the cool night air seeping through the living room win-dow and the traffic noises below reduced to only the occasional honk, these two will finally sit down at the cluttered table and contentedly nibble on leftovers while the eldest son tidies the apartment and re-turns the chairs. I wash up, take a sip of tea, and put on a clean apron. My hand reaches for a bean curd triangle, and I hum softly to myself while sedately scraping out a little crater. I tamp the edges of our bell jar down securely around us. We will not share another word the entire evening, but there will be no need for conversation.

After five minutes, my father-in-law looks over his glasses at the per-fectly hollowed-out piece in my fingers and rewards me with the slight-est of nods.

The Year of the Ram fades as the shadows on his desk lengthen. I pour my father-in-law a fresh glass of hot jasmine tea.

There is no hurry.

Loving Spoonful

By Zainab Shah

From *Saveur*

Pakistani-born fiction writer Zainab Shah parses the cultural
vagaries of a weekend with her parents in this essay, in which one
dish—*nigari* stew—becomes a stand-in for all the connections
that make a family a family, even in the worst of times.

Earlier this year I decided to get divorced. The whole process was
tough, but the hardest part of the ordeal, it turned out, was breaking the news to my conventional Pakistani parents. As soon as I told
them, they resolved to take a 14-hour flight from my hometown of Lahore, in Pakistan, to New York to set me straight. Luckily, my father
wasn't granted a U.S. visa, so they settled for meeting me at an AirBnB
apartment in Toronto instead. This was a relief; if they had come to
New York, they could have stayed at my place indefinitely. My plan was
to see them and assure them that I was an adult who knew what she was
doing before hurrying back to Manhattan.

I took an early morning flight and arrived at the apartment at 7:00
A.M. As soon as I saw my mother, I surprised myself by clinging to her
and crying uncontrollably. I hadn't seen her in two years, and when I
did, my adult demeanor dissolved. She started to cry, too, and I felt like
nothing would be okay, ever. She wailed and cursed herself for being a
bad mother, for not raising me to respect tradition, my husband, and a
woman's expected role. Finally, she stopped and asked me if I was hungry. I was. On the plane ride over, I had been craving *nihari*, a thick stew
of meat and spices she used to make for me in Lahore every Sunday.

My mother was taken aback to hear that I longed for such a traditional meal. After all, she'd just written me off as "too modern." She expected me to shun the food of my ancestors because I had rejected so many other traditions. But my desire for *nihari* transcended my cultural critique. When it comes to food, I don't discriminate.

Passed down to us common folk from the royal, Persian-influenced kitchens of Lucknow, in India, *nihari* is a laborious, time-consuming dish that is the ultimate proof of a cook's dedication. In requesting that she make it, I was testing my mother's dedication to me. I knew she would readily do it, though. She has always had time to cook for her loved ones. In fact, she claims that's why her family is still together.

"We should get to work if we want to eat it today," she announced at 8:00 A.M. As if on cue, my father, who was waiting his turn to talk to me, decided to take a nap. After a trip to a nearby market, she asked me to lay out the spices we needed. I knew the procedure, having grown up watching her: I placed fennel seeds, black peppercorns, cumin seeds, cardamom pods, cloves, cinnamon sticks, coriander, and nutmeg in front of her. She used her eyes and hands to measure the amounts needed. I cringed slightly as she put the spices into a whole-bean grinder, concerned for my next cup of coffee.

She held the machine under my nose, but she didn't have to, I could have smelled it a mile away. It was spicy, sweet, and bitter all at once, a reminder of my childhood, most of which was spent perched on my mother's kitchen counter. She smiled as I sneezed, and then asked the question I had been dreading: "So, what's the problem?" As I searched for the right words, she continued, "All marriages are hard work."

She lifted a heavy, cast-iron pot from the cabinet next to the stove as if to demonstrate her point. Her strength did not surprise me. She grabbed lamb shanks from the fridge, recalling how difficult her own marriage had been, and her sister's, and her cousin's. She talked about husbands who beat their wives, who cheated on them, and about marriages that lasted because of the loyalty of women. I began to wonder: Why did I have to request a dish that takes 7 hours from start to finish? Couldn't I have settled for a couple of scrambled eggs?

She heated some oil and placed the lamb shanks in it. The loud sizzling provided the appropriate soundtrack to her interrogation. I felt my face burn as I watched her add the ginger paste and spices. She cooked the meat until it was half done. Then she added water, brought it to a boil, and informed me that the lengthy stewing process had begun.

For the next several hours, as the *nihari* cooked, I listened to horror stories of divorcées—women who were miserable after their marriages ended, who were fated to lives of loneliness, poverty, and mental illness. "What makes you so special?" she asked.

There was no convincing my mother that I had tried hard, that there was no hope for my marriage, and that I was being rational when I asserted that no marriage at all was better than a bad marriage. She wouldn't hear it, and at some point everything became my fault. It was my fault for not wearing enough makeup, for not being a good cook, for being too independent. I fell silent, resigned to the fact that I would never change her mind. Meanwhile, the smell in the apartment had altered dramatically, from raw and meaty to tantalizingly spicy.

That night, when we sat down to eat, the rich, mahogany-hued *nihari* had thickened with the gelatin that had slowly seeped out of the lamb bones. Some of the meat had dissolved into the fragrant gravy and the rest melted in my mouth. I closed my eyes and imagined the stew clinging comfortably to my insides, and felt a warm fullness in my belly. When I opened my eyes, my mother was looking at me. "I worry for you," she said.

"I know," I responded, my voice sounding tiny. She went on, "I may never understand your reasons, but I just want you to be happy." As always, my mother didn't wait for a response. "How is it?" she asked, nodding toward the *nihari*. "It's great, Ama," I told her. But she already knew this. "Happy?" she beamed proudly. And at that moment I was.

Pakistani Slow-Cooked Lamb Stew (Dumbay ki Nihari)

A rich, spicy stew topped with bright cilantro leaves, a squeeze of citrus, and thin-sliced hot chiles, *nihari* is the ultimate comfort food for home cook and Lahore native Zainab Shah, whose mother makes this dish for her and her family. The dish's name is derived from the Arabic word *nahaar*, or "day," which makes sense considering the long, slow cooking required to coax the rich marrow out of the lamb bones.

Serves 4

For the Garam Masala

2 tbsp. poppy seeds
1 tbsp. coriander seeds
1 tsp. cumin seeds
1 tsp. fennel seeds
½ tsp. whole black peppercorns
¼ tsp. freshly grated nutmeg
5 whole cloves
3 green cardamom pods
1 black cardamom pod
1 star anise
1 stick cinnamon, halved

For the Nihari

1 cup canola oil
1 medium yellow onion, very thinly sliced
3 lamb shanks, halved crosswise
1 tablespoon cayenne
2 cloves garlic, mashed into a paste
1 (3-inch piece) ginger, peeled (1 inch mashed into a paste, 2 inches
    julienned, for serving)
Kosher salt, to taste
¼ cup flour
2 tablespoons ghee, melted
Chopped cilantro, lemon or lime wedges, minced Thai chiles, and
    naan bread, for serving (optional)

1. Make the garam masala: Purée poppy seeds and 1 tbsp. water in
a spice grinder into a paste; transfer to a bowl. Grind remaining spices
into a powder; stir into paste.

2. Make the nihari: Heat oil and onion in a 6-qt. saucepan over
medium. Cook until onion is caramelized, about 25 minutes; using a
slotted spoon, transfer onion to a bowl. Discard all but ¼ cup oil from
the pan. Cook lamb, turning as needed, until browned, 8–10 minutes.
Stir in reserved garam masala, the cayenne, garlic and ginger pastes,
and salt; cook 1–2 minutes. Add 3 cups water; boil. Reduce heat to

medium-low; cook, covered, until lamb has fallen off the bone, 5½–6 hours. Using tongs, transfer lamb to a bowl; keep warm. Stir flour, ghee, and ¼ cup water in a bowl and add to pan; cook until thickened, about 15 minutes. Return lamb to pan. Serve with the reserved onion, julienned ginger, and, if you like, the cilantro, lemon or lime wedges, chiles, and naan.

I'm Just Trying to Keep Everyone Alive

By Phyllis Grant

From Food52.com

Berkeley-based pastry chef Phyllis Grant illuminates the family
dynamic in her popular blog dashandbella.com, dedicated to
her two children and the day-to-day experience of cooking with
them—even when it seems that the whole shebang is going to
fall apart at the seams.

I ask my grandmother what kind of soup she wants. I need her to eat.
Butternut squash? No response. *White bean?* Nose scrunch. *Split pea
with a ham hock?* Her big smile brings me relief. She wants soup. She is
still here. But the tone in the nun's voice is enough to push me up and
over into tears: *We are not God, you know. But she is close.*

My friend Margi tells me that hospice knows. I don't want to believe
her. But it is enough to send me to the phone. To call my parents. To tell
them to fly home.

I am not hungry but I need to make a tart. I move into my kitchen
for the day.

I take dough out of the freezer, brown and cool some butter, tell my
son that if he doesn't take a bath he will have to move out before the
first of the month.

I pick up a rolling pin and *wack wack wack* the dough until it is soft
enough to handle. I roll. I try to let her go. I roll. I try to let her go.

My son dives underneath the bath water to see how long he can hold
his breath. His silence brings me running to the rescue. He is absolutely
still, floating face-down in the water. I scream. He pops up with a laugh.
What, mom? What? You worry too much.

As I arrange the apple slices in concentric circles and paint them with vanilla bean-flecked brown butter, I hear my dad telling me about this tart he had in Paris, somewhere slightly northeast of the Église Saint-Germain-des-Prés. It wasn't gooey like a tarte tatin. It wasn't doughy and gelatinous like a pie.

My daughter climbs up on the dresser to tape a series of cupcake photos to her wall. The house-shaking crash—drawers and clothes and child flying—sends me running.

I'm just trying to keep everyone alive.

I go back to my safe kitchen and finish up the tart with egg wash and turbinado sugar. I slide it onto a hot pizza stone. Thin and crisp. That's what my dad always said he loved about that tart in Paris.

I smile. This might be the closest one yet.

My parents land late. They are stressed. Anticipating death.

They find apple tart on their kitchen counter. They eat it with wine and cheese, turning it into dinner.

There is nothing else we can do.

Brown Butter Apple Tart

This is inspired by an apple tart that my father had in Paris many years ago. If possible, cook it on a pizza stone. This allows the crust to get quite crisp. The apples are so thinly sliced that they cook quickly. Make sure to leave on the skin because the border of the apple slices brown nicely in the oven.

Just know that in order to make lovely apple circles, you will need to sacrifice at least half of each apple. Just plan on using the scraps for a compote or snacking. You can even julienne it up right away, toss with lemon juice, and save for a salad. Or not all of the slices have to be circles. You could also play with making a pattern with all different shaped slices.

Serve with vanilla bean ice cream or crème fraîche. Alternatively, this tart makes a great dinner alongside cheese and a tangy green salad.

Serves 6

1 recipe of your favorite tart or pie dough (or puff pastry)
6 to 8 Granny Smith apples

3 tablespoons salted butter

½ vanilla bean, halved and scraped of its seeds

½ teaspoon vanilla extract

1 egg

3 tablespoons heavy cream

4 tablespoons turbinado sugar

3 tablespoons apricot jam, any large chunks of fruit finely chopped up

1. Take your dough out of the fridge 20 minutes before rolling it out (or 1 hour before if it's in the freezer).

2. Heat your oven to 450° F. Place your pizza stone or sheet pan in the oven to warm up. Melt the butter in a small saucepan. Swirl it around a few times. It will foam and spatter. After 3 to 4 minutes, it will start to smell nutty. Don't walk away. It's ready when the sizzling quiets down and you see little brown bits drop to the bottom of the pan. Cool. Whisk in vanilla bean seeds and extract.

3. Cut a piece of parchment paper that's about a 10-inch square. Roll out your dough into about a 12-inch round. It doesn't need to be perfect—you're going to fold over the edges. Roll dough onto your rolling pin. Unroll dough onto the piece of parchment.

4. Using a very sharp knife or a mandoline, with the apple stem facing north, very thinly slice about 5 circles off of two opposing sides of the apple. Stop once you hit the core. Repeat with the remaining apples. Save remaining apple and the outermost discs with lots of skin for applesauce or some other use.

5. Starting about 2 inches in from the border of the rolled out dough, make a circle with the apple discs, having them overlap. Continue with a second layer that overlaps the bigger circle. Do a third and smaller circle. And a fourth. Finish it off with a few discs in the middle in a flower pattern. Paint all exposed apple surface with the brown butter vanilla mixture. Fold the outer border of the dough in to enclose about half of the exterior edge of the outermost apple discs. Let it be funky!

6. Whisk together egg and heavy cream. Paint exposed border of dough with a thin layer of egg wash. Refrigerate any leftover egg wash and save for your next tart or pie (it will last a few days). Generously sprinkle the turbinado sugar all over the apples and the egg-washed dough.

7. Remove hot pizza stone or sheet pan from the oven. Quickly slide the tart (keeping it on the parchment) onto the hot surface. Bake until apples are golden brown and the crust is crisp, about 20 to 25 minutes.

8. Warm up the apricot jam. Using a pastry brush, paint surface of the cooked apples with warm jam. Serve immediately.

Life, on a Plate

Leaning in Toward the Last Supper

By Sarah Henry

From *Lucky Peach*

Host of the blog LettuceEatKale.com, Bay Area freelancer (and transplanted Australian) Sarah Henry writes socially-conscious food pieces for publications such as *The Atlantic, Chow,* and *Civil Eats.* When it comes to feeding her son, Henry treasures the meals that matter, always knowing that the clock is ticking.

My son is sixteen now. The other day I tried to recall the last time he nursed and I can't. Once he started walking—finally—at fourteen months, he moved quickly to running, everywhere, all the time. There was no time to hang around tied to a tit when there was a whole world out there to explore.

There was the time, nine months earlier, when I coaxed him to try cereal, most of which he was pushing out of his mouth with his tongue. A visiting friend, a parent of two, asked: "What are you doing?" And I said: "Introducing solids." And he shot back: "He's not interested." The dad was correct. What did I know?

There was the time he spat beets from his mouth and sprayed them all over the kitchen cabinet in our San Francisco apartment. I suspect some of that bright pink purée is still stuck there, ossified, for all time.

There were the years of carrying sources of nourishment in little containers. Who knew when hunger might hit? It proved a surefire way to ward off blood sugar–related meltdowns. I'm still the mom who's always carrying: fruit, nuts, bars, bagels, trail mix.

There were the visits home to Australia coinciding with his phase as a serial food flinger. When they saw us coming, his aunts would put newspaper under the high chair and hope for the best. My sister tried to feed him steak once and he ran screaming from the table.

There was a more recent trip back to the motherland, four months ago, when he was the designated plate cleaner. He's happy to do his bit in the war against food waste by eating everything in sight, as many sixteen-year-old boys do.

Back in my adopted home in Berkeley, I find myself fielding his texts at dinner time. I'm making a mushroom risotto on a Saturday night, expecting him to show up and devour a dish he loves. He texts me that he and a friend are making dinner before a party. They're wilting spinach and zesting a lemon and toasting walnuts for a pasta. It's all there in the text: the specific techniques, the ingredients. This makes me smile. The risotto will keep until Sunday.

And then I think about the last supper, the one that's coming, after he goes off to college. It's still a couple of years away, but I can feel the shift already. He's still delighted to come home to a Mum-cooked meal. When he sees supper set out or gets a whiff of what's on the stove, he'll emit an appreciative groan. But the dinner-table dynamic has changed during these high school years. There's less time for lingering and chatting about the day's events. Food is becoming more about fueling up for sport, study, or social life. Age-appropriate. What might take half an hour or more to prepare, he gobbles up in ten minutes, tops.

It's into the home stretch now—another transitional time that a mother can accept with grace and good humor, or ignore, or fight at her peril. What sometimes feels like a relentless task—this constant, daily cooking for a child—will soon be over. Then what?

I'm bracing myself for that first night, when there is no hungry son to feed. It's unsettling, because family meals matter to me. After my divorce, my angry boy would sometimes say, "Two people don't make a family." He was hurting. That first night in our new place a thoughtful gal pal delivered Cheese Board pizza. It hit the spot at our unfamiliar, smaller, dining room table. A family ritual had begun.

As a single parent who shares, I've had years of practice with the temporarily empty nest. There's the transition night when the kid is at his dad's and I'm free to eat whatever takes my fancy. Anchovies and broccoli rabe. Scrambled eggs. A glass of wine with cheese and crackers. A glass of wine, period. Nothing at all.

When the boy returns, we get back into our regular rhythms. He's a granola or porridge person for breakfast. On lazy weekends and late-Monday-start school days, it's waffles or pancakes. He's not much of a sandwich man, but willingly takes dinner leftovers for lunch. Rice and beans. Tofu stir-fry. Big salads loaded with cheese, nuts, and seasonal produce. Other kids, he tells me, think his lunches are odd. Then they eat some and say it tastes so good.

He's always been particular about the foods he eats. I was the same, although I grew up with five siblings, so I had much less input about dinner (read: none). My Mum, a terrific cook, would want a night off from the stove. Sometimes we'd have Australian Chinese takeaway, a genre all its own. Or McDonald's. On the burger nights, I'd boil an egg. I decided in my late teens to become a vegetarian. I've skipped red meat for most of the past thirty years, though I guess technically I'm a pescetarian, who lapses in her line of work every once in a while.

My son is a devout vegetarian by choice: He's never eaten meat. He's now in a strident teenage phase. He's horrified if I tell him I tasted lamb's tongue for a story, even though he's delighted that his Mum writes about food, and enjoys the sweet and savory treats that frequently find their way onto our table, and into his belly, as a result of that gig.

I have regrets about my own limitations in the kitchen and what I haven't given him growing up. I'm not a baker. My kid won't miss his Mum's cakes and cookies when he goes off to college, though we do laugh about my attempts (he dubbed one "lumps of goodness"). Given my line of work, there's some shame in having not yet taught him how to cook. He should have better knife skills. He doesn't know how to make stock. I'm not even certain he can peel the boiled eggs he likes (seven minutes, no gray). I've let him off the hook in the cooking department. I've tried, and failed, at different points to introduce a night a week when he cooks for us both. Maybe this summer.

There's an inherent tension as you nudge a child towards independence, with the expectation that he learn to fend for himself in the kitchen and elsewhere, especially when food is an essential way many parents express love. Guilty as charged.

After a recent evening visit to the ER—a big gash over his eye, courtesy of a baseball—I knew when we got home long past dinnertime that he'd want noodles, with just a faint dusting of Parmigiano-Reggiano, and a swig of good extra-virgin olive oil or a chunk of creamy butter. Comfort food after crisis.

His world and his palate are expanding. On a recent trip to Maui, he was thrilled to taste freshly picked pineapples, coconuts, and taro. He enjoyed street food, hole-in-the-wall joints, fancy-pants restaurants. When we returned from the trip and I asked him what he wanted for dinner he said: "Home food." I knew exactly what he meant.

This summer, he'll head to Madrid for a month. The child who never wanted to go to sleepaway camp—because, why, and what would you eat?—is now eager to fly halfway around the world to live with a family he's never met, for an adventure on a continent he's never been to, to practice a language he'd like to master. I see a lot of flan in his near future.

I did something similar, on a much smaller scale, at the same age. A gaggle of schoolgirls from Sydney on a weeklong French-class excursion to the Pacific island nation New Caledonia. I wasn't even taking French, but they needed to boost the numbers. We landed in Nouméa, promptly met the "locals,"—including a cadre of twentysomethings of French descent—and were educated in the language of pain au chocolat, red wine, eating late, and sex. Scandalous by today's sheltered school-trip-abroad standards. It was my first exposure to anything vaguely European, and it was delicious.

My teen will be away for his seventeenth birthday. I'll make him whatever he wants on his last night at home and whatever he's craving on his first night back. Since he's a California boy at heart, produce will figure prominently. But maybe he'll come home with a new recipe repertoire and ask for something he's discovered in his travels.

My Mum died just days ago—I found out as I was writing this piece. Not totally unexpected, but also a complete shock. I've been struggling to complete the most routine tasks ever since. I don't remember the last time she cooked for me, or even exactly the last time we ate a meal together. But I do remember preparing a plate of food for her and my father to share in the hospital last Christmas. I'd made curried eggs, an homage to my Mum, who always made them on the holidays. Hers were so creamy, with just the right amount of spice. Mine weren't nearly as good but she ate them hungrily, nonetheless.

That's the thing about last suppers. You don't always know when you're having one.

Infrequent Potatoes

By Elissa Altman

From *Poor Man's Feast*

Family connections can cut both ways, as blogger/author Elissa Altman knows all too well. Her memoir *Poor Man's Feast* delves into many layers of it; her upcoming book *Treyf: A Story of Family, Food, and the Forbidden* digs even deeper. Like a family scrapbook, this essay gives us snapshots of her growing up, haunted by her mother's own food issues.

I was a particularly tiny baby; my mother didn't know that she was pregnant for six months (being unable to get her antique garnet ring off was a clue; she went to the doctor at her teenage niece's suggestion) and the diagnosis sent her into a tailspin. In a shaky picture of my parents taken by my grandmother in Carl Schurz Park, the evidence is barely noticeable: there is my mother, the East River over her shoulder and Queens behind her in the distance, her wrists so slender and lithe even in her ninth month that her charm bracelet, heavy as Marley's chain, would slide off her hand until she had a few links removed. There I am, the incontrovertible affirmation of her pregnancy, and nothing more than a minuscule bump under her pink and white cotton blouse. My mother carried me to term, almost to the day; I weighed four pounds at birth which, for scale, is more or less the size of an average supermarket chicken.

The words my mother uses to describe me as an infant: *spindly, delicate, tiny, petite, exquisite, dainty, fine-boned, wispy*. Not being one to nurse—*I would have wound up with a chest like your grandmother's*, she says—she fed me tiny amounts of formula, botching the instructions given to her by my first pediatrician at New York Hospital. I screamed all day and all night for my first three months, until our next door neighbor in Yorkville, a gorgeous German woman with a face like Marlene Dietrich, told my mother that I was probably hungry; she instructed her to fill my bottle with thinned-out oatmeal, cut an X in the nipple, and let me eat. She did, and at last, I stopped crying. I also ballooned up like a scaled-down version of The Michelin Man.

Eventually, the oatmeal weight fell off me: like most middle class American children of the Sixties and Seventies, I was fed a regular diet of meat, chicken, fish, lamb, and, because I was almost always anemic, beef liver, which looks surprisingly like beef liver. I shuddered at its jiggling, squidgy presence; my grandmother, who cooked most of our meals, broiled it until it took on the consistency of a stiff brown sponge, and my mother served it to me on our heavy burnt umber earthenware next to two flaccid spears of canned asparagus; there was no bread at our kitchen table, no rice, no pasta, and infrequent potatoes. My mother and I drank Tab by the bucketful, going through a six pack every two days. By the time I was four, I had become an unwitting adherent to something resembling The Atkins Diet; I was so skinny that my mother shook me into my school leotards like a pillow into a pillowcase. When I went into first grade, I carried damp tuna sandwiches made on Diet White bread, which disintegrated into a dense brick of bleached mush that wrapped itself around my red plaid thermos by the time I arrived at school.

As I wrote in *Poor Man's Feast,* when my mother went off to have her hair done every Saturday, my father—not someone I would call corpulent, but certainly not thin—secreted me away for fancy lunches that were as enlightening as they were forbidden: I learned what happens when you apply a coating of egg and flour to trout, saute it in hot butter and bathe it in wine and lemon juice. I learned what happens when you slice potatoes to a filmy thinness, layer them in a shallow copper dish, and blanket them in cream. I learned what happens when you roll a crepe around warm apricot preserves and dust it with confectioner's sugar and chopped hazelnuts. And I learned to keep my mouth shut once I got home, because food was the enemy of the body.

My mother went back to work when I was eleven; my grandmother stepped in after school and fed me regular grilled cheese and bacon sandwiches, potato latkes, pizza, and, because she loved him, Arthur Treacher's fish and chips. All that food fueled my raging tennis addiction; I played it every day, for hours. My mother never noticed what I was eating because my grandmother chose not to tell her, but also because all that tennis turned my skin and bones into solid muscle. I became a swimmer and my shoulders broadened; I hit puberty and the chest that kept my mother from nursing me as an infant was suddenly mine. My mother's desperate, hysterical need for thinness, achieved by starving her teenage self in order to be the model and television singer she eventually became, was a blip on my genetic screen. My body rebelled in the most profound of ways: I was no longer skinny. As a teenager, I began to resemble almost every woman on my father's side of the family: thick-boned, solid, muscular, and zaftig enough to acquaint me with the bitter flavor of self-consciousness.

"You'll lose that chest if you drop some weight," my mother said when I started college, as though *That Chest* was a disembodied entity unto itself, with a mind and government all its own, like Texas. At school, the freshman fifteen worked the other way for me: with everyone gorging themselves on pizza and East West lasagna at the cafeteria, I ate nothing but taco-flavored Doritos and Diet Coke in my dorm room, but only when my roommate wasn't around. I came home that October, fifteen pounds lighter.

My mother was confused and irate a few years later, when I went to work for Dean & Deluca, and attended cooking school at night: I *wanted* food in my life. I wanted to *understand* sustenance, and to find that almost spiritual connection that comes from feeding your *self*, and others, thoughtfully and well. I wanted to re-create a family table of goodness and peace, where food was not the devil, and it didn't have to be hidden.

My body responded to the stress of her furious consternation with uncanny irony: surrounded as I was by masses of food every day and night, the pounds fell off me without my even trying to lose them. My nails went brittle and my hair thinned, and then fell out. My thyroid was off kilter and my heart rhythm wonky and I passed out twice—once in the walk-in, once on the loading dock while signing for a Sid Wainer delivery—but man, did my body look *great*: my fat jeans were a size two, my everyday pair, a zero.

"Okay," she said, as though I was competitively orchestrating my weight loss, "you win. You can stop now."

Over the years, my body has settled like a house; the *Title Nine* catalog invariably arrives when I'm feeling sluggish and thick. My knees and hips creak, and I have a bottle of Aleve in every bag. No matter what—no matter how many steps I take, no matter how dedicated to my FitBit I am, no matter how much yoga I do, no matter how often I go to the gym, no matter how much I cut out wine or sugar or infrequent potatoes—my weight travels along a five pound continuum: sometimes I'm up, sometimes I'm down. Like my mother when she was pregnant, I gauge change by how tight my rings are. On the days when I can't get them off, I don't go to see her; I don't tell her why.

Recently, she came to stay for Passover and Easter; I saved my beloved matzo brei—the crack cocaine of my people, which I make once a year—for the breakfast after our seder. That morning, we sat at my dining room table while she drank a cup of hot water and watched me lift my fork to my mouth; she glared violently at it, and me, like we were the devil incarnate. I pushed myself away from the table and took my plate into the kitchen; I stood at the sink and ate with my back to her, hidden from view.

Finding Home at Taco Bell

By John DeVore

From Eater.com

Satirist/critic/humorist John DeVore is managing editor of
Team Coco, the website for Conan O'Brien's late-night talk show.
Along the way, he's done a bunch of other stuff. (So Google him,
already) But he really isn't kidding when he says that Taco Bell
defines his mixed-up cultural heritage.

T aco Bell is the best Mexican food I ever ate. I will say this to your
face over a plate of enchiladas suiza. You will shake your head at
such transparent provocation. What a shocking thing to say at a restaurant that has the best tacos in New York City!

I won't even correct that assertion. There is no such thing as "the
best tacos in New York City." There are only two kinds of tacos in New
York City: adequate, and whatever is a little better than adequate. Unless we're talking Taco Bell. Which I will talk about, at length, even if
you haven't asked a question that has anything to do with Taco Bell.

Yes, fast food is unhealthy. It preys on the poor by offering
scientifically-engineered food products that are devoid of nutritional
value, but are richly emotionally satisfying. These products are intensely
tasty, and most of all, cheap. Why spend five bucks on groceries? What
can you get for five bucks at a grocery store anyway? A stalk of broccoli
and a jar of mayo? Since we're at dinner, and I'm busy proselytizing, I'm
not currently able to fact-check the following statement, but I'm pretty
sure you can buy ten tacos for one dollar.

Taco Bell tacos are crunchy, crispy, meaty sailboats of spicy chemical flavor. The Taco Bell Cool Ranch Doritos taco shell is the most important invention of this century. But we've come this far, and you're halfway through your plate of organic, locally-sourced, *New York Magazine*–celebrated Mexican tube casserole, so we have time to talk about Taco Bell. I'll order more chips and salsa. Now I'm going to hold up my fingers and wiggle them. This will signify we're flashing backwards in time.

The first meal I ate in New York City was a corned beef sandwich at a diner. When it was unceremoniously plopped down in front of me, I said to the waitress, "Thank you, ma'am."

I had just gotten off the plane from Texas. I was polite because good manners are the best way not to get shot in Texas. Politeness was nearly beaten into me. The waitress looked at me with dead eyes and said, "What do I look like, your fucking mother?"

Then she stormed away, kicked open the kitchen door, and I'm pretty sure beat up the chef just because. *What a colorful New York character*, I thought. *She is terrifying and I am weak*, my thoughts continued. So that's why I gave her a fifty percent tip. It was an expensive lunch.

Over the next few weeks I experienced New York cuisine. I would call my mother back in Texas from filthy payphones and tell her about all the delicious foods I was eating: dim sum, oysters, meatballs. Do you remember what it was like talking to someone on a pay phone? They always sounded so far away. As if one of you were standing at the bottom of a deep dark hole. There was a time when New York's only social network was a series of coin-fed boxes on the street connected by miles and miles of wires.

I'd end every conversation with my mother enthusiastically. I was going to gorge on kielbasa and pierogies! A job interview at a prestigious magazine company was coming up! It sure was a good idea to move to a city that didn't really want me there!

None of these things were true. Parents lie to their children about the cruelties of the world, and children grow up to return the favor to their parents.

This was the mid-nineties, a time when New York still went out of its way to make twenty-three-year-olds cry in public. I lived in an SRO and shared a bathroom with a ghost that left great gobs of green phlegm in the sink. I wasn't eating oysters; I was eating foods that didn't cost more than a dollar. Pizza slices, hot dogs, knishes.

My mother would finish each call saying, "Be safe, *mijo*." As a kid, I used to be so embarrassed when she'd call me "mijo" in front of my friends. It was bad enough that she looked different than me, but she also spoke in another language, a weird one.

As the weeks grew colder, I found myself blowing warmth into my hands like a forgettable Charles Dickens character. My work skills qualified me to answer phones or enter data into glowing green computer screens.

Then I moved to Queens. SROs are inexpensive places to die slowly, but moving to Queens is still cheaper. Queens is where America walks the talk. In school, we were taught that America is a country of immigrants. It's a nice idea, especially in comfortable suburbs where the lawns are mowed by workers who immigrate into the neighborhood at the crack of dawn and immigrate somewhere else by the time you get back from work.

Queens is an entire country of immigrants in 178 square miles. Hello, you're from Greece? Morocco? Bangladesh? Croatia? Senegal? I grew up in Virginia, but my family lives in Texas now. I guess I just emigrated from Texas to Queens!

In Queens, I found a small apartment with a toilet under a staircase buried deep in the borough. My neighbors were a large family of Mexicans. That large family probably would have liked an extra room to spread out. Which is probably why they always seemed to really, really hate me.

My mother spent years trying to get me to learn Spanish, but I never wanted to take the time. Besides, who was I going to speak Spanish with in Virginia? To most Virginians in the 1980s, Mexicans were just the guys who Clint Eastwood shot in the movies. If I had learned Spanish I could have turned to this family and said "My good friends, stop hating me. I am lonely and hungry. Also, I am half-Mexican!" Then we'd fiesta?

Those were dark, cold days. Some people called those days "winter," but not me. My phone calls home became more infrequent. I couldn't keep up the cheer. Every young person's mettle is tested when you move to New York. There were times I thought I should just pack up and die, which was just my way of saying move back to Texas.

Then, one weekend, instead of playing the game "Sleep All Day Because Sleeping Is Free," I went walking through the streets looking for somewhere to spend three dollars. I was hoping to find a street-meat cart that served something more than charred gristle on a stick.

And that's when I saw the most marvelous sight. Glowing! In the distance! Right there on Steinway Avenue! It was something I had never seen before. A fast food restaurant that combined two famous brands into one mighty, delicious Frankenstein's monster of empty calories. I beheld a restaurant that was, simultaneously, a Taco Bell and a Kentucky Fried Chicken. This didn't exist in Texas. But here, in New York City, these two franchises were turned into a two-headed snack shack.

Suddenly, I knew that everything was going to work out. I was home.

In elementary school, I had a stand-up routine I'd perform on the playground for my white friends. I'd tell them that I was what you'd get if you crossed a redneck with a wetback: a wetneck! Pause for laughter. My mom is Mexican-American, you see. My dad is a white guy. Which means when I grow up, I'll drive a truck and steal my own hubcaps. You know why Mexicans don't barbecue? Because the beans fall through the grill.

This was how I survived, because racism is easy. That's why it's so evil. Judging other people on the color of their skin is, literally, the least the human brain can do. Racism is the opposite of imagination.

I made fun of myself in order to keep my white friends laughing, because sometimes all laughter does is reinforce tribal integrity. I wanted to be part of their tribe, because my tribe—half-breeds—was a small one at my school. We numbered uno. And we were secret.

After all, I was white. My brothers were darker, like my mother. But me? I looked like a chubby little butterball. I was a spy under deep cover. No one suspected that I was different. Until they met my mom. My funny, feisty mom who loves books and paintings and movies and her family. She would passionately defend me when my teachers would question why I drew nothing but monsters. "He's an artist," she'd say.

During one of my birthday parties, to which I invited my friends from elementary school, I was asked who that brown lady serving cake was. I said she was my maid.

My mom and I were always followed by floorwalkers at department stores. Once she spoke up when a man cut in a grocery store line, and a racial epithet was muttered. When I got older, some people assumed I was the younger boyfriend of a foreign woman, not her son.

Many years later, when I was an adult, I would admit my birthday party betrayal to my mother. She laughed at my confession. She had always known I was ashamed of her.

I remember asking my dad once if I was white, and he told me I was one half him, and one half my mother. Simple. Then for dinner, mom made huevos rancheros. That was one of her quick dinners. The next night we probably had eggs again, only this time with biscuits and gravy. She was a good family cook. Nothing fancy. Big portions.

My dad was a Depression-era kid from the South, so he ate chicken wings like they were going to flap away from his mouth at any moment. He had terrible taste in food, but that's because when you grow up hungry, you'll happily eat food that tastes terrible.

My mother dutifully learned the Dixie dishes of his childhood, including exotic fare like spaghetti. Once upon a time, I think, spaghetti must have been an alien cuisine in lush, banjo-loving places like Louisiana. But what does a Latina from El Paso in the sixties know of such things? So with a little sleuth work, she invented DeVore Spaghetti. DeVore Spaghetti features a spicy salsa broth, boiled meatballs, and cheddar cheese. It is delicious because it tastes like everyone is home for dinner and we're all silly and happy.

She would also make the food of her own childhood. Flautas, soup studded with tiny *albondigas*, quesadillas. I loved a simple dessert that consisted of a tortilla fried in oil, then dusted with cinnamon and a drizzle of maple syrup. Her tamales were—they are—perfect. My favorite meal on Earth is my mom's chiles rellenos. A chile pepper stuffed with cheese is what a poor family makes when they can't afford meat because the chile flesh becomes tender, like a slow-cooked cut of beef.

Mom wouldn't always eat my dad's beloved foods; she hated the fried gizzards he'd beg her to make. But she loved my old man dearly, and never complained when he'd ask her to make beef tongue. I'd stare at that slab of meat and imagine a field of tongueless cows trying to moo.

She was also the kind of mother who never ate with her family. She was a tornado of knives and skillets and wooden spoons. But once the food was served, she just kicked back with a glass of milk. Sometimes she'd sit with us. If we were at a restaurant, she'd order something modest. She didn't adore food the way my dad did, and not because she didn't also come from humble beginnings; she was raised on the Texas border by a father whose rifle was used to shoot at wild dogs.

But she did love Taco Bell. A summer break treat was a quick trip to Taco Bell for tacos and burritos and a styrofoam cup of pinto beans, salsa, and cheese. When my mom was a kid, fast food was the dream. Imagine—literally anyone could afford to eat out! And not just boring and bland diner food, but high-tech food that was exploding with rainbows of taste-bud melting mystery powders! Food that you could eat not just at a table but in your car, the chariot of the future.

Taco Bell was easy, and inexpensive, and it was shamelessly Mexican. Emphasis on "shameless": its garish facsimile of an entire nation's culture was seemingly dreamed up by the type of white person who gets drunk on tequila and wears a sombrero for comedic effect. It was still Mexican, though. In fact, it was both Mexican and American. All under one greasy roof.

Go ahead and lecture on what true Mexican food is. My mom would probably just roll her eyes at you.

But even though the restaurant's cartoonish decor bordered on offensive, it was still a temple to a people and a cuisine that America couldn't ignore. Taco Bells were everywhere. In every strip mall. Off every highway exit. Even the racists, the immigrant-haters, the people who'd laugh at my elementary-school stand-up comedy routine would run for the border.

You can laugh or sneer at Taco Bell. Shake your head at its high fat and salt content. Go ahead and lecture on what true Mexican food is. My mom would probably just roll her eyes at you, and take a broken yellow shard of crispy taco shell and use it to scoop up the pintos, cheese, and salsa.

I stood before that Taco Bell–KFC hybrid in Queens and felt like I had come home. I went inside and ordered biscuits and a taco for three dollars, and filled my stomach. Finally, I thought to myself, a restaurant that represented my upbringing. My heritage. Maybe I wasn't the only person in Queens who silently ate at a Taco Bell–KFC and remembered parents who lived so far, far away.

We are now back in the present. So here we are, you and me, eating enchiladas at this restaurant. I think it's a little easier to be biracial today. I hope it is. I still can't believe the President of the United States knows what it's like to have a mother who looks different.

Taco Bell is still the best Mexican food I've ever eaten. Because when I eat it, I'm sitting with my mom, and her hair isn't gray, and my father's brutal death from cancer is so many years away, and she is so beautiful and I am so young and safe.

Just one bite of a seven layer burrito—not six, not five, but seven unbelievable layers of goop—and we're laughing because I won't stop saying "Yo Quiero Taco Bell," and she wipes guacamole off my face and says, "Oh, *mijo*."

The One Ingredient That Has Sustained Me During Bouts of Leukemia

By Jim Shahin

From the *Washington Post*

While *Washington Post** readers know him as the barbecue guru behind the column Smoke Signals, Jim Shahin has had a long and prolific career as a writer, editor, and occasional journalism professor. For years, though, he has waged a private battle in which food has played an entirely different role.

T he night before I began my first clinical trial for leukemia, my then-girlfriend Jessica and I argued about a hoagie.

"You know you can't eat that," she said. Clutching the classic Philly Italian cold-cut sandwich in my hands, I looked at her, uncomprehending. "You can't leave meat and vegetables under the Texas sun all day," she continued. "It's a salmonella hothouse."

We had just returned to the Houston home of a close friend, where we had been staying during the run-up to the trial at MD Anderson Cancer Center. We were there because my leukemia hadn't responded to the initial treatment and because my oncologist in Austin, where I lived, had said something alarming: "We may have to put you on a bland diet."

As the saying goes, sometimes the cure is worse than the disease.

When I told my oncologist about my interest in the interferon trial, he replied, "They just do a bunch of voodoo down there."

Voodoo? Beats a bland diet any day.

We got to Houston within a week. The following days were a blur: CAT scan, blood work, EKG, bone marrow biopsy, forms—lots of forms. And then came the night before the trial.

It was November. In Texas, that month can be hot, and this one was. The hoagie had been sitting all day in FedEx packaging on the stoop of my friend's house.

We didn't know it was a hoagie until we got inside and opened the box. This was not just any hoagie. It was a hoagie from my childhood shop, the Drexel House, in suburban Philadelphia, sent as a good-luck gesture by my brother, Ric.

I held the sandwich in my hands and gazed upon its beauty: the creamy tan long roll, crisp outside and squishy inside, encapsulating a perfection of ham, salami, hot capicola, sliced tomatoes, onions and lettuce, all sprinkled with salt and oregano and drizzled with olive oil and wine vinegar.

"It was sent with love," I told Jessica. "Nothing sent with love can harm you."

It can, though, emit a sour odor. I took a bite anyway. Then another. And another. The flavor was slightly . . . off. Yet each bite conjured, like Proust's madeleine, a blur of childhood memories. There was my father, with his wavy black hair and crooked smile, who would die of cancer at 43, when I was 17. My mother, young and beautiful, a 1950s housewife, in her apron at the stove of our tiny kitchen. Box hockey at my elementary school. Pinball at the pizza joint. Baseball in the back yard. The girl in fourth grade who swung her leg back and forth, flipping her shoe on and off her foot.

This was some hoagie.

I ate every bite, honoring the spirit in which it had been sent. The slight pang in my belly would pass, right? Wrong. Later, in bed, I was awakened by a horrible, sour rumbling in my gut. I raced to the bathroom, where I more or less stayed the rest of the night, throwing up.

The next day, I began the interferon treatments. I plunged a small vial of the protein subcutaneously into my upper thigh, an act I would repeat three days a week for months. I suffered no side effects. No head-aches. No fever. No nausea.

I credited the hoagie, but Jessica was skeptical. "You got lucky," she said.

Rallying with Food

That was 1985, and things since then have mostly gone well. My spleen was removed, but I haven't missed it. I've been in and out of remission, but mostly in.

The notion of hoagie as inoculation has stayed with me. Whether science would agree, I can't say. But there exists mystery and faith in this life, unquantifiable. Call it the placebo effect, if you like. I'd say it's out of reach of Big Data, but in fact the phenomenon has been backed up by plenty of research.

I don't know if anyone has researched the merits of believing in a hoagie, but believing in the power of love communicated through the offering of food strikes me as not as crazy as it sounds. I'm not talking about superfoods, like blueberries. Nor do I dispute a connection be-tween diet and disease.

I'm talking about the spirit with which a food is offered and received and the psychic healing it provides, like a jolt of unseen electrical cur-rent. Shortly after that first bout with leukemia, a friend suggested I go on a highly specific diet aimed, she said, at helping boost the immune system. I replied that, while I appreciated what she was suggesting, I was considering writing a book called "A Barbecue Way to Health."

I was joking. A little.

The last time I battled what I came to call Big Leuk was 1998. That episode was tough. I had moved on from interferon to chemo, and I reacted with uncontrollable chills, dry heaves and a high fever. My head lolled on my shoulders like a baby's, while Jessica—now my wife—rushed me to the hospital during a tornado. Emergency room patients were moved away from the windows, for fear the glass would shatter. Because of my low blood counts and susceptibility to infection, I was quarantined in a room under a heavy, thick "chilling blanket" intended to bring the fever down. The last thing I wanted was food. Which was good, because it was among the last things I could have.

When the worst passed, I regained an appetite. And the first thing my friends did was the first thing they should have done: rallied with food. I came across a notepad from that time. In it was a message from a longtime close friend: "Robb wants to bring you some chicken soup, he will drop it off this eve. Call me + give me a job!!" The job I gave her was to make one of her macrobiotic dishes. Not because I regarded the grain-and-vegetable-oriented diet medicinal but because she was good at making those dishes, and I wanted to eat whatever she wanted to make.

This has remained central to the way I have viewed food, in sickness and in health: It is a sharing of love.

This past January, during a routine visit, my doctor discovered I had fallen out of remission again.

After the diagnosis was confirmed, the first thing I did was go back to the childhood well, so to speak, and a variant of my brother's kindness. On my way home from the hematologist's office, I beelined to Taylor Gourmet and ordered a cheesesteak.

I've ordered countless cheesesteaks over the years: in Philly, mostly, but also in the District and elsewhere. I love them so much, in fact, that it was Taylor's 2008 opening that first drew my attention to the H Street NE neighborhood, where Jessica and I ended up buying a house.

The cheesesteak on this morning struck me as among the best ever. The roll was overstuffed with flavorful, tender, well-seasoned meat, gooey with melted American cheese. (Taylor doesn't offer Cheez Whiz, or I would have ordered it. I like the way its silken texture seeps into the very membranes of the grilled meat.)

It was 11 a.m., and no one else was in the place. I had arrived 20 minutes earlier and waited in my parked car until Taylor opened. A guy believes what he believes, know what I mean?

The problem was, I could barely eat the thing. I was feverish. Achy. Deeply fatigued. Not just not hungry, but frankly revolted by the idea of eating. I nibbled, hoping to tap into the magic of restorative nostalgia.

The magic barely flickered. And over the next few days, I uncharacteristically picked at my food, forcing a couple of spoons of breakfast granola and yogurt into my system just to eat something, neglecting lunch altogether, and scarcely touching dinner.

Dispirited and weak, I returned to the clinic for a blood transfusion.

After I returned home, my temperature rose into the low 100s, which sometimes happens immediately afterward. Through the afternoon and evening, Jessica tended to me with Advil and cold compresses, but my temperature continued to go up. My hematologist had instructed me to return to the ER if my temperature hit 100.5.

Around 5:30 that evening, a close friend named Lou stopped by with an enormous pot of homemade beef stew. "Wish I felt up to eating it," I told Jessica after he left.

My temperature hit 102, and Jessica called the doctor, who said I had to go to the hospital. "If I can bring the temperature down within the next hour," I pleaded, "can I stay home?" I could.

I furiously drank ice water and continued the compresses. Jessica brought me a bowl of stew and insisted I eat something. I glowered at it, but to appease her, I took a spoonful. "Wow," I said. "Wow. That is amazing."

The aroma went from off-putting to intoxicating. I had another bite, then another. Meanwhile, my temperature gradually declined. Within the hour, it was at 98.7. "That," I proclaimed, "is a magical stew." I had it for breakfast the next morning, and again for lunch.

Meanwhile, as word was getting out about my situation, friends and relatives sprang into action. Melissa and Aileen, colleagues at Syracuse University, where I teach journalism, had a pastrami sandwich from Katz's Deli in New York shipped to me. My close friends Tim and Carrie dropped by with an enormous cache of groceries that included Bolognese sauce, rustic bread, and bone broth from Red Apron. My cousin Kathy and her husband, Yoram, brought a dozen bagels with all the fixin's. Longtime bestie Marion, who had been through this with me before, brought barbecue from Baltimore, where she lives. For his part, my brother Ric eschewed the hoagie idea but stayed true to our sentimental hearts, having three loaves of Italian bread shipped from DiCamillo Bakery in Niagara Falls, where our father grew up.

Our son, Sam, who lives in New Orleans, lifted my spirits with a surprise visit. He lifted them even higher by making his spicy tomato-based cabbage soup, a dish I find addictive in the most healthful sort of way.

On a brutally cold day, a homemade chocolate babka showed up on my porch. It was from a colleague. Having eaten only a couple of babkas in my time, I am no expert on the Jewish pastry immortalized in a

Seinfeld skit. This one, though, was larger than any I had ever encountered, its sheer bulk worth a riff on a sequel episode.

I sliced off a hunk and dug in. I savored every bite because it was good, yes, but more so because the baker had made me something from her heritage, which, to me, was kind of like her hoagie.

At the time, I was due for another blood transfusion, and would get one in two days. Eventually—this month, in fact—I am scheduled to participate in a clinical trial at the National Institutes of Health in Bethesda.

Until then, I know in my blood that, whether it's handmade or purchased, hand-delivered or shipped, beef stew or babka, an offering of food rejuvenates the psyche and, in turn, the body.

Science calls it the placebo effect. I call it hoagie voodoo. And I thank my lucky stars that it exists.

Yeast Are Never Depressed

By David Leite

From Leite's Culinaria

Founder and editor-in-chief of this award-winning
gastronomical website, David Leite is also the author of the
cookbook *The New Portuguese Table.* Though he's known for the
humorous spin he puts on food writing, Leite is now writing a
book about his struggles with another, darker side.

I am depressed.

I can't choke it down any longer. Like a fat birthday boy demanding the largest chunk of cake by moving his hands farther and farther
apart, my depression has eyed me, everyday wanting a bigger and bigger
piece. This morning it took all of me.

Maybe I'm still sick with the flu, I think when I awake. It's possible.
I'd been pummeled for more than twelve days with it. That could be
the reason. I consider calling my assistant, Annie, and telling her not
to come to work. Annie is cheerful. Sometimes relentlessly cheerful. I
want to murder relentlessly cheerful people when I'm depressed. But I
flutter the idea out of my mind. Isolation is the worst thing, I've learned
from a lifetime of experience. Then I remember the bread dough that
has been rising on my counter for almost twenty hours. I'm happy until
I walk to the bathroom and forget I'm happy.

A walk. I will take a walk. And at the unholy hour of eight in the
morning, I am outside, walking down the gentle slope of our road. I
smell wet: damp leaves, sweet; soaked bark, earthy and dark. Crows
caw and warn the others of my approach. My stomach clutches. When

I'm depressed, everyday pleasures cause me such angst and guilt. I'm reminded that I'm constitutionally unable to be buoyed—no matter how momentarily—by something outside of myself. I prefer dark, obliterating skies, or better yet, night; the cold shoulder of winter; lashing storms, like yesterday's downpours—anything that a normal person would consider depressing because I find refuge in them. Unlike an animal that changes its appearance to blend into its surroundings, I am camouflaged by bleak, gloomy, and untoward surroundings, and I don't have to explain myself to others. Doesn't everyone get down on rainy days and Mondays? They even wrote a song about that.

Depression is cunning, I think, watching the floodwaters gush over the falls down at the bottom of the hill. It first figure-eights between my feet like a cat trying to trip me up. I can usually outmaneuver it—a few quick steps and I fox-trot out of the way. But then the seduction begins. It slithers up, licking my calves, the insides of my thighs. For the past several days, I've felt it trying to lace its fingers between mine, wanting to pull me to it so we can waltz. Me listless, feet dragging while it, haughty and victorious, sweeps us through the rooms. When this happens, The One usually steps back, watching from a distance. He knows I will, in one vicious swipe, attack him. Twenty-two years of trial and error has shown him that only when I reach out should he comfort me. And I like to call him to me when I'm sitting down. He wraps his arms around me and strokes and kisses my head. The thrum of his voice deep in his chest soothes. At these times, I need to feel smaller-than, to feel someone bigger in whom I hold the childlike hope that he can make it all go away. When I am well, I will again tower over him, but not before this leaves.

Back from my walk, I turn on the oven and inspect the bread dough. The top is a riot of bubbles, like winking eyes. Although I'm a baker of sweets, I turn to bread when I'm down. Single-cell microscopic fungi springing to life, not just surviving but thriving, give me hope. For each loaf, they have the equivalent of a frat-house kegger, gorging themselves then farting, belching, and gorging some more. I think how apt that "yeast" rhymes with "feast," for that's what they do, that's their sole job. To feast.

"Yeast are never depressed, I bet," I say to no one. I fold the dough over itself several times, place it on a floured towel, and cover it. I sit watching, knowing I will grow too distracted to notice it rising. It will take more than two hours to double in size, but I hope some of the party atmosphere will rub off on me.

I write. I clean. I sigh deeply. I miss my mania. I want somehow to ignite those fireworks that have sparked and exploded in me, whispering, "You can do anything," making plans for me that I will never keep. I want to sing; singing is always a sign I feel good. But no song comes. Just two lines from *Hedwig and the Angry Inch:* "I put on some make-up, I turn on the eight-track . . . " loop through my head. I try to divine meaning in it, but there isn't any, just some detritus left over from a Times Talk.

After the dough has risen, I flip it into the searing-hot Le Creuset pot, and it sticks to the dish towel. I try to shake it off, but the clump hangs above the pot, pendulous. "This dough is a piece of shit!" I yell, which expands to include *this recipe is a piece of shit,* and inevitably bleeds into *I am a piece of shit.* I am a screw-up. I claw the dough from the towel, throw it into the pot, and slide it into to the oven. Any joy I had derived from baking the loaf is gone. It will be a mess, look freakish, and I will have failed. I will feel no modicum of accomplishment, which can, sometimes, lift me, just for a moment, when nothing else will.

Pulling the loaf from the pot 45 minutes later, I marvel, *yeast is amazingly forgiving.* The loaf is not even misshapen, and it's richly brown, with pockmarks and desert-like cracks ripping through its surface. That's why I turn to bread when depressed, I believe: It bears no grudge. Puff pastry, brioche, and *pate à choux* are punitive doughs. But this ordinary bread, with its punch-drunk yeast, can cope with being cursed at and mangled. Bread is the dough of the depressed, the worried, the anxious, the burdened.

I am still depressed, but at least I now have the carbs. I cut myself a slice.

Mexico in Three Regrets

By John Birdsall

From Chow.com

In this impressionistic travel piece, John Birdsall—once a cook, now a food writer based in Oakland, California—repeatedly visits Mexico on vacation and keeps on making the same classic tourist mistake. Sometimes off the beaten path really is where you want to go.

Cancun 1997

We're on our honeymoon. Perry and I got married last month at an art gallery in Chicago; we had a Southeast Asian theme and served lemongrass Kamikazes and Singhas and everyone got drunk. Perry said, "Let's go to Mexico." Neither of us had ever been. We bought the all-inclusive plan at Caribbean Village, maybe the homeliest hotel on Boulevard Kukulkan, Cancun's *zona gringo*. It's cheap. There's a swim-up bar and a cluster of country boys with the jug-eared look of U.S. military.

The swim-up bartender has a nametag: *Eloy*. Eloy sets up the drinks in plastic cups that hold a lot of ice (they say the water goes through some big filter they bought for the tourists so nobody gets sick). You'd need to drink a lot of Eloy's margaritas to get drunk, maybe more than you could take (Perry says they're watering down the booze). The country boys are amazed, they're chugging. I want to chug but feel bad bothering Eloy so I pace it. I think I'm starting to feel a little wasted, then I don't—it's like the tequila's on a Slip 'N Slide that goes dry near the end, just before the alcohol can go skimming into my brain.

That night Perry and I take the hotel shuttle as far as it goes, to the very end of Boulevard Kukulkan. We walk the rest of the way into Cancun City where the hotel workers live, including, probably, Eloy. I smell the charcoal grills of the taco vendors on the street, the savage scent of tallowy beef grilling over *carbon*, of corn masa blistering on portable comals in the darkness. I'm afraid to eat (I don't want to get sick). We end up at Señor Frog's, where I lie back in a dentist's chair as a girl pours tequila in my mouth. Hey! I'm buzzed! But the ghost smell of meat on charcoal—that dogs me like a hangover.

Puerto Vallarta 2001

Perry finds this gay guesthouse (a guy named Craig owns it—he's from San Francisco). It's in the hills above town, beyond where the paved road ends, a beautiful old adobe casa with *cupulas* and a pool, views, and a monkey raiding the mango tree that hangs over the terrace. It's off-season and we're the only ones here besides Craig, who's always on his laptop. We take a swim.

Craig comes asking if we want mango margaritas; we feel like we have to say yes. Meanwhile I'm thinking *How much are these going to cost?* but they taste good and we order a couple more. Next day we decide to go to a gay beach-bar and hangout you have to take a boat to; it's called Paco's Paradise. We get to the beach and a boatman looks at us and says, "Paco's Paradise?" I think *It's that obvious?* He drops us off on a rocky inlet where a couple of boys with a net are catching small fish. An old man has a pair of bigger fish he's split and impaled on sticks in the sand, roasting over a little fire.

Paco's place is up the beach: a few lounge chairs and a tattered volleyball net. There's a wide-open casa that feels abandoned, except Mariah Carey is blasting and a couple of girls are mopping the floor. They look up and smile. We decide to bail—down to the beach and across an outcropping of tumbled slabs jutting into the sea. Beyond, where the stones end, we can see another beach; there are people there. When we get to it, we realize it, too, is an isolated place you get to by boat, except this one's not gay. I think it's some eco theme park. You have to pay to get there and everything's included, only we didn't pay, we crashed it.

A woman in an embroidered campesina costume waves us to the

lunch buffet, a waiter in a straw hat brings us beers. There's no bill, no cashier when we leave to go lie on the beach. Bells clang. "Are you part of the green group?" a man asks. "Your boat is leaving now." We file onto the boat. I'm thinking *When they figure out we are not part of the green group we are so busted* but we don't get busted. We help ourselves to more beers from the cooler on deck—we have no clue where we're getting dropped off until we see it: the cruise ship pier! We're laughing.

After a long ride in a taxi on unpaved switchbacks we're at Craig's again, but no longer alone: Two Latino guys are sitting by the pool, holding hands. They're from LA. "Get the mango margaritas," I say. "They're good." We tell them about Paco's, and right about then it hits me: Why didn't I buy that old man's roasted fish?

Tulum 2012

Roberto, our one-armed driver, is taking us down the narrow highway on the way out of Merida, languorous capital of the Yucatan. He's driving us to Tulum, a 3½-hour trip by road, through long stretches of dry tropical scrub. Perry and I have reservations at Adonis, a gay resort with a name that kind of embarrasses me when I have to repeat it to Roberto but whatever; we're going for it. "*Ahhh*, A-DOAN-isss," Roberto says, his inflection signaling that he gets what's up, as if we'd asked him to take us to a brothel and don't worry, amigos, because he'll be totally discreet about it.

Roberto is an enormous man in a crisp white guayabera, the redundant sleeve pinned to its tunic. He has a deep, sonorous voice, and sings while driving—I think the entertainment is considered part of the ride service. After a couple of hours we approach a town, actually a pretty little colonial city, Valladolid. "I'll take you around so you can see it," Roberto's voice booms in the cramped headspace of his Jetta. "Then perhaps we can eat." The car creeps through streets of narrow sidewalks and high stucco walls, past machine-gun *federales* with faces like Mayan temple glyphs, to pause before the 16th-century Convent de San Bernardino de Siena, jagged and fortress-like. "I know a little place where we can have a *sneck*," Roberto says. "Nothing fancy."

He parks on the street, leads us to a covered arcade with tables in the middle, ringed with tiendas and loncheras. The one he stops at is a sloppy counter peppered with flies, with a line of plastic buckets holding sauced meats and salsas in shades of red and amber. Perry gets a couple of tacos. I follow Roberto's lead and get panuchos, craggy corn-masa purses filled with refried black beans of a mineral potency and a lardish gloss, piled with pink pickled onions and shredded, achiote-stained turkey with the deepest flavor you can imagine. They're amazing. I go get another, and one for Perry.

A couple of hours later we've said goodbye to Roberto and dropped our bags in our room at the Adonis, which is enormous and austere, all hard stone surfaces and AC nobody knows how to turn off. We retreat to the pool, where everyone's eyeing the pair of fleshy-looking French guys with tattoos, Russian lesbians are chain-smoking, and the big American bear and his buddy will not get out of the churning spa pool.

By the end of the night we'll have paid San Francisco prices for a mediocre dinner with the other tourists at Hartwood, which offers a little bit of Brooklyn on a boutique stretch of beachfront. In the dark, as we'll try to flag a taxi to take us back to the frigid charms of the Adonis, we'll wonder why we aren't in Valladolid, drunk out of our minds on panuchos and bottles of beer. Maybe next trip we'll learn.

Beach Town

By Anthony Bourdain

From *Lucky Peach*

In 2000, Anthony Bourdain's *Kitchen Confidential* roiled the restaurant industry, inspired a gonzo school of food writing, and launched his own career as a TV host and food personality (his current gig is The Travel Channel's *No Reservations*). But he isn't always the culinary bad boy—here he waxes mellow and downright nostalgic.

F rom one end of town to the other, one-pound bricks of butter melt slowly into metal crocks—thick layers of white froth gathering on the surface. In the bars, the seasonal visitors drink Heineken out of chilled bottles. The townies drink Bud Light.

The smell, when you walk down the street, is of french fries, cooked in the same hot grease as the clams—though CLAM STRIPS is what it says on the #10 cans they come in. They are dunked into banks of deep fryers by the same people who do the roofing and house painting in the spring. French fries and clam strips are joined in the bubbling oil by scallops and shrimp, flounder fillets, and rings of squid, all coated in the same universal breading. By the town pier there are funnel cakes and the fudge shop, adding a sickly sweet note to the airborne miasma of atomized fat. As you walk down Main Street after the dinner rush, past the Shell Shop, the Shirt Shop, the Dinghy Dock, Neptune Lounge, Olde Towne Tavern, Cap'n Barnes Galley Bar, Candles 'N' Things, Reggie's Pizza, the Scupper, you hear the clatter of hundreds of lobster carcasses scraping against heavy Buffalo China plates.

Tomorrow morning, former cheerleaders from the local high school will cut lemons into wedges, fill bowls with pilot biscuits in little plastic wrappers, pluck sprigs of curly parsley and float them in ice water. They'll line up monkey dishes and ramekins, top off the ketchup bottles, restock the lobster bibs, fold napkins, and gather around garbage stockades in rear parking lots to smoke and gossip about last night.

I'm six years old, playing with molded plastic army men in the beach grass of the dunes. Here comes the truck that sprays insecticide in a huge, smoky cloud from its rear; I join the other children from the block, running in its wake. For dinner, there will be mussels and steamed lobster, corn on the cob, Jersey tomatoes.

I'm twelve years old, same dunes, smoking pilfered menthol cigarettes with some girls who are older than me. For dinner, there will be pan-fried tails of the blowfish I caught off the dock, or takeout pizza. Somebody's dad will fire up the grill and cook hamburgers and hot dogs in a backyard of pebbles and crushed seashells. The adults will get tipsy and play charades or rummy or Mille Bornes or whatever game is popular that summer. The kids will slip off into the dark to build fires on the beach.

I'm seventeen years old, "wrapping the bakes" in the cellar of the RipTide Lounge—there's a sinkful of potatoes I am detailed to seal in portion-controlled squares of tinfoil, which I'll then pierce with a fork. After that, I'll pull the muscles off a bushel of sticky sea scallops, wash the spinach and romaine, dodge the pots and pans the cooks throw into the pot sink next to me. Then it's bust suds, dive for pearls (wash dishes) from five to midnight, then mop the kitchen, strip the stove, drag the mats out into the parking lot to hose them down. Then it's the glorious walk home. The town's other restaurants are closing down too—dishwashers running their last loads, bar customers with raised voices laughing at unheard jokes, the clatter of plates loaded into trays, boat whistles, the occasional foghorn.

I'm eighteen years old and the menu is clam chowder, kale soup, shrimp cocktail, lobster salad, Caesar salad, oysters on the half, clams on the half, broiled fish, fried fish, fisherman's platter, steamed cherrystones, squid stew, cioppino, steamed mussels in red sauce, steamed mussels in white wine, steamed lobster, broiled lobster, stuffed lobster, stuffed flounder, broiled bluefish, haddock amandine, New York strip, ribeye. I can cook the whole menu and think I'm fucking Escoffier.

The striped bass are running and I score a twenty-pounder off the manager, who's got more than he can use. A storm is kicking up, and the big rollers are coming in just outside our summer rental, the ocean foaming and hissing past and around it onto the county road. My girl-friend, my friends, and housemates gather, and I roast the whole bass on foil, haul it out onto the deck where we squeeze lemons over it, tear at it with our fingers, gape in wonder at the dark and ferocious surf.

Out on the highway (the old one, not the new one), between Tum-ble Town and the miniature golf, there's Ed's Lobster Roll, the A&W Root Beer stand, and the Dairy King. At the pier, the Hurricane ride has been closed since a rumored decapitation a few years back but the bumper cars still run. The terrifying Zipper still separates its customers from the contents of their pockets and their stomachs.

Sullen, no-longer-young men stand all day at Skippers on the board-walk, shirtless—bellies protruding over their jeans, all faded tattoos and disappointment—wearing work boots and drinking beers out of sixteen-ounce plastic cups, glaring ever more menacingly at passersby as the day wears on.

I'm fifty-seven. Another beach, a very different town, a long time and a long distance from the beaches of my childhood. My daughter's strapped in the car seat behind me and we've come from shopping. To-day, I walk into the surf with her on my shoulders, the way my father once did with me. The waves are big—a little too big—and as we get deeper, she wears that same mix of terror and delight on her face that I once felt as a child. I hear myself saying the same things my father used to say: "Uh, oh! Here comes a big one! Hold your breath!"

We get knocked down. I lose her for a second, reach into the foam, and pull her, spluttering, back into my arms. "We got wiped out," I say. "Creamed. Are you okay?"

She wants to cry but doesn't.

"You did everything right," I say. "You held your breath. You stayed calm."

"My eyes sting," she says. And I hug her tight. Later, we stand at the kitchen counter of our summer rental, and I show her how to husk corn.

I let her salt the water in the big pot, show her how to tap the garlic with the side of the knife, slip it out of its skin. I put the steamers we bought at the store in another pot with a little white wine and crushed red pepper and the garlic, then put the lid on top.

When the corn is done, I put her to work rubbing each ear with a hunk of butter on the end of a fork. When the clams open, I strain off the liquid, run it through a cheesecloth.

We cover the table in newspapers, and put out the food. I show her how to pop the cooked clams from their shells, slip off the dark, sock-like layer covering the foot, dip them first in the broth to wash off the grit, then in the clarified butter. She takes her first taste of my childhood.

"They're good, Dada," she says.

And I am very happy.

Recipe Index

Permissions Acknowledgments

About the Editor

HOLLY HUGHES is a writer and editor, the former executive editor of Fodor's Travel Publications, and author of *Frommer's 500 Places for Food and Wine Lovers*. She also blogs about music at TheSongInMy HeadToday.blogspot.com

Submissions for
Best Food Writing 2016

Submissions and nominations for *Best Food Writing 2016* should be forwarded no later than May 1, 2016, to Holly Hughes at *Best Food Writing 2016*, c/o Da Capo Press, 44 Farnsworth Street, Boston MA 02210, or emailed to best.food@perseusbooks.com. We regret that, due to volume, we cannot acknowledge receipt of all submissions.